Culture Change and the New Technology

An Archaeology of the
Early American Industrial Era

CONTRIBUTIONS TO GLOBAL HISTORICAL ARCHAEOLOGY

Series Editor:
Charles E. Orser, Jr., *Illinois State University, Normal, Illinois*

A HISTORICAL ARCHAEOLOGY OF THE MODERN WORLD
Charles E. Orser, Jr.

CULTURE CHANGE AND THE NEW TECHNOLOGY: An Archaeology of
the Early American Industrial Era
Paul A. Shackel

Culture Change and the New Technology

An Archaeology of the Early American Industrial Era

Paul A. Shackel

Harpers Ferry National Historical Park
Harpers Ferry, West Virginia
and University of Maryland
College Park, Maryland

PLENUM PRESS • NEW YORK AND LONDON

Library of Congress Cataloging-in-Publication Data

On file

Cover illustration: "Harpers Ferry—Scene of the Last Insurrection." *Harpers Weekly*, Vol. 3 (1859), p. 692.

ISBN 0-306-45333-9

© 1996 Plenum Press, New York
A Division of Plenum Publishing Corporation
233 Spring Street, New York, N. Y. 10013

Printed in the United States of America

To Luigi Pepe and Maria Michaela Russo and
Damian Shackelovich and Kristina Hluchy, the founders
of two working-class families whose values and ethics
I cherish

Preface

For centuries, Native Americans seasonally inhabited the shorelines of Harpers Ferry. During the 1780s, the area first received prominent recognition from Thomas Jefferson. Sitting on the cliffs of Harpers Ferry, he wrote his *Notes on the State of Virginia*, in which he described the vast beauty found at the confluence of the Shenandoah and Potomac rivers. Jefferson (1954 [1789]:45) claimed that it was "one of the most stupendous scenes in nature" and that it was "worth a trip across the ocean" to see. At that time, the area had a ferry operated by Robert Harper and only a few buildings, including a mill and a tavern. George Washington, a land speculator along the Potomac, seized the opportunity to capitalize on the region's waterpower and created a National Armory at Harpers Ferry in 1796.

In the early nineteenth century, manufacturing proceeded slowly, but not quietly. At the Harpers Ferry National Armory, interchangeable parts were perfected by John Hall, much to the displeasure of many of the armory craftsmen. The creation of uniform parts became known as the American system of manufacturing, and eventually many other industries adopted this method. Interchangeable parts, mass production, and low-paid immigrant labor eventually became the norm for most American industries.

Harpers Ferry is most widely known today for the attempted slave revolt led by John Brown. While his venture to capture weapons and to free slaves failed, he became for Northern abolitionists a martyr and a symbol for the fight against slavery. Devastated by the Civil War, the economy of Harpers Ferry rose from its ashes by the 1880s. Small industries played a part in its revival, although the town increasingly catered to tourists. Many people traveled to Harpers Ferry on the Baltimore & Ohio railroad, taking daily excursions to visit the railroad-built amusement park, as well as to see the remains of the armory, Civil War fortifications, and John Brown's Fort.

Harpers Ferry was devastated yet again, by floods and the great economic depression of the 1930s, but it has again risen to become a popular tourist attraction in America's growing heritage tourism industry. Part of the town is now a national park, visited by about half a million people a year. While the town is most readily recognized as the site of John Brown's raid, other nationally significant themes are celebrated and interpreted to the public, such as industry, transportation, African-American history, and the Civil War.

These themes help shape America's views of progress, democracy, development, and equality. Unfortunately the value of the National Parks Service has been questioned by the 104th United States Congress, and the Service has received substantial budget cuts. Over 250,000 federal workers will lose their jobs by 1999, and the National Park Service must share in this burden. These cuts have already affected public educational and community outreach programs. Visitors to the national parks increasingly find educational exhibits closed rather than open, as parks no longer have the personnel to staff them.

Therefore, much of the new social history, which has been the norm in academic pursuits for several decades, but only recently pursued by the National Park Service, is not being conveyed to the public. In the past, national parks have provided accounts of the achievements of the "great men" of history, but have neglected to mention the contributions of laborers, craftsmen, boardinghouse keepers, and other subordinate groups. We celebrate industrial innovations as progress and development, but these changes often occurred at the expense of the workers, and their households. Industrial work compromised a worker's self-value as well as his household's health and welfare.

Over the past decade, however, some National Park Service projects have integrated the story of the working classes into nationally significant themes. They have been telling the story from the bottom up, being inclusive rather than exclusive. Even as parks were increasingly being used as outdoor "laboratories" for public educational purposes, however, much of the research budget is now being diverted to even more basic needs, such as maintenance and upkeep on buildings. Research projects are becoming a luxury of the past.

It is the history from the bottom up that I hope to convey in this book. While many of the archaeological assemblages analyzed are from anonymous households, it is the story of these people that I integrate into one of the nationally significant themes of Harpers Ferry, the development of the United States Armory.

I grew up in a household of immigrant grandparents and first-generation Americans, where it was the norm to work nearly twice as many hours a day as an average laborer toils today. The average work week was six and one-half days. Pay was often below the average American wage, and sometimes it was only through the generosity of family and community that families such as mine were able to make ends meet. The brutality of the working conditions took its toll, and the clash between capital and labor was often intense.

I find it unfortunate that as Americans proceed into the twenty-first century, they increasingly overlook historical accounts of the harsh working conditions found in the preunion era. Today, Americans have an attitude that we can never experience those days again, but as the average workday increases and real wages shrink, I fear that some of the progress made to better our working conditions over the past 60 years will be lost. We will have to regain them in the new work world of the postindustrial era.

Hard work, unions, Franklin D. Roosevelt's reforms, the G.I. Bill, and the Great Society allowed my family, along with millions of others, to obtain their share of the middle-class dream. I owe my values and good fortune to the founders of my American family. I admire their difficult struggles, and their accounts will live forever in my memory. Their story is very much part of my life, and it is also a part of the national story of working-class families in America. For the founding members of my family—Luigi Pepe and Maria Michaela Russo, and Damian Shochalevich and Kristina Hluchy, I dedicate this book.

Acknowledgments

Over the course of my tenure at Harpers Ferry National Historical Park, there have been many professionals who helped to make the archaeology program a success. I am indebted to all of them, including Ellen Armbruster, Janet Blutstein, Anna Borden, Brett Burk, C. Gary Butera, Karen Coffman, Vikki Cornell, Tina Daly, Susannah Dean, Gwyneth Duncan, John Eddins, Diane Fenicle, Benjamin Ford, Mark Goleb, Jill Halchin, Nancy Hatcher, Jean Harris, Jill Harris, Deborah Hull Walski, Marcy Jastrab, Kenneth Kulp, Eric Larsen, Michael Lucas, Erika Martin, Mia Parsons, Kelly Passo, Amy Peters, Devon Pyle, John Ravenhorst, Andrew Schenker, Dennis Scott, Jennifer Shamberg, Priscilla Smith, Kimberly Sprow, Nancy Turner, Frank Walski, Dave Warren-Taylor, Susan Trail, Anna-Marie York, and Cari YoungRavenhorst.

The program also had a strong volunteer component, and I am grateful for the efforts of Allan Alexander, Sandra Anderson, Daniel Ballas, Jason Beard, Howard Beverly, Hilary Chapman, David Christy, Jeffery Cogle, Douglas Dammann, Carolyn Gates, Theresa Grob, Logan Johnson, David Larsen, Katrina Larsen, Ryan Levins, Guian McKee, Stephanie McSherry, Thomas Neff, Bob Newnham, Janina O'Bien-Trent, Anne Marie Parsons, Jane Rago, Marcia Robinson, Douglas Sause, Karl Smart, Jack Smith, Mary Beth Williams, and Terrie Wise.

It was also a pleasure working with and receiving feedback from the park's Historian team, comprised of Patricia Chickering, Michael Jenkins, Mary Johnson, Stan Bumgardner, and John Barker. The Cultural Landscape team comprised of Maureen Joseph, Perry Wheelock, and Steve Lowe provided considerable input into this project.

Susan Winter Trail served as the original principal investigator for the Harpers Ferry construction project that began in 1989, and I commend her efforts in beginning the research project. John W. Ravenhorst provided the Autocad drawings, and Cari YoungRavenhorst produced many of the photographs. Frank Schultz-DePalo provided guidance in facilitating the curation of artifacts, and Bruce Noble provided helpful feedback. Dennis Frye also provided advice.

The following persons provided expertise and advice through the course of the project, and I appreciate their assistance: Louise Ackerson, Joanne Bowen, Gregory Brown, Charles Gunn, Elise Manning, George Miller, Stephen Mrozowski, Paul Mullins, William Pitman, Karl Reinhard, Irwin Rovner, Linda Scott Cummings, Kathryn Puseman, and Mark Warner. I drew upon their specialization and synthesized their results for this book. I am especially grateful for the hard work and dedication of Brett Burk, Linda Scott Cummings, Eric Larsen, Michael Lucas, and Irwin Rovner for their synthesis of complex data sets that I used. Their efforts, which are found in many technical reports, are greatly appreciated.

Robert Gordon and Carolyn Cooper were very instrumental in the analysis of gun parts from the armory workers' site. They introduced us to Smithsonian curator Edward Ezell, and they all spent considerable time helping us identify these objects.

The archaeology project could not have proceeded without the strong commitment of Park Superintendent Donald Campbell. He has always provided strong support and leadership for the project. Members of the park's administrative staff were also very helpful; they include Peggy Smallwood, Gayleen Boyd, Julie Johnston, Rita Mihalik, Ann Shuey, Judy Coleman, Joyce Howe, Kay Kenney, and Dori Lent. Special thanks to Facility Manager Richard Fox and Grounds Foreman Dennis Ebersole for providing staff and equipment throughout the excavation process. Paul Lee indexed many of the armory letters, and his work was very useful to this project. I appreciate the friendship of Vernon Smith, who always provided helpful suggestions during the archaeology project.

Stephen Potter, chief archeologist for the National Capital Area (NCA), provided helpful technical oversight throughout all phases of this program. NCA staff archaeologists Marian Creveling, Deborah Hull-Walski, Robert Sonderman, and Matthew Virta also provided assistance for archaeology projects. I am thankful to Perry Wheelock and Diana Duncan for their comments on various drafts of the manuscript. I truly appreciate their insights and helpful suggestions.

I appreciate the helpful guidance and suggestions provided to me by Chuck Orser and Eliot Werner. Barbara Little read several drafts of the manuscript. She gave encouragement and suggestions throughout the entire process of writing the volume.

Contents

Tables and Figures

Tables

Figures

Culture Change and the New Technology

An Archaeology of the
Early American Industrial Era

Introduction
Industry and Interpreting the Past

WORK AND THE GLOBAL ECONOMY

The industrial revolution is a global phenomenon that has had and is having far greater effects on our daily lives than many of us realize. This case study of Harpers Ferry armory workers and their households examines the interrelationship between industrial and domestic life. While the social and political circumstances of Harpers Ferry are unique to this community, there are many phenomena that are universal in incipient industrial communities. The effects of the industrial revolution in the United States had significant implications that changed work life and domestic relations to those that we know today.

Nineteenth-century Harpers Ferry was one of this country's earliest and most significant industrial communities. From 1796, the town was the site of the United States Armory, an early American experiment with new industrial ideals. Various immigrant groups came to the Potomac valley in search of jobs provided by the iron industry, milling, the construction of the Chesapeake and Ohio canal, and the Baltimore & Ohio railroad. Groups also flocked to Harpers Ferry to meet many of the needs of the growing industrial community. While a melting pot never truly existed, neighborhoods based on ethnic and class distinctions were rare. Harpers Ferry is a unique place in which to examine ethnic and interracial development in a craft-based economy that transformed to an industrial economy.

As the industrial revolution developed in eighteenth-century England, many Americans feared that life in the new nation would degenerate to the squalor and substandard living conditions found in England. Although many entrepreneurs assured the public that such conditions would not arise in America, industry developed rapidly, and by the 1840s, living conditions in growing urban centers were similar to those found in England. People lost control of their means of production, and the work of laborers, rather than being task-oriented, was

1

dictated by the clock and done to the rhythm of machines (see Thompson 1967). New domestic relations were also created, and inequality was increasingly expressed in many ways, including the material culture possessed by the household.

In the United States, industry reached its peak in the late nineteenth through mid twentieth centuries. As labor became powerful in twentieth-century United States, industrialists encouraged third world nations to develop industry and pay workers relatively lower wages. In the present-day global economy, it is more cost-efficient to manufacture products oversees and ship them back for sale to American consumers than it is to manufacture products in this country. Even though most Americans' livelihoods are no longer driven by the factory, our work and daily routines are still driven by the industrial process. The clock, which drove the armorer's production in the gun factory, and the weaver's day in the cotton factory in the mid-1800s, still drives production and daily life today. Time-efficiency and increased production are key to industry's success.

During the 1990s, as production steadily increases, large businesses are continually "downsizing" to become more cost-efficient, and workers continually struggle to keep their salaries in step with inflation. It is common to read newspaper headlines such as "Gain in Workers' Pay, Benefits Is Smallest Since at Least 1981" and "U.S. Finds Productivity, But Not Pay, Is Rising" (*Washington Post* 26 July 1995:A1, A9). These headlines are nothing new. In fact, from the beginning of the industrial era, workers in all parts of the globe continually struggled for increased wages. Strikes, sabotaging of machinery, and arson were common through the nineteenth and early twentieth centuries as an expression of workers' discontent with wages and working conditions. Today, explicit forms of workers' discontent are for the most part less extreme, but many of the problems of inequality still exist.

It was common to find women laboring in factories next to men during the birth and development of the early industrial revolution. It was a way to justify industry in such a way that farmers were not threatened by a competing workforce. An ideology developed in the mid-nineteenth century to create a domestic sphere controlled by women, thereby removing women from the paid workforce. In the late twentieth century, domestic relations are once again changing. As workers' earning powers are steadily declining, women are once again becoming a major component of the workforce, and it is now increasingly common for both members of middle-class couples to be working full-time to support the household—a concept foreign to most middle-class Americans just a few decades ago.

The growth and development of industry is a global phenomenon that increasingly affects the world's population every day. As Western society moves into the postindustrial era, we are increasingly committed to understanding and celebrating industrial progress, as well as the ingenuity and entrepreneurship associated with industry. Western countries are increasingly encouraging the development of organizations, scholarships, displays, monuments, and parks that venerate industrial progress. Many historical parks that commemorate the industrial era, whether national, state, provincial, or local, do not recognize how human relations changed with the introduction of industry. I will address this issue, examining the effects of the early industrial revolution on domestic life, in the following chapters.

Harpers Ferry serves as an excellent site in which to confront these questions. There, industry displaced craft, craftsmen revolted, entrepreneurs developed new industrial surveillance technologies to control workers, and nineteenth- and twentieth-century citizens commemorated the glories and success of the industrial revolution. Recent archaeological excavations at Harpers Ferry have concentrated on the domestic sites of the early industrial era. This work complements the growing literature on industry and sheds additional light on changing domestic relations during this era.

The development of Harpers Ferry National Historical Park has been committed to the monumentalization of key events in American history. A history of this monumentalization provides a context for the current archaeology program at Harpers Ferry and the relevant topics for park interpretation.

MONUMENTALIZATION AND HISTORIC SITES

Historic sites help affirm Americans' connection with a particular heritage and disseminate critical messages that create an American identity. Preservation, reconstruction, and stabilization of public symbols and interpretation of past events in civic arenas influences people's beliefs about historic legends and the current attitudes they serve (Bodner 1992; Linenthal 1993:87–126; Patterson 1989:138ff; Rainey 1983; also see King 1994).

Commemorating the industrial past is inherent in the National Park Service's interpretation of Harpers Ferry today. Through exhibits, wayside signs, and brochures, visitors are told about industrial advancements and modern life. Recent work at Harpers Ferry has changed the emphasis of interpretation and has focused on the everyday lives of those who labored in this industrial community. Commemorating this history by creating exhibits, stabilizing ruins, and incorporating this message in everyday interpretation is one method of creating and reinforcing this national ideology.

Since the town became Harpers Ferry National Monument in the 1950s and National Historical Park in 1963, archaeology and the use of archaeological remains changed as different avenues of inquiry became important to our national heritage. Harpers Ferry National Historical Park today stands as a monumental landscape that emphasizes different interpretive themes. Some of the early National Park Service interpretations that use material culture to interpret the past can still be seen today. Other older exhibits have been modernized and new ones have been created. Together, these exhibits provide a material cultural history of what was considered important in the national agenda several decades ago, what is meaningful today, and what will be taught to our children tomorrow.

THE CREATION OF HARPERS FERRY NATIONAL HISTORICAL PARK

In 1944, Congress passed legislation to create Harpers Ferry National Monument. Between 1944 and 1953, the states of West Virginia and Maryland acquired lands that were given to the federal government to fulfill this legislation (Figure 1). Archaeology and architecture played a significant role in the National Park Service's interpretation of the town's historic events to the public. Early decisions to emphasize and interpret a portion of the town's history significantly altered the physical appearance of this mid-twentieth-century town.

In 1955, the National Park Service assessed the conditions of the town's buildings. While the country prepared for the Civil War centennial, telling the story of John Brown and the Civil War became a major interpretative thrust at Harpers Ferry National Monument. The monument, along with the rest of the National Park Service, adopted a preservation ethic similar to that found at Williamsburg and Mount Vernon. These historic sites originally chose to interpret only those histories related to prominent times or specific people. In the case of Williamsburg, the original archaeology was performed to re-create the eighteenth century, when Williamsburg became an affluent town and the capital of Virginia. At Mount Vernon, archaeology is currently being performed to interpret George Washington's 1799 landscape. In both

Figure 1. View showing the poor condition of buildings along Shenandoah Street, circa 1955. (Courtesy of Harpers Ferry National Historical Park, HF311)

cases, histories predating or postdating the era in question are often overlooked. Williamsburg has recently taken steps to correct this bias (Shackel and Little 1994:10).

At Harpers Ferry, much as at other historic sites of the era, the National Park Service removed any buildings that did not fit into the proposed 1859–1865 time period. Between 1956 and 1959, 22 structures were eliminated from Lower Town. During the 1960s and 1970s, the National Park Service determined that any structure with a pre–Civil War construction date with later renovations was to be restored to the Civil War era. Interpretive exhibits as well as archaeology also focused on this era (C. Gilbert et al. 1993: 3.125–3.129).

In the late 1950s and into the 1960s, the National Park Service began restoration of the Harper House, named after the founder of the town (C. Gilbert et al. 1993:6.2). Harper began construction of the building in the 1780s, but he died before he was able to occupy it. Today, the house, with an original eighteenth-century core, exhibits a cross section of living conditions of Harpers Ferry residents in the 1850s. On the first floor is an armory worker's apartment; the second floor contains a middle-class apartment; the upper floors display upper-class

Figure 2. View of Lower Town Harpers Ferry from Maryland Heights, circa 1900. The buildings mansard roofs (*center*) were constructed upon the arsenal yard foundations. (Courtesy of Harpers Ferry National Historical Park, HF96).

living quarters. The occupancy of specific apartments by specific families, or groups of people, is not certainly known on the evidence of the historical documents. These interpretive exhibits of living quarters, with the poorer group inhabiting the bottom floor and the wealthiest group inhabiting the upper floor, metaphorically reflect the inequality that has become accepted in our society today.

The restoration of a row of buildings, known collectively as Marmion Hall, was also accomplished during this era (C. Gilbert et al. 1993:6.3). Many other buildings were restored to their 1850s facades, including stores and taverns. Other structures that postdated the Civil War were dismantled.

Some of the first restorations of the townscape included the removal of several Victorian structures that stood in the former arsenal yard (Figure 2). This work was accompanied by the first archaeological excavations in Harpers Ferry, which included the search for the armory arsenal. The arsenal was the structure that John Brown hoped to seize in order to capture weapons to supply newly freed slaves. Edward Larrabee (1960a) (see Cotter 1959, 1960) excavated several trenches during the summer of 1960 and found the walls of the arsenal building located about 5 feet below the present surface (Figure 3). The northeast

Figure 3. Excavations of the arsenal square, circa 1960. (Courtesy of Harpers Ferry National Historical Park, NHF3239).

and western walls from these excavations are at present exposed for public interpretation.

Larrabee (1960b, 1961, 1962) also performed the initial excavations on Hall's Island and located some foundations belonging to the United States Rifle Works. Using a resistivity and seismic survey, Hamilton Carson (1963) located anomalies on Hall's Island. Excavations, in the form of trenches, found 2 1/2- to 4-foot-wide shale walls of the United States Rifle Works of the 1840s at about 6-feet beneath the current ground surface. Carson (1963) also uncovered a headrace and channel that led to a 9-foot wide turbine pit that powered the machinery in the rifle works.

David H. Hannah (n.d.) produced the first assessment of cultural resources on Virginius Island in the mid-1960s and briefly described aboveground historical features. In 1966-1968, he directed a Job Corps project to uncover the foundation walls of the large cotton mill ruin and to open part of the raceway on the north side of the mill (Figure 4). This work exposed three basement chambers within the mill. Within the narrow center chamber sat four well-preserved, in situ Leffel turbines positioned in a wooden floor (Figure 5). Flour-milling machinery parts also were recovered near the base of the excavations (Hannah 1969).

William Hershey (1964) performed excavations around the Lockwood House on the site where John Hall, a prominent arms manufacturer, had lived. The structure was later destroyed, and the armory

Figure 4. Excavations of the turbine chamber at the cotton/flour mill, 1968. (Courtesy of Harpers Ferry National Historical Park, NHF3120)

built a house for the armory's paymaster in its place in the 1840s. After the Civil War, the United States Government deeded the paymaster's house to Storer College, an African-American institution of higher learning established after the Civil War. The purpose of the excavations was to locate outbuildings and graves related to the Civil War, but the work was unsuccessful in attaining the original objectives. Archaeologists located postwar features, such as privies, but they kept only a sample of the objects from these features, since, at the time, postbellum occupations were not considered archaeologically significant. During the Victorian era, the college put a mansard roof on the Lockwood House. During the 1970s, the National Park Service removed the mansard roof and restored the building to its appearance in the 1850s, an era that saw the house occupied by the paymaster of the United States Armory.

Generally, the first goal of Harpers Ferry National Monument was to restore the town to its appearance prior to the Civil War era. The

Figure 5. Excavations of the turbine chamber at the cotton/flour mill, showing exposed Leffel turbines, 1968. (Courtesy of Harpers Ferry National Historical Park, NHF3119)

archaeology complemented this objective. Most of the excavations centered around the town's early industry and the Civil War era. Usually, significant industry related artifacts were kept and objects that postdated the war were not kept for inclusion in the park's collection.

THE 1970S AND 1980S AT HARPERS FERRY NATIONAL HISTORICAL PARK

During the 1970s and early 1980s, the questions related to archaeology remained just as limited. The goal of much of the archaeology was compliance-driven for updating facilities and restoring buildings and yards to the Civil War era.

The Wager Block served as the core of the Harpers Ferry commercial district from the early nineteenth century through the twentieth century. The site contained mainly hotels and associated businesses and later diversified into mixed commercial use. In the 1970s and 1980s, major excavations were done around these buildings with the goal of restoring the structures and surrounding landscape to the 1850s. William Gardner (1974) performed preliminary work that identified major archaeological features in preparation for architectural and landscape renovations to the Civil War period. Other excavations on this block followed. They provided information regarding the functions of buildings (Blee 1978) and furnished a more diachronic assessment of the cultural resources that extended into the late nineteenth century (Pousson 1985).

Other archaeological work was done in several commercial dwellings along the northern side of Shenandoah Street and west of High Street in the commercial district (Seidel 1985). The excavations identified cultural resources for future restoration, stabilization, and rehabilitation of buildings that currently contain exhibits on the industry and the commercial use of the town.

James W. Mueller conducted testing around the Shenandoah Canal wall in 1983 as part of an expanded restoration effort (Mueller et al. 1986). The canal lies on Virginius Island, a once vibrant, mid-nineteenth-century community that grew as entrepreneurs capitalized on waterpower. Excavations also revealed a deeply buried wall that formed part of the tailrace for the original flour mill constructed circa 1824. Additional work defined the mouth of an early iron foundry/tannery tailrace. In 1986, the archaeology staff monitored additional construction activities around the foundry tailrace (Frye and Young-Ravenhorst 1988). This fieldwork uncovered the foundation of a massive, previously unrecorded, building that adjoined the canal wall on the west side of the iron foundry/tannery tailrace. The building is a new iron foundry constructed around 1860 to replace the old foundry established in the original oil mill.

Work has continued through the 1980s documenting cultural resources throughout the park. A major survey effort documented the rich and diverse nineteenth-century cultural history found on Maryland Heights (Frye and Frye 1989) and Loudoun Heights (Winter and Frye 1992). In the early nineteenth century, both Maryland Heights and Loudoun Heights served as major charcoaling areas. These heights are best known, however, for their strategic role in the Civil War. In the postbellum era, the area was inhabited by small farmsteads. Today, the heights serve as educational and recreational areas in which their historic significance for both Civil War and charcoaling is highlighted through wayside signs and brochures.

RECENT YEARS AT HARPERS FERRY NATIONAL
HISTORICAL PARK

From the early 1980s, the restoration philosophy has changed in Harpers Ferry National Historical Park. Restoration to a specific time period is no longer seen as valid, since time-freezing provides one history at the expense of other histories (Lowenthal 1985). Since the 1980s, Harpers Ferry National Historical Park has expanded its interpretive thrust to include the entire nineteenth century. Today, any restoration or archaeology projects must consider not only the armory and Civil War histories, but also the later Victorian contributions. While John Brown is a major focus of the park, archaeology has made significant contributions to telling the story of the everyday interactions between people of varying status and racial affiliation during the nineteenth and early twentieth centuries.

In many cases, this changed philosophy has guided the most recent renovation projects at Harpers Ferry. Since the new interpretive themes now include the entire nineteenth century, a post–Civil War structure removed in the 1950s was rebuilt using most of the architectural materials saved during its earlier dismantling. Four major archaeological excavations and over a dozen smaller projects have been undertaken since 1989, all of which include late-nineteenth-century remains. Archaeology in the center of the commercial district has focused upon the everyday lives of residents who lived, prospered, struggled, and worked in this small industrial town. Excavations were performed at armory workers' houses, a hotel, boardinghouses, stores, and private dwellings. In 1990, archaeology was performed in a parking lot that was built over several domestic ruins. Today, the outline of these foundations stands in the former parking lot. The cultural landscape report for Lower Town Harpers Ferry (C. Gilbert et al. 1993) recommends the outlining of the Victorian house foundations that covered the old arsenal yard. A trail through Virginius Island interprets life and industry on the island from the early nineteenth century through the turn of the twentieth century.

The recent archaeology has concentrated on domestic sites related to armory workers as well as their managers. The archaeology shows clear differences of adaptation and resistance to the new industrial order (Lucas and Shackel 1994; Shackel 1993a, 1994a). Excavations in the yards of a commercial district, adjacent to a hotel that coexisted during the armory's operations, located a wide range of consumer goods that were probably used by a variety of social, business, and economic groups. The variety of material goods found may reflect a conscious effort by the hotel owners to maximize business potential (Halchin 1994; Larsen and Lucas 1993, 1994).

Examination of a late-nineteenth-century boardinghouse privy and its comparison to an entrepreneur's household assemblage illuminates some differences in material wealth and health conditions between groups in industrial society (Cummings 1993, 1994; Larsen 1993; Lucas 1993b; Reinhard 1993, 1994). More recently, excavations have focused on the nineteenth-century industrial island known as Virginius Island, located adjacent to the commercial district of Harpers Ferry (Figure 6). Since 1992, three sites, the inhabitants of which cross-cut the social, cultural, and economic structure of Virginius Island, have been excavated. These excavations provide a balanced picture of life in an industrializing community.

In 1992, National Park Service personnel designated the reclamation of Virginius Island, an overgrown, desolate portion of Harpers Ferry, as a top priority to help interpret the community's nineteenth-century industrial past. Virginius Island served as a major private industrial center that complemented the public establishment used for arms manufacturing. Virginius Island thrived in the nineteenth century, and manufacturers produced cloth, flour, pulp, leather, and an assortment of many other products. Floods, economic decline, and the growth of coal-fueled industry hampered the island's economic growth in the late nineteenth century, and entrepreneurs eventually abandoned this once thriving industrial community. Since public interpretation is a major thrust of the park's mission, landscapes have been redesigned to highlight domestic and industrial historic cultural resources. The ruins are maintained and protected with shallow-rooted vegetation, and they provide the image of a site in decay. Protecting the sites and maintaining the image of perpetual decay helps to instill the notion of continuity. Wayside signs or placards explain the anomaly in the topography and the site's history (see Joseph et al. 1993).

The chapters that follow examine the interrelationship between industry and domestic life. Chapter 1 provides a context for understanding the role of material culture in a consumer society. Scholars have traditionally focused on production during the industrial era and hold the Protestant Ethic of Max Weber (1930) to be a prime mover of the industrial consciousness. While work consciousness is a stimulus for production, it does not necessarily explain why people desired new consumer goods (see McCracken 1988). I use sociologist Colin Campbell to help explain this new consumerism by addressing the development of the Romantic ethic. The Romantic ethic is rooted in the nineteenth-

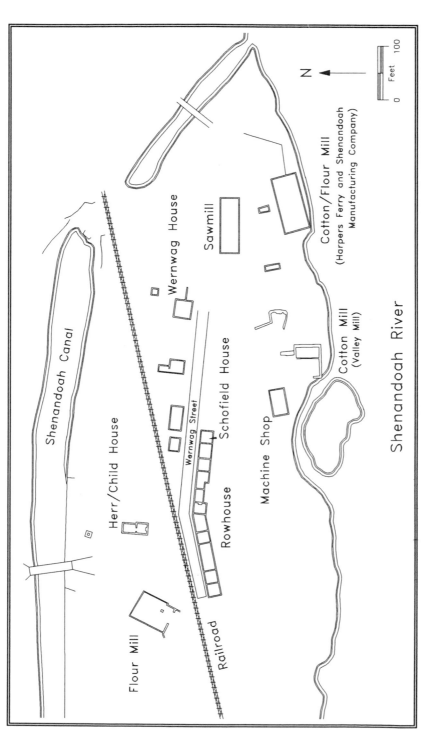

Figure 6. Site map of Virginius Island showing locations of major features and of excavations. (Drawn by John W. Ravenhorst)

Shenandoah Canal

Flour Mill

Railroad

Herr/Child House

Wernwag Street

Rowhouse

Schofield House

Machine Shop

Wernwag House

Sawmill

Cotton Mill
(Valley Mill)

Cotton/Flour Mill
(Harpers Ferry and Shenandoah
Manufacturing Company)

Shenandoah River

N

0   Feet   100

century transcendental movement which created an environment for people to consume goods and aspire to a social class that they would never truly be members of. The Romantic ethic operated closely with the Protestant ethic to stimulate a new consumer society.

Chapter 2 creates a context for studying early industrial Harpers Ferry. The histories of Harpers Ferry have changed considerably from the late nineteenth century to the twentieth century. Histories in the late nineteenth and early twentieth centuries focused on Harpers Ferry's historic and noble past, as well as on the town's national role in industrial progress. Legislation to create Harpers Ferry National Monument was enacted in 1944, and in 1963 it became Harper Ferry National Historical Park. While the park's enabling legislation is over 50 years old, the histories told by the National Park Service have changed dramatically in just these few decades.

Chapter 3 discusses how the town plan of early nineteenth-century Harpers Ferry developed haphazardly. Factory buildings were constructed wherever and whenever needed, and although early maps show a linear configuration of factory buildings on the Potomac River, the construction process did not necessarily move successively from building to building. On the Shenandoah River, John Hall, an inventor from Maine, perfected the development of interchangeable parts. On Hall's Island, a short distance from the gun factory on the Potomac River, the work process did not flow from building to adjacent building; rather, structures were scattered in no particular pattern throughout his industrial complex. With increased factory discipline and the change in management from civilian control to military control in the 1840s, new order and realignments were created in the factory as well as in the entire town.

Chapter 4 further describes landscapes of specific house lots, and I note how these spaces are an indication of how communities and individuals ordered their world. Landscapes not only reflected residents' behavior, but also shaped and reinforced behavior. Connections between increased factory discipline, commercial endeavors, and domestic needs are related to the changing landscape. This work is placed within the context of the struggle between the "garden and the machine" and roles individual households played as they ordered their environment around themselves.

Chapter 5 examines the extent to which households of different socioeconomic status relied on regional and national networks for their daily existence and how they were influenced by the development of a new factory discipline. All households examined contained men, women, and children; the two master armorer families owned male and female slaves, both adults and children. There was no universal acceptance of fashionable consumer goods and Romantically inspired products of the industrial revolution. Examination of ceramic acquisition patterns of the master armorer's household reveals the relationship between the diversity of the ceramic assemblage and the penetration of a modernizing discipline into the households during the first decades of the industrial revolution. Pieceworkers' and wage laborers' household material acquisition patterns also changed during this era, but in a very different way from the master armorer's assemblage. Diet patterns complement the material findings regarding each household's changing reliance on industrial systems for survival. Here again, managers and workers acquired similar foods, but in different proportions. The reliance upon home production of foods was quite common among all armory families, but the amount of self-sufficiency varied among households. The different consumer goods and foodways strategies may have been specific survival techniques or coping mechanisms in a new industrial order.

Chapter 6 describes how home production and limited managerial control at the armory in the 1820s and 1830s transformed piecework into a successful republican ideal among workers. Piecework in the armory was traditionally assumed to have occurred solely within the factory, and armory workers were allowed to come and go as they pleased as long as they met their monthly quotas. Material goods found around a pieceworker's house lot challenge this assumption, and new evidence may indicate that pieceworkers had more freedom in the armory than originally assumed. The home appears to be a viable setting for piecework production of weapons.

Generally, this material analysis of households among armory workers of various status provides insights into the everyday life of early-nineteenth-century Harpers Ferry residents. From the advent of the industrial revolution, tensions grew between conflicting world views. Confrontations grew between the ideals of republican freedoms in the workplace and the concept of new factory discipline dictated by managers. Simplicities of the material world, another republican ideal, collided with Romantic consumer behavior. On one level, Harpers Ferry is an example of a working-class manifestation of Romanticism. On another level, its material manifestations are a reflection of local political factionalism and changing industrial structures. Material goods and the built environment play an enormous role in structuring and responding to society, and they provide a valuable means to discern the various ways in which households coped in this very turbulent era in American history.

Chapter 7 provides additional context and a summary for the book. It examines the connection between the formal introduction of public schools and churches and their relationship to the new industrial order. The interrelationship between these institutions and work and domestic life were all vital factors that helped changed the everyday behavior and the material culture of working class families.

"At the Mercy of the Capitalist"

1

—DANIEL WEBSTER

SOME OF THE QUESTIONS THAT COUNT

Since the publication of two of the most influential works on early industrial America, *Harpers Ferry Armory and the New Technology: The Challenge of Change* by Merritt Roe Smith (1977) and *Rockdale: The Growth of an American Village in the Early Industrial Revolution* by Anthony F. C. Wallace (1978), historians and historical archaeologists have increasingly paid attention to the local social and cultural context of technological change. Smith's and Wallace's works are part of a larger trend in history and anthropology that does not focus on great men or firsts in technological development. Smith and Wallace are more concerned with the impact of the new technology on ordinary people. Their works focus on individual beliefs and the relationship between cultural attitudes and the acceptance of new industrial technology. These histories are based on the correspondence, diaries, and personal papers of literate managers and the local elite.

To a large extent, both studies lack evidence regarding the relationship of work life and the material and behavioral manifestations of domestic life of the factory operatives and their families. By way of making up for this deficiency, I provide additional material anthropological analysis of Harpers Ferry to provide evidence on the interrelationships between industrialism and domestic life among households of varying social and economic status during the early industrial era in America. To carry out this task, I use some of the sources used by M. R. Smith (1977) in his Harpers Ferry history as a complement to new and additional historical information gathered since his original study. I also analyze domestic archaeological assemblages from the house lots of managers and workers.

Harpers Ferry serves as an excellent example of early industrial history, since it was one of only a few major industrial areas that devel-

Figure 7. A view of the United States Armory in Harpers Ferry. (From Edward Beyer's *Album of Virginia*, 1857. Courtesy of Harpers Ferry National Historical Park, HF256)

oped, struggled, and flourished south of the Mason-Dixon line. It was also one of only two national armories (the other was at Springfield, Massachusetts) developed for the production of arms after the American Revolution (Figure 7). Despite the tremendous amount of literature and archaeological material remains from Harpers Ferry, few scholars have paid attention to the labor, economic, or social and political development of the Harpers Ferry Armory since the study by M. R. Smith (1977). My work is by no means the definitive work on Harpers Ferry, nor is it compiled to refute the labor history produced by Smith. Rather, I use archaeologically retrieved data and historical documents to provide another history—a history of the town's industrial and domestic landscape and the domestic life of armory workers and their households in the first half of the nineteenth century.

It is the laborers, craftsmen, women, and minorities who are often mute in our interpretations of the past. This analysis of Harpers Ferry addresses research questions about the relationship between people and a new, disciplined behavior that is associated with industrial society. To understand how these people survived and interacted with each other on a daily basis, it is essential to link the material correlates and the growth of an industrial town to issues related to the new ideology of industrial capitalism.

NATIONAL CONTEXT FOR AMERICAN INDUSTRIALISM

Socioeconomic transformations occurred at an increasingly rapid rate during the early nineteenth century in the United States. Change meant different things to the workers and the industrialists; therefore, it is necessary to understand the workers as individuals struggling to come to grips with a changing society. Most American workers in the early nineteenth century subscribed to a republican ideology; they saw themselves as citizens who could participate in the daily affairs of their community. They believed that government would act as an arbitrator between labor and capital and correct any inequalities, thus rejecting the development of working-class parties often found in Europe. Mainstream organizations such as Democrats, Whigs, and Republicans promised to abide by these republican ideals (Ross 1985:xix).

This republican ideology inhibited the growth and implementation of industrial discipline in the early decades of industry. Many citizens remembered Thomas Jefferson's advice that the well-being of the government depended upon the commitment that a society made to "independent and virtuous husbandmen" (quoted in McCoy 1980:14). Jefferson also cautioned, "Let us never wish to see our citizens occupied at the work-bench. . . . For the general operations of manufacture, let our work-shops remain in Europe" (Jefferson 1954[1789]:165).

When Jefferson and Benjamin Franklin proposed a new republican technology sensitive to human perfection, enthusiasts of industrialization, such as Alexander Hamilton and Tench Coxe, argued strenuously that industrialization would strengthen American society. They asserted that farmers would benefit because new markets would be created for their goods and industry would ensure their prosperity. In some cases, manufacturers would aid merchants by generating goods for local and international trade. Industrialists insisted that manufacturing was necessary for the new republic's independence from European manufactured goods. The survival and security of the country depended upon the prosperity of manufacturers. Coxe believed that American independence relied upon economic independence. Since the early republic was dependent upon other countries, he proposed that manufacturing would solve its political problems. He noted that manufacturing would be the means to the country's "political salvation." In many cases, early industrial supporters did not abandon their commitment to agriculture, as many of them still supported themselves by farming (Prude 1983:61; M. R. Smith 1994:4).

The development of factory work created contradictions in the republican ideology. Daniel Webster, a federalist and staunch supporter of the development of industry, even admitted that a factory worker could not be an independent and good citizen because he was "at the mercy of the capitalist for the support of himself and his family" (quoted in Ross 1985:13). Republicanism was favorable to the skilled craftsmen who dominated production in the early decades of the Harpers Ferry Armory. This philosophy dominated early arms production and helped to minimize tensions between labor and capital. As long as craftsmen had some control over their production, they felt that they could dictate the terms of their livelihood.

While the increasing division of labor was an industrial necessity, some early managers at the national armories frowned upon the idea of creating machine-tenders rather than complete armorers. An inspector at the armory in 1819 noted that occupational specialization undermined the future of the armorers (Dalliba [quoted in Lowrie and Franklin 1834:543]):

> The general arrangement of the workmen to their work is the best that can be adopted for the United States, but not so for the interest of the workmen; that is, each man is kept at one particular kind of work, and is not shifted. . . . By this arrangement, it will readily be perceived that each workman becomes as adept at his part. He works with a greater facility, and does the work much better than one could who worked all the parts. This is undoubtedly the best method for Government. The consequence, however, to the workmen is, that not one of them becomes a finished armorer. If he is always employed at the Government factories, it is no matter for him; he is, in fact, the better for it, for he does more work, and gets more money; but if he wishes to set up business for himself, he has got no trade, he cannot make a fire-arm.

Many armorers agreed with the inspector's statements, and they resisted many changes toward mechanization.

The transition from craft production to piecework accelerated in the 1820s, although this new work system allowed armorers to maintain some of their liberties and sustain faith in the republican ideology. The piecework system gave armorers the freedom to work when they chose, as long as they met their quotas. Through the 1820s and into the 1830s, some pieceworkers maintained farms or garden plots to supplement their livelihood. Changes in the factory that increased mechanization did meet with some resistance, and individual skirmishes between managers and workers sometimes developed. Operations of the facility changed from civilian to military management during the early 1840s, and the desire for the armory to create a well-rounded armorer was no longer a management concern. Republicanism was only a past ideal as the armory became increasingly mechanized, and many of the operatives who were pieceworkers became machine-tenders. An ordnance official wrote in praise of the new management and machinery in 1841 (Talcott [quoted in Benét 1878:395–397]):

> The difficulty of finding good armorers no longer exists; they abound in every machine-shop and manufactory throughout the country. The skill of the eye and the hand, acquired by practice alone, is no longer indispensable; and if every operative was at once discharged from the Springfield armory, their places could be supplied with competent hands in a week.

AFRICAN-AMERICANS IN THE ARMORY SYSTEM

Though they were an exception rather than the rule, some African-American slaves were employed in menial tasks by the United States Armory (National Archives Record Group 217; Snell 1959a). An 1845 armory slave roll indicates that local slave owners rented slaves to the armory. Their occupations are listed as one carman, four laborers, one carpenter, and one horse and cart driver (Snell 1959a:Form No. 18, March 1846). With the exception of the carpenter, these slaves performed unskilled work. Similarly, the January 26, 1847, account of expenditures from July 1845 to June 1846 also indicates that slaves were primarily used in menial positions. The voucher states that $1160.49 was spent on miscellaneous slave labor, while $346.35 was spent on slave workmanship (Snell 1959a). There is no evidence to suggest that these slaves were actually working on guns (Shackel and Larsen in press).

Armory records reveal that free African Americans were also employed by the armory. A voucher from January 1842 listed John Butler, a free African-American, as a lock keeper for the armory canal. The same voucher indicates that another free black man, Thomas Spriggs, was a wagoner. Other pay records show Jeremiah Harris, a plasterer, as frequently working on government projects (Snell 1959a). John Gust, a stonemason and contractor, is one of the most striking and successful examples of free African-Americans working for the armory. Armory pay records from 1824 to 1831 provide copious evidence of Gust and his crew quarrying, hauling, paving, building embankments, and laying stone (Shackel and Larsen in press; Snell 1959a; National Archives, Chief of Ordnance, Springfield Armory, Record Group, 1830–31 8R:3).

By at least 1850, Superintendent John Symington realized that the employment of slaves in the United States Armory did not coincide efficiently with the wage labor system. He noted that while "masters or agents signed the rolls" for the slaves' labor, it would be desirable to abolish this system "in order to have uniformity throughout" (HFNHP Microfilms 1850).

While the nation industrialized and became firmly rooted in and adhered to the standardizing and disciplining requirements of industry, bondsmen and free African-Americans were increasingly pushed to the periphery of industrial capitalism, and they became a support group for the new industrial culture. Even though the African-American's economic role changed through the nineteenth century, ideological mechanisms ensured their subordinate status in an industrializing society and disenfranchised them from the growing dominant industrial culture. Many African-Americans created varying meanings and uses for goods from the mainstream as they participated in the culture of capitalism on their own terms (Fields 1985).

CONSUMERISM: THE RISE OF ROMANTICISM AND THE DEMISE OF REPUBLICANISM

Due to poor transportation networks, many towns and cities inland from the east coast ports, including Harpers Ferry, participated in a market economy in a very limited way until the 1830s. As Ross noted, market possibilities expanded with the construction of roads, railroads, and canals (Ross, 1985:30–31):

> While the broadening of transportation networks and markets brought greater wealth to large numbers of citizens, the expansion of commercial capitalism within commerce, manufacturing, and the crafts gradually undermined earlier working-class sensibility of a mutualistic and cooperative economy.

The economic sectors became very distinctive and highly specialized and independent of one another. While traditional craftsmen saw the development of industrial discipline as a symbol of dependency, other younger workers saw the new technology as an opportunity and a chance for upward mobility. Classical republicanism discouraged the excessive accumulation and display of wealth. The preservation of the republic was dependent upon citizens to hold an approximate equality of wealth (Ross 1985:16). As the republican ideals faded, however, consumer patterns changed, and people accumulated material wealth. This phenomenon is easily visible in the archaeological record. Archaeologists working on east coast urban sites that have an occupation from 1790 to 1840 have encountered massive deposits of ceramics, and to some extent glassware (e.g., Agnew 1988; Herman 1985; Mrozowski 1984). The same pattern is also true in Harpers Ferry (see Halchin 1994; Shackel 1993a, 1994a). Many scholars have associated these deposits with changes in households or life cycles. These changing consumption patterns may also be explained by the declining influence of republican ideology and the rise of Romanticism.

Romanticism served to facilitate the emergence of modern consumer behavior in the late eighteenth and early nineteenth centuries. It legitimated the consumer ethic. Colin Campbell (1987:8) questions the long-standing explanation of describing the new industrial society as a product of the Protestant ethic. The Protestant ethic is production-oriented, and there is no emphasis on consumerism. In order to ignite the industrial revolution and the new consumer society, a desire for new consumer goods needs to be created. Campbell (1987:31) notes:

> Puritanism, even today, is recognized as a tradition of thought which, out of a basis in intense moral and religious concern, condemns all idleness, luxury and indulgence, espousing in contrast an ethic of asceticism and industry— and this, it must be assumed, was the primary source of the moral objections levelled against the new propensity to consume.

Campbell (1987:31) continues by noting that the consumer revolution was carried out by the section in society with the strongest Puritan traditions, such as the middle classes, artisans, and yeomanry. This consumer behavior would most likely have incurred disapproval from a Puritan outlook. Therefore, he claims that there were two ethics, a consumer ethic and a Protestant ethic, that coexisted.

Consumerism and a demand for nonessentials, and leisure and leisure-time pursuits, are closely linked to the reading of novels, the demand for fiction, and the cult of romantic love. This phenomenon was almost exclusively a middle-class phenomenon (Campbell 1987:34). Since women's role was increasingly being redesigned into that of domestic engineers, especially in the middle classes, women became the proponents of this new Romantic consumerism.

The spirit of modern consumerism is more than materialistic; it is a growth of modern, autonomous, imaginative indulgence. Individuals do not seek satisfaction from products; rather, they seek self-illusory experiences that they construct from their associated meanings: "Imaginative pleasure-seeking to which the product image lends itself, 'real' consumption being largely a result of this 'mentalistic' hedonism" (Campbell 1987:89). Campbell (1987:89) continues:

> The idea that contemporary consumers have an insatiable desire to acquire objects represents a serious misunderstanding of the mechanism which impels people to want goods. Their basic motivation is the desire to experience in reality the pleasurable dramas which they have already enjoyed in imagination, and each 'new' product is seen as offering a possibility of realizing this ambition.

Puritanism was hostile to this thought of opulence. Anything that was seen as not glorifying God or being useful to humans, and as serving only to promote human pride, was seen as sinful. Romanticism legitimated the search for pleasure as good in itself and not merely of value because it restores the individual to an optimum efficiency. Romanticism ensured the widespread basic taste for novelty, together with a supply of "original" products necessary for modern fashion to operate (Campbell 1987:201). Continuing this line of thought, Campbell (1987:216) wrote:

> Romantics were not necessarily wrong in assuming that people could be morally improved through the provision of cultural products that yielded pleasure. Nor indeed were they wrong in seeing this process as one which relied upon individual dreaming about a more perfect world. Such activity can reasonably be viewed as creating opportunities for the generation of idealism.

Romanticism encourages people to pursue imaginative pleasures. In North America, the Romantic movement took the form of transcendentalism as expressed through the writings of Emerson, Melville, Thoreau, and Poe. They criticized the immoral nature of Franklin's utilitarianism and the ideals of republicanism (Barbour 1979. Campbell 1987:218; Wyllie 1954:140).

In many cases, when economics allowed, middle-class white women spent most of their time in the home devoting themselves to household management in what Tilley and Scott (1978) call a "family consumer economy." Women, who were becoming increasingly more involved in household management, were also the prominent readers of romantic and sentimental fiction. They also became associated with activities with Romantic values, such as child care, welfare work, and fine art. The family unit no longer served as a productive unit, but primarily as a consumer of goods. Household goods and foods prepared for family consumption became symbols of domesticity (Ryan 1981; Wall 1985, 1994) and a reflection of the growth of Romanticism (Campbell 1987).

Men therefore became the principal carriers of "puritan" values and women the carriers of "romantic" values. The Puritan and Romantic ideals represent contrasting models, but they were incorporated into one system of modernity. (Campbell 1987:224–25).

AN ARCHAEOLOGY OF HARPERS FERRY

Since the 1980s, the work of Eric Wolf (1982) has stimulated many researchers to rediscover the uses of history in anthropology. Recently, Bruce Trigger (1991) has called for the rediscovery of historical approaches in archaeology. It is the rediscovery of historical anthropology that has facilitated historical archaeologists' use of social context and meanings in their analyses. An understanding of social context reveals the complex situations in which goods operated and can therefore provide an understanding of the inequalities produced in society, especially since the advent of the industrial revolution and the creation of the Romantic philosophy.

Historical archaeological studies of nineteenth-century urban settings have also increased since the 1980s (e.g., see Dickens 1982). Generally, these studies focus on issues related to the development of hierarchies, changing social relations, and the existence and naturalization of inequalities (see Paynter 1989). On a city or regional scale, archaeologists are asking questions that address the relationship of space to social inequality in areas such as the Connecticut River valley; Alexandria, Virginia, Lowell, Massachusetts; and Harpers Ferry, West Virginia (Beaudry and Mrozowski 1989; Cressey et al. 1982; Paynter 1982; Shackel in press). The growth and development of neighborhoods and settlement systems in New York City is also discussed (see Rothschild 1990). Others examine large-scale land modification and its connection to urban development and commerce (Kelso and Beaudry 1990; Mrozowski 1987; Ostrogorsky 1987). Issues of ethnicity have been addressed in the development of the West as well as urban centers in the East (DeCunzo 1982; Praetzellis et al. 1987; Staski 1990). Others explore diet (Henry 1987) and the relationship of diet to dining practices (Lucas 1994b). Changing perceptions of health and hygiene have been discussed for areas such as the mill town of Lowell, Massachusetts, and the armory town of Harpers Ferry (Ford 1994; Larsen 1994a; Mrozowski et al. 1989). Archaeologists have also addressed issues of domestic reform movements in New England (Spencer-Wood 1991), as well as gender relations in urban areas such as New York and Annapolis, Maryland (Little 1993; Wall 1991, 1994).

This book addresses the interrelationship between changing work relations and domestic life. I examine historical context and material remains of armory workers' households to provide a cross section of early industrial life in Harpers Ferry. One archaeological site was inhabited by two different master armorer households, one from approximately 1821 through 1830 and the other from 1830 through 1850. The master armorer was responsible for the daily management of the gun factory. The other site was inhabited by armory workers and their households. From about 1821 through 1841, pieceworkers probably inhabited the structure, while later heads of households, from 1841 through 1852, usually consisted of mechanics and wage laborers. Excavations of these house lots provide insight into how domestic relations were transformed within the context of changing work discipline.

The various households that occupied these armory dwellings are easily discernible in the archaeological record, since documented floods are visible in the soil stratigraphy, and they neatly separate the different occupational zones. Documented construction of armory dwellings also provides exact chronological markers. The multiple and changing uses of these house lots serve as a microcosm of the changing lifestyles of various groups of people and how they dealt with the conflicting republican and Romantic ideologies and the onslaught of the industrial revolution.

"The Most Eligible Spot on the Whole River"

—GEORGE WASHINGTON

Harpers Ferry—The Early Years

EARLY SETTLEMENT

Harpers Ferry is situated at the gap in the Blue Ridge Mountains at the confluence of the Shenandoah and Potomac rivers. In 1733, landowner Lord Fairfax allowed Peter Stevens to settle on lands and to establish a ferry that crossed the Potomac River. Stevens's appearance is part of a larger migration to the lower Shenandoah valley and western territory by German, Quaker, and Scotch-Irish from southeastern Pennsylvania and the tidewater region seeking agricultural and commercial opportunities. The ferry operations facilitated travel through the Blue Ridge Mountains as the area became a major nodal point for two major transportation routes, one connecting Frederick and Winchester, the other connecting Charles Town and Antietam (Gutheim 1949; Noffsinger 1958:5) (Figure 8).

After 14 years of squatting on Lord Fairfax's land, Stevens sold Robert Harper his log cabin, corn patch, and ferry equipment (Figure 9). Harper subsequently received three patents from Lord Fairfax that allowed him to control lands on both sides of the river to facilitate his ferry operations (Noffsinger 1958:6, 221–223). Harper originally occupied Stevens's cabin, but he later constructed his dwelling a mile down the Shenandoah River near his gristmill and sawmill. He later began the construction of a tavern at the rivers' confluence, but he died in 1782 before it was completed. His property was divided between Sarah Harper (the only child of his brother Joseph) and Robert Griffith (a relative of his wife's). Sarah Harper married into the Wager family, and they owned what later became the town of Harpers Ferry (Barry 1988; Noffsinger 1958).

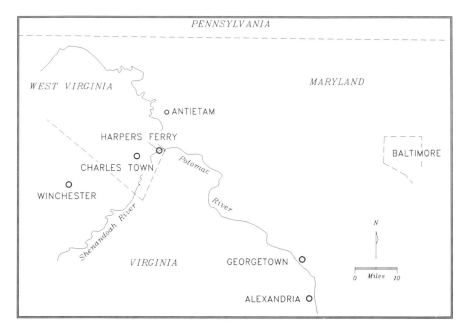

Figure 8. Location of Harpers Ferry. (Drawn by John W. Ravenhorst)

Figure 9. A view down the Potomac at the confluence with the Shenandoah showing the early ferry operations prior to armory construction, by William Strickland, circa 1795. (Courtesy of the New-York Historical Society, New York City, HF1195)

Thomas Jefferson traveled through northern Virginia in October 1783 to investigate and write about the region's resources. He came to Harpers Ferry and in his *Notes on the State of Virginia* wrote that it was "one of the most stupendous scenes in nature" (Jefferson 1954[1789]:45). George Washington was also enamored with the setting of Harpers Ferry, but for a very different reason. From the end of the French and Indian War, George Washington speculated on land along the Potomac River (Mitchell 1977:59, 127). Washington became deeply involved in the affairs of the Potowmack Company and dedicated himself to improving navigation along the river. Such improvements, he believed, would attract trade to the ports of Alexandria and Georgetown and would create economic growth in the new Federal City and the Potomac valley region (M. R. Smith 1977:27–28). It was also a place that could not be easily reached by enemy troops.

DEVELOPMENT OF AN ARMORY TOWN

Prior to the American Revolution, England supplied arms to the colonies, and France became a major supplier during the war. During the 1790s, the new nation was in a dangerous situation. Spain was on the southern and western boarder, holding Florida and the Louisiana Territory, and England controlled Canada. The English often encouraged Native Americans to attack bordering neighbor settlements and supplied them with arms. In 1794, England and the United States signed a treaty of peace, but the French claimed that it violated the Franco-American alliance of 1778. Tensions grew between the two countries, and Washington was eventually called from retirement in order to prepare for any new hostilities (Brown 1968:9–10).

This political unrest threatened the stability of the newly formed nation, so in 1794 the United States Congress legislated the establishment of armories for the manufacture and storage of arms. President Washington was determined to build an armory at Harpers Ferry, and he received endorsements from Georgetown and Alexandria merchants who stood to profit from hinterland trade (M. R. Smith 1977:29–30). In a letter, Washington noted that Harpers Ferry was the "most eligible spot on the whole river in every point of view . . ." (HFNHP photostats 1795). French military engineer Colonel Stephen Rochfontaine, who studied the site for placement of a future armory, disagreed with Washington. He claimed that the area lacked convenient grounds to establish manufacturing, and power would be unpredictable since the area tended to flood (C. Gilbert et al. 1993:3.8; HFNHP photostats

1795). Washington prevailed, and the acquisition of all lands in Harpers Ferry necessary for construction of the armory was completed by 1796. By agreement, the Wager family kept a 6-acre reserve (known as the Wager Reserve) adjacent to the armory, as well as the rights to monopolize mercantile trade. The Wagers also retained a 3/4-acre ferry concession and the rights to transport all traffic across the Potomac (M. R. Smith 1977:147) (Figure 10).

In 1798, Congress appropriated funds for the development of federal arsenals and armories. Construction of the armory began in 1799, although the government was continually plagued with the lack of skilled mechanics and laborers. A temporary force of 100 soldiers under the command of Major General Charles C. Pinckney was stationed at Harpers Ferry to protect the town from possible invading forces. Soldiers also provided necessary labor for construction of the armory canal.

Early manufacturing did not proceed smoothly. Though the armory canal was completed by 1802, it often leaked and slowed production. Poor health conditions continually plagued armorers and their families. The government did not provide sufficient housing to accommodate all its workers. Armorers could not construct dwellings on the Wager Reserve; therefore, most workers constructed dwellings on the low-lying riverbanks because inland areas were too hilly or mountainous to build on. These areas were havens for various diseases, to which many of the inhabitants were prone. Many armorers lacked housing and, for the lack of any other alternative, slept in the attics of machine shops (M. R. Smith 1977:137–138). In order to accommodate these workers, the superintendent often purchased blankets for the single men, who were given last priority for housing (HFNHP microfilms, 1818a).

In 1803, Thomas Jefferson commissioned the Lewis and Clark expedition, and much of the equipment was made or procured at Harpers Ferry. Lewis wrote to Jefferson that "my rifles, tomahawks, & knives are preparing at Harpers Ferry" (quoted in Brown 1968:30). Also made for the campaign at Harpers Ferry was a collapsible iron canoe (Brown 1968:30).

In the early years of the nineteenth century, the town developed quickly. An observer described the town in 1805 as consisting of a post office and about 15 houses (Joseph Scott 1805). By 1810, it had "a good tavern, several large stores for goods, a library, one physician, and a professor of the English language" (Vale [quoted in Noffsinger 1958:20]). The town had increased to 700 people and included 197 armory workers and 12 workshops. The neighborhood adjacent to the armory and located on the Wager Reserve developed into a commercial area. The Wagers constructed the Harpers Ferry Hotel in 1803 and

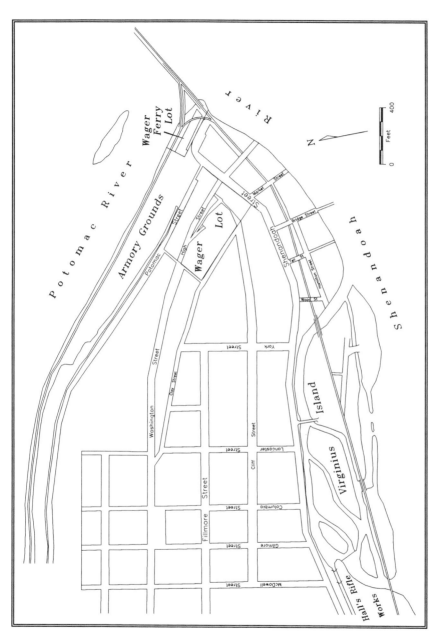

Figure 10. A mid-nineteenth-century map of Harpers Ferry showing the Wager lot, Wager ferry lot, armory grounds, Virginius Island, and Hall's Rifle Works. (Drawn by John W. Ravenhorst)

eventually leased the structure to various innkeepers. While the armory developed on the Potomac side of the town, the area along the Shenandoah shore contained stables and was used for grazing the armory horses (HFNHP microfilms 1813a). Houses were scattered throughout the town, and construction conformed to the topography rather than to any formal plan.

In the 1810s, the town developed many urban characteristics. Entrepreneurs continually petitioned the government to allow them to construct businesses on public lands in order to serve the growing armory community and related businesses. For instance, one tavern keeper asked to construct a tavern and hotel, since Harpers Ferry was "now a resort of many travellers" and a good house of entertainment was wanted (HFNHP microfilms 1915a). During this era, about 86 dwellings of various sizes and different forms were constructed without much attention to their placement throughout the town. Workshops and two arsenal buildings were also erected. Harpers Ferry developed as a major regional spectacle as the industrial works thrived. One person wrote, "There are a large number of respectable persons who come here at particular seasons of the year to view the natural curiosities and the public works" (HFNHP microfilms 1915b). Another observer described the armory (Anonymous 1821):

> ... the public buildings of the workshops built of brick, two stories high, in two straight lines, leaving between them an area of about 70 ft., and forming a handsome street. Above these buildings a canal, at the head of which is a dam, this water for use of the shops. The public buildings are thirteen— eleven of brick, one stone, one frame.

The commercial district, based on the Wager Reserve, developed along Shenandoah and High Streets. The area consisted of one warehouse and a store on the ferry lot and one hotel and five stores along Shenandoah Street. One commercial building was located on High Street (C. Gilbert et al. 1993:3.24). The Wager Reserve was adjacent to the armory grounds, and tavern keepers sold liquor to armorers, who were "frequently in a state of intoxication" (HFNHP microfilms 1816).

West of the Lower Town commercial district, private manufacturing blossomed with the exploitation of waterpower on Virginius Island. Virginius Island was not conveyed to the United States in 1796, nor was it controlled by the Wager family. The 1751 land grant to Harper did not include the island; therefore, the island could not be claimed by either the government or the Wagers. Since neither entity could claim ownership, the land was squatted, and Armory Superintendent Stubblefield eventually acquired the land. He subdivided and sold the island, making a substantial profit. Sparsely inhabited in the 1820s and early 1830s, the island developed as a mill village and contained industries that catered to the armory, such as a machine shop, sawmill, oilmill, gristmill, and tannery. The industries focused on local markets, both domestic and armory-related, making machinery, tools, and replacement parts for the latter.

FAMILY TIES AND INTRUDERS

During the early decades of the nineteenth century, the Beckham, Stephenson, Stubblefield, and Wager families dominated almost every aspect of daily life in Harpers Ferry. Armisted Beckham served as master armorer, and his brothers were wealthy merchants, entrepreneurs, and landowners. Fontaine Beckham attained even higher standing in the community when he married the daughter of Major James Stephenson. Stephenson served ten years as a Berkeley County magistrate, six years in the Virginia House of Delegates, and eight years in the United States House of Representatives. At Harpers Ferry, Stephenson operated an inn on the Wager Reserve on Shenandoah Street and owned a distillery with Stubblefield. His influence as a well-respected politician played a major role in facilitating the Beckham–Stubblefield operations of the armory. To complete the connection between the town's power brokers, Mrs. Stubblefield's niece, whom she raised from childhood, married Edward Wager, the eldest son in the Wager family. While Edward helped to manage the family's business, he served as the chief clerk to the superintendent at the Harpers Ferry Armory. Together, these four families formed a powerful oligarchy, referred to by some contemporaries as the "Junto." They had every intention of keeping the status quo so that they could monopolize and dominate Harpers Ferry life (M. R. Smith 1977:145–149). Laborers who did not support the Junto, or did not remain silent, risked unemployment and harassment by other armory employees.

Generally, production at the armory was done by skilled craftsmen during the first several decades of the facility's operations. This task-oriented production required the armory worker to have a high degree of manual skill and knowledge of many different aspects of gun making. While armorers were adept at the production of the entire gun, a form of division of labor existed whereby artisans made a particular part of the gun, such as lock, stock, mounting, or barrel. One of the master armorer's principal duties included coordinating the output of each part and determining work assignments so that an equal number of parts would be made simultaneously. In 1807, Harpers Ferry gun manufacturing consisted of six separate branches: barrel making, lock forging, lock filing, brazing, stocking, and finishing (M. R. Smith 1977:78–79). During the late 1810s and through the next several decades, piecework became a prominent form of production in the armory. One armorer became responsible for the production of one part or completing one stage in the production of a gun component. Prior to 1816, the two national armories made no effort to standardize their products. In fact, many of the pre-1816 weapons show a great deal of variation, often reflecting the whims and skills of the artisan rather than deviation from an official plan (Brown 1968:13–14).

During this era, John Hall, an inventor and manufacturer from Maine, established workshops west of the Lower Town commercial district. He was contracted by the United States government to produce breechloading rifles comprised of interchangeable parts at $25 each. Hall's manufacturing ideas endangered what remained of craft production and threatened to make armorers tenders of machines. Threatened by this intruder, who could eventually change the work method in the armory, Stubblefield wrote the Ordnance Department: "[I] think [the rifles] will cost much more than $25 a piece. If Mr. Hall would agree to make them at $25 at his own establishment it would in my opinion save the govt. $10,000 in that number of rifles" (HFNHP 1819a). The Ordnance Department ignored Stubblefield's request and urged him to accommodate Hall and his operations.

When Hall arrived at Harpers Ferry, he consulted with Stubblefield regarding the equipment and materials that he would need to start production. Stubblefield offered him some of his most decrepit buildings, including a dilapidated sawmill operated by Robert Harper in the 1780s. Hall and Stubblefield estimated that $4000–$5000 was needed from the Ordnance Department to update the facilities and provide Hall with the necessary machinery to begin production. Unfortunately, they were told that "the erection of any new buildings is out of the question as it was not included in the appropriations and there is no money to spare" (Letters: Wadsworth to Stubblefield 22 July 1820 and 11 Oct 1820 [quoted in Huntington 1972:29]). Many of the buildings that Hall obtained from the armory were old and in need of repair, and they did not follow any systematic plan (Figure 11). Some were described as in a "state of decay as renders it disreputable in its appearance, and uncomfortable & unwholesome to the workmen" (Letter: Hall to Bomford 5 October 1835 [quoted in Huntington 1972:96]).

Between 1821 and 1827, Hall created a makeshift operation and developed an impressive array of new machinery for manufacturing.

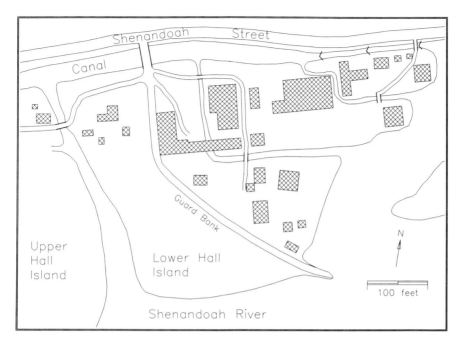

Figure 11. A plan of Hall's Rifle Works, circa 1835. (Drawn by John W. Ravenhorst)

He had to make do with only a few metalworking machines and limited workspace. Each machine had to be readjusted by a machinist each time a different piece needed to be manufactured, causing a delay between the manufacture of each piece and the rifle's eventual assembly. Hall completed an entire run of about 1000 parts before the machines could be readjusted for the manufacture of another piece. This inefficient process meant that machine-tenders often had to be released from their duties for a time until the machines were set to make the next piece. To complicate matters and increase Hall's frustrations even further, the raceway system and water supply were insufficient to operate all the machinery simultaneously. "Whereas it took eight months or more before Hall could turn out his first finished arm after starting production, the Musket factory could arrange its work so that all branches of the business progressed simultaneously, and completed arms could be produced in a short space of time" (Huntington 1972:36).

An 1826 inspection of Hall's rifles noted that he successfully completed the first weapon with fully interchangeable parts ever made in the United States. The manufacturing was completed without skilled

craftsmen tending machinery. Hall noted that his machines were so ac-
curate that they could be run by a "boy of but eighteen years of age, who
never did a stroke of work in his life" (quoted in M. R. Smith 1977:239).

During the inspection, 100 rifles were disassembled, and the parts
were scattered "promiscuously over a large joiner's bench." Parts from
the new rifle were placed on the new stocks. As the rifles were reassembled, they were handed to the commissioners, who "were unable to dis-
cover any inaccuracy in any of their parts fitting each other." The
commissioners expressed a "doubt whether the best workmen that may
be selected from any armory, with the aid of the best machines in the
elsewhere, could, in a whole life, make a hundred rifles or muskets that
would, after being promiscuously mixed together, fit each other with
the exact nicety that is to be found in those manufactured by Hall"
(quoted in Brown 1968:70).

By late 1828, Colonel Bomford of the Ordnance Department recognized the success and popularity of Hall's rifle. Breechloading arms
were increasingly being requested by state militias throughout the
country. Since Hall could produce only about 1000 arms a year at Harpers Ferry, Bomford decided to expand production by contracting with
Simeon North for the production of more rifles.

Many armory workers considered Hall an intruder and a threat to
the status quo of craft production. He often felt threatened by the local
townspeople, and on occasion he wrote about the necessity of training
others to perform his tasks in case of his death, "an event not improb-
able anywhere at my time of life, and still less in this neighborhood"
(HFNHP microfilms 1831). The Junto worked to gather congressional
support to expose the high cost of the project in an attempt to withhold
congressional support for Hall's project. "In 1839 Superintendent Rust,
a proponent of the craft system, wrote 'I avail myself of the present
occasion, to state it as my opinion, as I have often done before, that
arms cannot be made, that will interchange, & at the same time fit
closely and accurately, at a reasonable price, & without sacrificing other
& greater advantages—and the sooner the attempt to accomplish it be
dispensed with, the better—this opinion is almost invariably enter-
tained by competent workmen & judges, at this Armory" (Letter: Lucas
to Bomford, 6 September 1839 [quoted in Huntington 1972:79]).

While the Junto made life miserable for Hall by threatening to withhold funding and harassing him in the streets, they failed to discourage
him. Hall's breechloaders continued to be produced in the Harpers Ferry
factories after his departure in 1840 due to ill health. His contribution to
arms manufacturing eventually led the way to the manufacture of the
Model 1842, the first musket developed with interchangeable parts.

Hall's innovations revolutionized manufacturing on a global scale, and manufacturing with interchangeable parts became known as the "American system of manufacture" (Huntington 1972; M. R. Smith 1991).

NEW TRANSPORTATION, INDUSTRIAL GROWTH, AND REDESIGNING THE ARMORY

The growth of private and public industries was stimulated by the development of new forms of transportation, as it heightened Harpers Ferry's importance as a center between the Ohio and Shenandoah valleys and the East. Linking Harpers Ferry to regional and national networks was instrumental to its continued economic growth (Everhart 1952:22).

One of the first developments in transportation was the development of the road system. The Harpers Ferry, Charles Town, and Smithfield Turnpike Company, organized in 1830, connected Harpers Ferry with the West. That same year, the Frederick and Harpers Ferry Turnpike Company constructed a toll road linking those two towns. In 1834, two stagecoach companies competed in Harpers Ferry—the Baltimore and Winchester Mail Stage Company and the People's Line of Troy Coaches (Snell 1973:11–13). As a result of these transportation systems, Harpers Ferry's service industry expanded. The *Virginia Free Press* (VFP 8 August 1831) noted

> that the fine road from Charles Town to Harpers Ferry, passing directly by this mill, is now very nearly completed, by which many of the farmers, particularly those quite near thereto, will be enabled for several months in the year to carry 100–125 bushels of wheat at a single load—this too will be a great advantage.

The arrival of the Chesapeake and Ohio Canal in 1833 offered cheaper transportation for people and goods. By December 1, 1834, the Baltimore & Ohio Railroad was completed to a point opposite Harpers Ferry on the Maryland side of the Potomac, thus reducing travel to Baltimore to 6 hours. Four months later, in March 1835, the Winchester and Potomac Railroad made its first trip from Winchester to Harpers Ferry. In 1837 the Baltimore & Ohio Railroad constructed a bridge across the Potomac River that allowed the joining of the head of the Shenandoah valley with the main Baltimore & Ohio line to the east (Bushong 1941:83–84) (Figure 12). Harpers Ferry became a regular stopping place for passengers to dine and lodge. By the 1840s, the

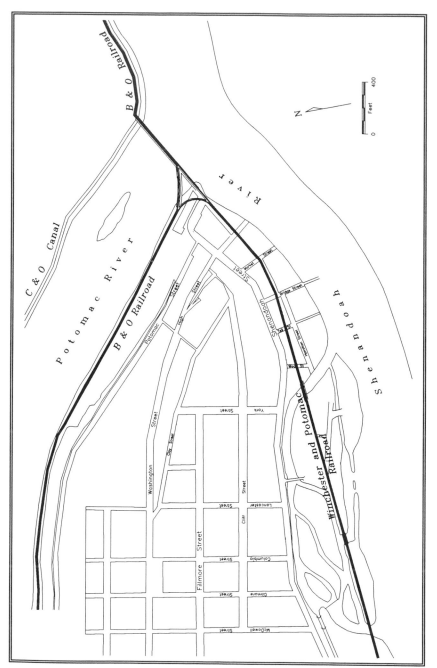

Figure 12. Map showing the major transportation routes that connected Harpers Ferry to major trade routes. (Drawn by John W. Ravenhorst)

hotels located nearest the junction of the Baltimore & Ohio and Winchester and Potomac Railroads thrived. Those more distant either closed or converted to other mercantile functions (Snell 1973:14–15).

The diversification of the economy of Harpers Ferry was stimulated not only the increase of transportation networks, but also by the demise of the Wager family monopoly over their 6 acres in Lower Town Harpers Ferry. In 1834, James Bates Wager found himself in financial difficulties. In order to settle his affairs, the reservation was divided into thirds and portions auctioned in 1836. The most dramatic increase of business occurred immediately after the selling of the Wager property (Snell 1973:19). Despite the auction, the Wager family still controlled a large portion of the town. In fact, over 20 years later, Gerald B. Wager and a fellow townsperson, Noah H. Swayne, who married a Wager, owned about one third of the town (Snell 1973:8).

Lower Town had 7 businesses in 1825, 18 in 1835, and 33 in 1840. Eventually, business establishments increased to 40 in 1850 and 43 in 1860. With the increase of businesses, there was a tremendous increase of available consumer goods. The number of dry-goods stores, which comprised the greatest number of businesses, more than doubled in the 1830s, from 3 to 7. The number of these establishments rose to 8 in 1840 and peaked at 10 in 1850 (Snell 1973:19).

The Winchester and Potomac Railroad ran through Virginius Island, and it allowed entrepreneurs to develop large-scale industries and produce goods that could be shipped to regional and national markets. For instance, the gristmill originally served as a custom mill, catering to the local population. It was transformed into a merchant mill, probably with upgraded machinery, supplying the larger regional and national markets (*Jefferson County Deed Book* 14, 3 September 1825:43).

As the gristmill thrived through the first half of the nineteenth century, waterpower and close connections to the railroad line encouraged the development of another industry—cotton factories. The Harpers Ferry and Shenandoah Manufacturing Company changed the labor orientation on the island from predominantly craft to wage labor. The owners sought to exploit regional and larger markets. A second and smaller cottonmill was leased to Valley Mill upriver and on Virginius Island (Bergstresser 1988:13). During this era, Virginius Island grew to 182 inhabitants living in 28 dwellings (Figure 13). Over 20% were foreign born, most of them probably weavers from England, Ireland, and Scotland. A small proportion of the inhabitants on the island consisted of slaves and free African Americans (Johnson and Barker 1993:38–41).

Figure 13. Lithograph of Virginius Island. (Sachse Co. 1857, HF490)

In the 1840s, major revisions of the armory labor and manufacturing systems were under way. The facilities contrasted sharply with the orderly layout of the New England factory system. Most of the armory buildings were unsuited for the implementation of a division of labor because they lacked architectural and functional unity. In 1844, Superintendent Major John Symington, an engineer, created a plan for the armory's renovation of architecture, town plan, and labor system. As part of the plan, Symington demolished Hall's Rifle Works, filled in the lands, and erected a new rifle factory. Other buildings were also replaced in the musket factory on the Shenandoah River.

Along with the new buildings came the introduction of new machinery and a new work discipline. Armory workers protested these innovations, fearing that they would become tenders of machinery, which is how they saw their New England counterparts (VFP 31 March 1842:3). The armorers' discontent did not prevent the reorganization of the daily customs of workers and the rebuilding of the factory. By the 1850s, 25 new structures were built, all according to a unified architectural plan (M. R. Smith 1977:275–276). Even the weapons were manufactured with interchangeable parts. In 1851, the two national armories were tested for their interchangeability. Parts matched their counterparts from the opposing armory with great success, although the front end of the lock plates differed slightly. Interchangeability was tested once again in 1852 in Harpers Ferry, the testing being done this time because of the opportunity presented by a flood that submerged 20,000 stands of arms, of which 9000 were the Model 1842 muskets. The muskets were " 'completely dismantled, their parts being thrown into great masses,' and after the parts were cleaned and dried, 9,000 muskets were put together from the parts" (Brown 1968:93). Mass production and interchangeability were now part of the daily manufacturing process in the armory.

By the 1850s, Harpers Ferry was a sprawling industrial town containing the United States Armory and Arsenal, along with private manufacturing establishments, such as a textile mill, flourmill, sawmill, iron foundry, machine shop, and carriage manufactory, as well as over 40 mercantile shops (D. Gilbert 1984:1). An 1855 account described the town (Edwards [quoted in Noffsinger 1958:43]):

> The village is compactly, though irregularly built around the base of a hill, and is the center of considerable trade. It contains four or five churches, several manufactories and flour mills, a United States armory in which about 250 hands are employed, producing, among other articles, some 10,000 muskets annually, and a national arsenal. In the latter are continually stored from 80,000 to 90,000 stand of arms.

JOHN BROWN: TERRIBLE SAINT

While private and public industrial enterprises thrived in the late 1850s in Harpers Ferry, the small industrial town became a key component in John Brown's militant abolitionist plans. Brown had built a reputation as being a great abolitionist while fighting in the Kansas Territory Civil War, and in 1858 he revealed his secret plan of attacking the South to a select few, including Frederick Douglass and Franklin Sanborn, two staunch abolitionists. He would first attack Harpers Ferry, where thousands of weapons were stored after their manufacture in the armory. He believed that once he attacked, slaves would revolt and join his cause. As slaves revolted to join his cause in Harpers Ferry, he would arm them. If his plan failed, he believed, it would at least serve to consolidate Northerners' emotions for their hatred for slavery and thus promote a crisis (Douglass 1881; Sanborn 1885:440ff; Oates 1970:224–279).

Brown rented a farm on the Maryland side of the Potomac River, and on the night of October 16, 1859, Brown and his party of 21 men

Figure 14. Marines storming the engine house to capture John Brown and his men. (Courtesy of Harpers Ferry National Historical Park, HF222)

approached Harpers Ferry. They easily overpowered the armory guard and captured the federal arsenal with relative ease, taking hostages. The next day, Brown was on the armory grounds, but refused to escape when he had the chance. Trapped in the armory with a growing and increasingly intoxicated crowd gathering around the complex, Brown, his volunteers, and the hostages took refuge in the armory's engine house, which later became known as John Brown's Fort. A group of marines under the command of Colonel Robert E. Lee finally overthrew Brown at the engine house (Figure 14). Not a single slave had come to Harpers Ferry. Some of the slaves Brown forcibly liberated during his raid refused to fight with him; others escaped and returned to their owners (Anderson 1972[1861]:36; Hinton 1894:311ff, 709ff; Oates 1970:293–300; Villard 1910:440).

Brown was hanged for treason on December 2, 1859. During his imprisonment, Northern abolitionists intensified the John Brown martyr myth, and they used his image in their antislavery campaigns. John Brown's attack on Harpers Ferry did much to polarize this country on the issue of slavery. Scholars claim that his actions were among the most notable deeds to have ignited the Civil War.

Figure 15. Sketch from *Harpers Weekly*, April 18, 1861, depicting the burning of the United States Arsenal at Harpers Ferry. (Courtesy of Harpers Ferry National Historical Park, HF533)

HARPERS FERRY DURING THE CIVIL WAR

After the bombardment of Fort Sumter and Lincoln's call to raise 75,000 troops in April 1861, Virginia seceded from the Union. Seizing the armory and arsenal at Harpers Ferry became a major objective for the Confederacy. Lieutenant Roger Jones, stationed at Harpers Ferry with 50 regulars and 15 volunteers, feared that an advancing force of 360 Confederates would capture the town. Before these forces arrived on May 18, 1861, Jones set fire to the federal factory buildings and abandoned the town. The arsenal, along with 15,000 guns, was destroyed, although the townspeople, in an attempt to salvage their livelihood, saved the machinery (Figure 15). The local newspaper, *Spirit of Jefferson* (SoJ 4 May 1861:2), claimed the burning of the arsenals and workshop was a criminal act. It noted that the event would be remembered as being similar to John Brown's Raid. John Brown, the paper claimed, deceived the community under the assumed name of John Smith, saying that April 18, 1861, would henceforth be associated with Lieutenant Jones of the United States Army "as the very prince of smooth faced deceivers." The newspaper also claimed that the "demon of destruction is abroad along our entire border. If the first fortnight witnesses such destruction, what are we to expect from the northern vandals if they be not checked?" The Confederates shipped the armory machinery to Richmond and Fayettesville, where it was used to make arms for the South (Noffsinger 1958:45–46; Snell 1960b:5).

Private industry suffered in Harpers Ferry as well. Even though Abraham Herr, the main proprietor of the Virginius Island flourmill owned four slaves in 1860, he supported Union troops when they arrived in Harpers Ferry in 1861. The commanding officer ordered the flourmill partially destroyed to prevent Confederate troops from using it. When the Confederates arrived several weeks later, they forced Herr's partner, James Welch, to torch the mill. This action, they claimed, was in retaliation for wheat donated by Herr to the Union army (Barry 1988:131–134; Johnson and Barker 1993).

Southern forces occupied the town for 2 months, using private buildings for barracks and hospitals. They vacated the town on June 14, 1861, burning the B&O railroad bridge and the musket factory shops. The B&O railroad bridge was destroyed and rebuilt nine times during the war. The Confederates returned shortly after and burned the trestle bridge that crossed the Shenandoah River and the rifle factory that lined the same river (Marmion 1959).

From 1861 to 1863, Harpers Ferry was occupied alternately by Union and Confederate troops and at times was left unoccupied Joseph Barry, a local historian, characterized the town as a "no-man's land" (Barry 1988[1903]; also see Snell 1960b). The town was mostly deserted, and portions were in a ruinous state (Drickamer and Drickamer 1987:124). Annie P. Marmion, a resident of Harpers Ferry, stated in her memoirs that the town's population during nonoccupied times declined from a prewar total of 2500 to "less than 20 families" (Marmion 1959:4). Food and safety during these periods were the major concerns: "The great objects in life were to procure something to eat and keep yourself out of sight by day, and your lamps or rather candle light hidden by night, lights of every kind being regarded as signals to the Rebels were usually rewarded by a volley of guns" (Marmion 1959:7).

In 1862, a Union soldier patrolling the Maryland shore was killed by a Confederate sniper in Harpers Ferry. Union troops retaliated by burning 14 buildings in town, including hotels, stores, taverns, warehouses, the B&O depot, office, and restaurant, and the toll house (Figure 16). The land mass at the confluence of the Shenandoah and Potomac rivers, which once thrived with commerce, was a barren wasteland (Barry 1988[1903]:119–121).

Figure 16. Federal troops on Camp Hill, Harpers Ferry, 1862. (Courtesy of Harpers Ferry National Historical Park, HF31)

The Union reoccupied Harpers Ferry in February 1862. General Robert E. Lee believed that taking Harpers Ferry was a necessary first step in his invasion of the North. He dispatched 23,000 soldiers, who easily took control of undefended Maryland and Loudoun Heights, and fired down on Union troops. On September 15, 1862, 12,693 Federal troops surrendered to Stonewall Jackson. Two days after this surrender, Union and Confederate troops fought to a stalemate at Sharpsburg, Maryland. On September 18th, General Lee retreated into Virginia, and two days later the Army of the Potomac regained possession of Harpers Ferry and fortified Maryland and Loudoun Heights. They evacuated these fortifications on June 28, 1863, as a result of the Gettysburg campaign, but Union troops reestablished their presence several days after the battle (C. Gilbert et al. 1993:3.54–3.55).

In 1863, Union forces returned to Harpers Ferry on a large scale for the duration of the war and revived the town's economy. Feeling that they were safe because of the presence of a large Union army, civilians, families of officers, and newly freed slaves flocked to Harpers Ferry (Marmion 1959:11). Jubal Early attacked the town in July 1864 on his way to Washington, DC. Union troops held the high points and retained possession of the heights and therefore control of the town (Frye and Frye 1989:71). During the last year of the war, General Philip Sheridan fortified Harpers Ferry to secure supplies for his army. His men re-roofed the burned musket factory and established a supply depot in the building (Snell 1960a:39). From August 1864 through February 1865, Sheridan's army used Harpers Ferry as a base of operations to attack the Confederate stronghold in the Shenandoah Valley. Trains of up to 1000 wagons left town to supply troops and returned carrying prisoners and wounded. John Mosby, a Confederate committed to guerilla warfare in the Harpers Ferry region, constantly badgered these wagon trains. These actions necessitated the deployment of large numbers of Union troops to Harpers Ferry to protect shipments from further harassment (Snell 1960a:3, 38). During these last two years of the war, many offices, boardinghouses, restaurants, and other businesses opened to serve the expanding military and civilian populations (Drickamer and Drickamer 1987:130).

Union clerk Charles Moulton noted in 1864 that ". . . while the supply depot was stationed here, there was nothing but a perfect jam all day and night in the streets, army wagons blocking up the streets and large number of soldiers were coming in continually and goodly share of them getting drunk" (Drickamer and Drickamer 1987:213). This military occupation produced a thriving but unstable economy.

POSTWAR RECOVERY AND TRIALS BY FLOOD

Immediately after the Civil War, Harpers Ferry citizens were optimistic about the prospect of revitalizing the armory. In August 1865, a small operation was reestablished. Daniel Young, former foreman of the rifle factory, aided by Zadock Butt and about 40 workmen, set up shop to repair damaged guns (VFP 24 August 1865:2). Townspeople wanted the government, if the armory was not reestablished, to place the property on the market (VFP 7 December 1865:2). With no economic base, the town was characterized as "Next to Dead" and a "Village of Paupers" (VFP 25 November 1869:2). In 1867, General Grant reported to the Secretary of War that the United States no longer required the Harpers Ferry grounds and recommended against rebuilding the armory at Harpers Ferry. He suggested that the lands should be sold or, if not, leased (VFP 19 December 1867:1). In 1868, Congress passed an act to sell public lands, buildings, machinery, and waterpower privileges to the Shenandoah and Potomac rivers (Figure 17).

Figure 17. View of armory ground ruins and some Lower Town buildings after the Civil War, circa 1870. (Courtesy of Harpers Ferry National Historical Park, HF45)

Some of these lands were donated for the establishment of an African-American college. Northern Baptists under the direction of the Reverend N. C. Brackett played a major role in establishing schools for recently freed blacks in postbellum Shenandoah valley. In February 1867, John Storer of Sanford, Maine, donated $10,000 to establish such a college in Harpers Ferry. On October 2, 1867, Storer College began classes with 19 pupils. The institution originally occupied the armory paymaster's house (now called Lockwood House), which served as a dwelling, school, and church. After petitioning James Garfield in the Office of Education in 1868, the college acquired the former residences of other armory officials on Camp Hill along with several acres. Additional contributions from the Freedman's Bureau facilitated the erection of Lincoln Hall, a dormitory (Everhart 1952:122–124; Noffsinger 1958:49–50) (Figure 18).

Throughout its existence, the college's mission was dictated by whites, who controlled the administration and the governing board. The goal was to provide technical skills and an education for African-Americans so they could provide for themselves in a segregated society. Racial tensions flared during the college's early years, and students and

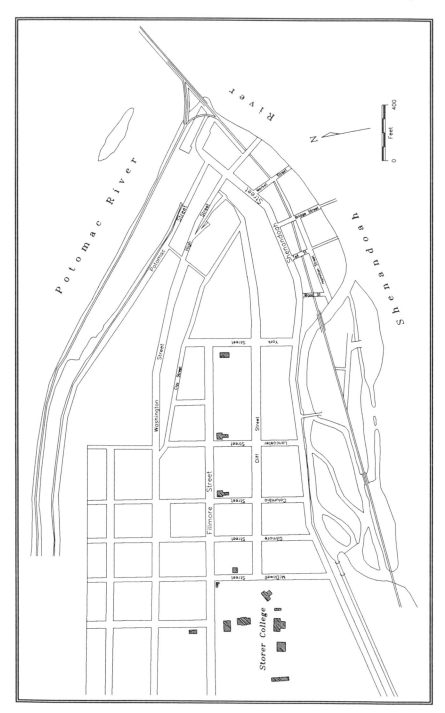

Figure 18. Map of Harpers Ferry showing Storer College buildings. (Drawn by John W. Ravenhorst)

teachers were threatened by the Ku Klux Klan. One teacher was "hooted at" when she went to the local post office because of her affiliation with the college; she was also stoned in the streets several times by residents. Therefore, it became necessary for armed militiamen to escort women teachers in the town (Anthony 1891:10–11).

In 1869, additional government lands were sold at public auction, at prices ranging from four to five times their true value and on easy credit, with no cash down (VFP 7 October 1869:3; Snell 1979:32–48). Many townspeople purchased properties at inflated prices on the basis of speculation that entrepreneur F. C. Adams would vigorously redevelop the waterpower industry. Adams and a set of investors purchased the federal armory grounds without having to deposit any money, although the deed would not convey until the transaction was paid in full. Adams's intention was not to redevelop the lands, but to legally challenge the Baltimore & Ohio Railroad's right to establish a route through the former armory lands. He hoped for a large court settlement from the railroad, since any realignment would hinder the use of the former armory canals (Snell 1981a:93). Not knowing of Adams's scheme, many entrepreneurs began to build stores in the Lower Town commercial district; other buildings were renovated, and new "cottages" were built. Prosperity was once again in sight.

Waterpower had been the catalyst for much of the industrial growth prior to the Civil War in government and private industries; but fewer industrial initiatives developed in the post-war era. Residents waited for Adams's industrial initiative. Abraham Herr, the sole proprietor of a privately owned community known as Virginius Island, was the principal owner of the community's flourmill industry, which was damaged substantially during the Civil War. In 1867, Jonathan C. Child and John A. McCreight, industrialists from Ohio, purchased the properties, buildings, watercourses, and water rights from Herr for $75,000. These two men entered into partnership with others and converted a brick cotton factory into a flourmill (Joseph et al. 1993:3.46–3.50).

Child and McCreight renovated the workers' domestic dwellings and surrounding grounds, although they allowed the substantial ruins of Herr's flourmill to stand, and they incorporated them into the vernacular landscape of the island. The great flood of September 30, 1870, devastated Virginius Island, extensively damaging the new flourmill facilities and obliterating the foundry, machine shop, sawmill, a number of houses, and outbuildings. The flood also ravaged any hopes of revival in Lower Town.

Adams lost his battle against the railroad in 1874, because the court ruled that the easement granted in 1838 was still binding and the lands reverted to the government since he had not made any down payments, or subsequent payments. Another flood in November 1877 caused considerable damage to the redeveloping community. Many of the buyers from the 1869 auction filed applications for abatement, claiming they had paid inflated speculative prices and that their new, flood-damaged property had lost considerable value. An Act of Congress on June 14, 1878, allowed purchasers of lots to make application for abatement as part of their 1869 bids. Twenty-nine purchasers who had originally paid a total of $39,755 for their properties were abated to $9668.35 (Snell 1979). The flourmill on Virginius Island was reopened and operated intermittently into the 1880s.

Upstream from the flourmill, Thomas Savery purchased the armory grounds on the Potomac, the rifle factory site, and water rights of the Shenandoah River in 1884. In 1887, he organized the Shenandoah Pulp Company and began construction of a dam, lake, and pulp mill upstream on Hall's Island, the former site of John Hall's workshop as well as the federal rifle works. Eventually, the pulp company purchased Virginius Island and leased the remaining dwellings primarily to company employees. In 1890, Savery developed the Potomac shoreline and created the Harpers Ferry Paper Mill. He incorporated the old armory rolling mill, armory dam, and armory canal into his operations (Joseph et al. 1993:3.81–3.87).

Although waterpower slowly recovered, the commercial district of Harpers Ferry was rejuvenated by the early 1880s and 1890s. Citizens in Lower Town developed and rebuilt the main business district on Shenandoah Street. New businesses flourished, and several substantial domiciles and businesses were added to the community. Accompanying this rejuvenation was a concern with the development of urban services related to health and hygiene (Chickering and Jenkins 1994). Three men—Hurst, Tearney, and Trail—incorporated the Harpers Ferry General Improvement Company in 1884 to "encourage manufacturing, community hygiene and beautification, and promote Harpers Ferry as a permanent place of residence and summer resort" (Chickering and Jenkins 1994).

In the mid-1880s, merchants expanded and diversified their enterprises. For instance, in 1888, James McGraw expanded his business and constructed a bottling plant abutting his store and dwelling. In a newspaper advertisement, he announced the shipment of Milwaukee Lager Beer to his establishment, where it was bottled. Like many other merchants, McGraw prospered in the 1880s and early 1890s. The *Spirit of Jefferson* often publicized his affluence, and once claimed that the

Figure 19. Shenandoah Street looking west, showing damage from the 1889 flood. (Courtesy of Harpers Ferry National Historical Park, HF82)

interior of his house "is probably not excelled by any in the Shenandoah Valley" (SoJ 28 January 1890:3).

Harpers Ferry suffered again during the 1889 flood, as many of the improvements constructed over the preceding decade were either damaged or destroyed (Figure 19). Merchants once again rebuilt the business district. For instance, McGraw had built a substantial addition to the rear of the old master armorer's house with the intention of operating a hotel or boardinghouse. In April 1892, McGraw advertised his new venture for rent as a "large, new stone and brick dwelling, 26 rooms, fine location. A splendid opening for a first-class Boarding House" (SoJ 22 March 1892:2). That same year, the *Spirit of Jefferson* described the building as containing "fifty-seven doors elegantly grained in walnut and other items to correspond" (SoJ 17 May 1892:3). The McGraw family had established themselves as leading entrepreneurs in the Harpers Ferry community. In 1895, the *Spirit of Jefferson* (SoJ 16 April 1895:1) reported:

> If Harpers Ferry had a few more enterprising men like Mr. McGraw it would not be long before we would have our town supplied with water and electric lights, and then what a delightful place this would be.

Figure 20. A late-nineteenth-century view looking up High Street. (Courtesy of Harpers Ferry National Historical Park, HF648)

During this same era, many new structures were erected on Shenandoah and High Streets, the center of the town's commercial district. The Hotel Conner was constructed on a portion of the former arsenal grounds south of Shenandoah Street. It consisted of three stories that accommodated both boarders and tourists. Adjacent to the hotel was a restaurant for its patrons. Close by, Murther Walsh constructed a new building that he used for his store and residence. Garland Hurst purchased and refurbished the master armorer's house, which had been constructed in the 1850s, and he and his wife occupied it for over 30 years. On High Street, many smaller commercial establishments developed, and in 1895, a brewery began operating on the north bank of the Shenandoah River (Figures 20 and 21).

COMMEMORATION AND TOURISM

Beginning in the 1880s and 1890s, touring battlefields and other areas of historical importance became a popular recreational activity among Americans. Visiting these places served as a continual reminder

Figure 21. View circa 1900 of Lower Town Harpers Ferry from Maryland Heights. (Courtesy of Harpers Ferry National Historical Park, HF92)

of patriotic acts and civic duties (Bodner 1992). The early preservation movement surrounding sites of the Civil War era began with a patriotic motive to preserve a tangible past and to provide a coherent cultural identity (Rainey 1983). Patterson (1989:138ff) and Linenthal (1993:87–126) outline the preservation and commemorative movement related to Civil War sites. For some sites, like Gettysburg, the earliest stage of preservation was biased toward Northern sentiment. After 1895, Confederates became increasingly represented. Rather than remaining a monument to the Northern cause, the Gettysburg battlefield eventually became a symbol of reunion, progress, and peace.

Harpers Ferry became a popular tourist spot along the B&O Railroad and the Chesapeake and Ohio Canal. After the war, citizens developed and rebuilt the main business district in the Lower Town area to cater to tourism. New enterprises, such as restaurants, hotels, and boardinghouses, flourished (Fenicle 1993; Shackel 1993a; Winter 1994). Many portions of the early- and mid-nineteenth-century commercial district were either renovated or replaced by new and imposing Victorian structures. In some cases, the materials used for renovation were "salvaged" from the town's industrial ruins (Chickering and Jenkins 1994).

The B&O Railroad played an influential role in the development of tourism in Harpers Ferry. In 1880, the railroad constructed on an island in the Potomac River a 20 acre amusement park that provided recreation for residents and tourists (SoJ 6 July 1880, 12 July 1898). In an oral history, Mayor Gilbert E. Perry (Wentzell 1957; also see C. Gilbert et al. 1993:3.91) recollected:

> "That was island park," he said. "You wouldn't believe it, but when I was a boy, it was every bit as gay as Coney Island. Downtown on Saturday nights," the mayor said, "you couldn't find a post to hitch your horse anywhere on Shenandoah Street. It was a savory street then. Saloons flourished; swinging doors, gambling, tin pan music, and cancan dancers—we had 'em all in the Gay Nineties. But we weren't all wild," Mayor Perry hastened to add. "We had our straight-laced side, too, in those horse-and-buggy days. Society people came from the city for the whole summer, or for a week or two during the racing season over at Charles Town. They lived in boarding houses here on the hill."

Visitors to Harpers Ferry were either day travelers or those who owned or rented cottages in the community. Tourist brochures described several important landmarks, including the site of John Brown's Fort and the ruins of the United States Armory (Taft 1898) (Figure 22). William Savery, owner of the armory grounds where John Brown's Fort stood, sold the structure in 1891 to a group of entrepreneurs. They dismantled the building and moved it by rail to Chicago to be displayed several miles away from the 1893 Chicago Exposition. Several years later, the fort was relocated to Buena Vista, a farm outside Harpers Ferry. There, many African-Americans and curiosity seekers visited the structure.

Savery sold a right-of-way to the Baltimore & Ohio Railroad and, after 1891, 14 feet of railroad berm fill covered the fort's original foundation on the musket factory grounds as the railroad through Harpers Ferry was realigned. The first thing tourists saw as they crossed the Potomac and entered town was an obelisk monument erected by the railroad to mark the fort's original location. Adjacent to this monument, the federal government placed iron tablets commemorating the Confederates' 1862 siege of the town in which 12,500 Union troops surrendered (Figure 23). The tablets were mounted there for "the enlightenment of travelers concerning the fighting that took place in the capture of Harpers Ferry by the Confederate Army in September, 1862" (quoted in C. Gilbert et al. 1993:3.93) Also visible from the tracks were several remaining foundations of the former musket factory. In

Figure 22. Late-nineteenth-century tourists visiting John Brown's Fort. (Courtesy of Harpers Ferry National Historical Park, HF57)

Figure 23. Obelisk marking the location of John Brown's Fort, and five tablets commemorating the Confederates' capture of Harpers Ferry. (Courtesy of Harpers Ferry National Historical Park, HF1041)

Figure 24. Landscaping of the armory foundations done by the B&O Railroad to commemorate early industry in Harpers Ferry. (Courtesy of Harpers Ferry National Historical Park, HF1220)

1916, the B&O Railroad landscaped the grounds around the musket factory foundations with trees and shrubs. By 1923, a large parklike garden filled the remains of the old armory grounds (SoJ 16 May 1896:2; C. Gilbert et al. 1993:3.101). The garden's design "incorporated the embankment, the matured trees and ornamental shrubs planted along the old river wall, and the rectangular outlines of old building foundations, creating a distinctive gateway of monuments, history, and ornamental landscape" (C. Gilbert et al. 1993: 3.101; SoJ 16 May 1916:2) (Figure 24). Many of these landscape changes made by the railroad were celebrated by the town as they were incorporated into an unofficial "public square."

Harpers Ferry remained a small industrial town supported by mercantile businesses and tourism through the beginning of the twentieth century. In 1906, the town was in the national spotlight again as Storer College hosted the Second Niagara Movement. The movement eventually led to the creation of the National Association for the Advancement

Figure 25. Photograph showing the destruction of both highway bridges after the 1936 flood. (Courtesy of Harpers Ferry National Historical Park, HF1219)

of Colored People (NAACP). In 1909, during the 50th anniversary of John Browns' Raid, and at the height of Harpers Ferry's tourist industry, Fort was purchased by Storer College and was moved the following year to its campus, where it served as a museum and a monument.

Floods in 1924, 1936, and 1942 greatly hampered any further development of the town (Figure 25). Vehicular and pedestrian bridges, connecting the town to Virginia and Maryland, were also destroyed, and temporary ones were erected, although the railroad bridge, constructed in 1894, survived. A 1945 *National Geographic* article (Atwood 1945:49; also see C. Gilbert et al. 1993:3.119) described the town:

> Thus it has suffered so grievously from a succession of floods that the lower part of the town looks like an Italian hill village after the Nazis left, almost bereft of residents and trade alike. The little town is one of steep, and tall narrow gabled houses, almost stately in their old time simplicity of line, even though half in ruins on their hillside perches.

It was not until 1947 and 1949 that permanent river crossings for vehicles were finally constructed. United States Route 340, which had served as Harpers Ferry's main artery, bypassed the town. Businesses

dwindled, and many residents moved to Bolivar, an adjacent community. By the 1960s, Harpers Ferry began to revive, centered around the
development of Harpers Ferry National Historical Park. Today, about
500,000 people visit the town, every year, and it has become a lively and
energetic place once again.

"Under a Malign Influence"

—GEORGE TALCOTT, Ordinance Department

3

Factory Discipline, Political Factionalism, Corruption, and the New Technology

NATIONAL CONTEXT OF WORK AND THE SEARCH FOR WORKERS' FREEDOM

Work in the early nineteenth century took many forms. In some instances, wage earners readily accepted jobs as a means to acquire the necessary funds to live—as a means of survival. On the other hand, the increasing number of factory jobs was also seen by others as a threat to workers' autonomy and craft pride. Workers' resistance to their loss of control over their means of production took many forms.

Factory owners often characterized unproductive workers as unreliable, careless, or lazy. This obstinacy can also be interpreted as a deliberate attempt to resist the domination of a machine-based system of production, as it left operatives with little room for personal autonomy or craft pride. While craftsmen often owned their own tools and machinery and treated them with care, factory workers had little loyalty to the machines that someone else owned. "Some workers abused their machinery to show that they had little traditional pride in or attachment to their machines or to the products they made" (Zonderman 1992:48). Breaking machinery in various acts of sabotage was an effort by workers to reassert the primacy of human beings over machines (also see, Paynter 1989; Paynter and McGuire 1991).

Goods were sometimes stolen even though operatives knew they could be fired if they were caught. Pilfering was a measure that workers took to "even the score" and compensate for low wages. "If they were denied what they saw as the full value of their labor, they would find a way to get what they thought was due them" (Zonderman 1992:196). Operatives were also rumored to have taken revenge by setting fires to factories. While they might have destroyed their jobs in destroying the factory, they could have easily found another one at another factory in a neighboring town, but the capitalist lost his investment, at times an insurmountable financial loss. Suspicious fires occurred at the Springfield Armory in 1842, when the armory management was shifted to military control. Documentation of the incident notes that neither the armorers nor the surrounding community helped to extinguish the fires (Zonderman 1992:196; Whittlesey 1920:n.p.).

Absenteeism was also characterized as another form of resistance. Sometimes dissatisfaction prompted workers to find other opportunities. The words of one song (In Foner 1975:44) captured this thought:

> They've cut my wages down,
> To nine shillings per week,
> If I cannot better wage make,
> Some other place I shall seek.

Factory workers' search for freedom and their expression of grievances against entrepreneurs were expressed by quitting and moving to other jobs, rather than staying and fighting for change to alleviate the boredom, tediousness, and low wages of factory labor. In some ways, the workers' transient state undermined their stability and strength, as they lacked the cohesiveness for social and labor change. This does not mean that protests were nonexistent. They did occur, but often they were less collective and less overt than the militant unionism that was to follow. The earliest organized strike at a large manufacturing company was at Waltham, Massachusetts, in 1821, catalyzed by a reduction in wages. In 1824, female weavers in Pawtucket, Rhode Island, led a strike against lower wages and increased hours. In this case, the factory was shut down for two weeks and a portion of one of the mills was set on fire. In December 1829, mill operatives in Dover, New Hampshire, walked off their jobs on a Friday because of "obnoxious regulations." They fired guns in the street and were released from their jobs by the mill owners, but they were back on the jobs the following Monday without any concessions made by the owners. Other known strikes occurred throughout the decade, and in many cases workers returned to their jobs without any substantial gains (Zonderman 1992:197ff).

By the 1830s and 1840s, regional labor organizations were created in the Northeast, and strikes increased dramatically. New ideological strategies were used to gain the sympathy of workers, community, and mill owners for concessions. In Lowell, for instance, operatives in an 1834 strike rooted their actions in the tradition of the American Revolution. They called themselves the Daughters of Freemen and invoked the traditional ideals of respect, justice, and equity. By calling themselves the Daughters of Freemen, they called attention to the dangers of factory bondage. They no longer wanted the role of dutiful daughters to their paternalistic managers in the mill structure. It was imperative that workers unite in order to gain more labor freedoms (see Dublin 1977, 1979; Foner 1977; Stansell 1986; Vogel 1977; Zonderman 1992:200–203). "Thus, their strikes were justified by blending the ideology of citizenship, republican rights, and self determination (all patriotic and mainstream democratic themes) with the language of class- and gender-consciousness and the solidarity in support of working women's rights" (Zonderman 1992:204).

Workers clung to the ideal of republicanism, which called for freedom from exploitation and oppression. This included individual liberty, respect, decency, and dignity. Protest was necessary to restore the balance of power and the fundamental rights of workers—a heritage of equality (Dublin 1979:106).

Eventually, some operatives realized that they could not will the factories away. In fact, they received a needed wage to sustain themselves and their families. They were not looking for a mythical place where they had absolute freedom; rather, they sought to control the terms of their labor. The answer was to master the factories through self-ownership. While operatives had little money to invest in such an enterprise, one such scheme developed in Boston in 1847. The idea was to create a producers' cooperative. No further documentation exists, and it appears that the idea was never carried through to fruition (Prude 1983:234; Zonderman 1992:295–296).

ADAPTATION OF FACTORY DISCIPLINE AT HARPERS FERRY

Resistance to factory discipline, political factionalism, and corruption all played a role in the slow adaptation of factory discipline in the Harpers Ferry Armory. Traditions were difficult to alter, and the persistent use of alcohol on the armory grounds hampered operations. In 1810, the armory's paymaster, Joseph Annin, requested soldiers to be stationed at the armory in order to control raucous behavior and alcohol consumption around the grounds: "Many mechanics, as well as soldiers, are given too free use of spirituous liquors; in such cases, unless the officer was a very prudent person, disputes might arise and be attended with serious consequences" (HFNHP microfilms 1810a). Joseph Barry

(1988 [1903]:30–31) reports an attempt to regulate the consumption of alcohol on the armory's premises. While whiskey was commonly found in some industrial shops, Superintendent Stubblefield prohibited spirituous beverages in the Harpers Ferry shops. The armorers countered by hanging buckets of whiskey outside the shop windows and leaning out the open windows to take nips. Apparently Stubblefield did not push this regulation any further. Colonel Wadsworth of the Ordnance Department wrote to the Secretary of War and stated that the workmen were "not as sober and orderly as at [the] Springfield [Armory]" (HFNHP microfilms 1817). M. R. Smith (1977:150) suggests that Stubblefield actually encouraged drinking on duty as well as after work hours, since he owned an interest in a local distillery and increased alcohol consumption meant a boost in income.

Stubblefield was not alone in his struggle to control workers' behavior. Like those at Harpers Ferry, the Springfield armorers had a long-standing debate with their managers as to what was proper behavior in the workplace and what was grounds for dismissal. In Springfield, the armorers also felt threatened that the managers were increasingly taking away their rights as craftsmen. When Stubblefield visited the Springfield Armory in 1815, the facility was continuously praised by the Ordnance Department as being more efficiently operated. During the visit, Superintendent Lee dismissed two men for wrestling in the armory yard. His action was an effort to remedy the undisciplined behavior found in the armory operations. The workers insisted that it was tradition for the two expelled operatives to buy everyone a drink around the flagpole or "liberty pole." Some armorers insisted that they cut down the flagpole, since their right to wrestle had been abolished by the superintendent. The superintendent and the master armorer had to intervene personally to prevent the act. Lee subsequently fired 11 more armorers immediately after the incident, and he issued new regulations that banned such customs as ball playing and conversation (Zonderman 1992:159; Whittlesey 1920:n.p.). The actual degree to which these regulations were enforced is not known.

Management in the armories fought against organized labor, and in 1816 the Springfield Armory prohibited workers from attempting to organize, under penalty of fines or dismissal. In 1834, the regulation was restated, but with only dismissal as the penalty (Deyrup 1948:104,165; Hindle and Lubar 1986:233).

While there is no evidence that the Harpers Ferry armorers organized into a formal union, they tended to be united against the notion of outsiders making changes in their daily routines. In 1818, the Springfield Armory asked Thomas Blanchard, a local mechanic, to help devise lathes to aid in the production of guns. While fitting both the Springfield and Harpers Ferry armories with machinery, he turned his attention to the manufacture of gunstocks in 1819. His machinery, which used eccentric turning, was unique for the time. The machinery traced a master pattern and reproduced it, thus making the reproduction of gunstocks no longer a craft but a mechanical process. Creating a gunstock with machinery also shortened the manufacturing process considerably (M. R. Smith 1991).

In addition to his patented lathe, Blanchard designed 13 additional woodworking machines for gunstocking. By 1826, stocking was completely mechanized, eliminating any need for skilled labor. Although Stubblefield wrote in 1819 that he was impressed with the machinery as a labor- and time-saving device, he apparently changed his attitude and hesitated in introducing new lathing machines in the following decade. His brother-in-law, Master Armorer Armisted Beckham, led a group of armorers to protest these "Yankee notions" and any introduction of additional new machinery. Skilled gunstockers feared that these changes would compromise their craft and make them machine-tenders. Stubblefield stayed clear of any potential strife and did not adopt Blanchard's improvements. Even though the price for stocking was relatively higher than at Springfield, the musket stockers' craft was saved, at least temporarily, and they petitioned the Ordnance Department for a pay increase (HFNHP microfilms 1819b). Stubblefield also continually failed to pay Blanchard the royalties he was due for the use of the machinery he had installed in 1818 (M. R. Smith 1977).

Criticisms of the Harpers Ferry operations for its lack of industrial discipline reached the halls of Congress in 1827, and Secretary of War James Barbour ordered a court of inquiry. Stubblefield was temporarily removed from his position, and the hearings convened on April 26, 1827, and ended eight days later. Roswell Lee from the Springfield Armory introduced Blanchard's machinery to Harpers Ferry while he acted for the suspended superintendent (M. R. Smith 1977:124–138). The armory continued to advertise for musket stocks into 1831 as local private contractors supplied roughed-out stocks; therefore, the machinery was not in full operation until the 1830s (VFP 19 January 1831:3; Brown 1968:9).

During Stubblefield's hearings, Charles Staley, an unemployed armory worker, noted that Master Armorer Beckham played cards with the men during working hours. Thomas Copeland, an armorer, stated that he remained on the government payrolls while working privately for Superintendent Stubblefield. Other armorers claimed that they used government property for their own private purposes. The report of the investigation noted that (HFNHP microfilms 1827a).

> Mr. Stubblefield has discharged his duties as Superintendent, with fidelity and integrity for twenty years—and that, if in the progress of this trial, some few instances of neglect of minor importance shall have been exposed, they are to be attributed to the state of things at the time and to the necessity, in the multifarious duties of a Superintendent, of confiding some things to the discretion and fidelity of subordinate agents.

Stubblefield was reinstated on June 1, 1827, and was given the authority to dismiss any armorers who disseminated false or malicious reports about the armory. Stubblefield wasted no time acting and released armorers who testified against him, including Thomas Copeland (HFNHP microfilms 1827b; also see M. R. Smith 1977:174.)

In 1828, additional inquiries were made into Stubblefield's ability to oversee the armory. Edward Lucas, who eventually became the armory superintendent in 1837, as well as other gentlemen from Shepherdstown, approached the newly appointed Secretary of War, John Eaton, regarding the improprieties at Harpers Ferry. Former armorers also wrote to the secretary, as well as to the president of the United States regarding mismanagement at the armory (M. R. Smith 1977:177–179; also see HFNHP microfilms 1829a,b).

Stubblefield faced another trial in May 1829, and he was found to have lacked the vigilance and efficiency required of his position. He resigned August 1, 1829 (HFNHP microfilms 1829c,d). Throughout the trials, the real culprit in the armory's inefficient operations and unethical treatment of workers and contractors appeared to be Master Armorer Beckham. For instance, a document based on several sworn affidavits reports the mistreatment of a Mr. Polley Barnard, who supplied gunstocks to the Harpers Ferry Armory. In one incident in March 1825, about 1500 stocks were destroyed by the inspector. "He would throw or strike the stock down upon the rocks or logs" and those that didn't break "were split with hatchets." In another incident in March 1827, about 4600 stocks were offered, and the inspector rejected about 2000. Master Armorer Beckham said that Barnard "had better not bring stocks there, as he would not suffer them to pass." At the same time, a Mr. Patrick McCorley was offered a contract for 5000 stocks at 22–23¢ each "if he would not let the Barnards have any part in it." The following May, McCorley delivered the stocks, which were cut from the same lot as Barnard's stocks, and received a fair inspection and avoided harassment (HFNHP microfilms 1929e).

M. R. Smith (1977:179) summarizes:

> The master armorer's name seemed synonymous with corruption, turmoil, and intrigue at the Ferry. He had taken bribes, falsified records, intimidated workers, played favorites, condoned the use of violence against those who threatened to expose his activities, and even attempted to have [an armorer] jailed on fictitious charges to prevent him from testifying [against Stubblefield].

Thomas Dunn's appointment as superintendent pleased most members of the Ordnance Department and the manufacturing community, as they claimed that he could "restore peace and correctness to the Establishment." Local politicians and community leaders feared the changes that might be imposed by the manager (M. R. Smith 1977:254). Dunn initially released several incompetent workers and rehired those who were unjustly fired by Stubblefield. Dunn reinstated many of the rules and regulations established by Roswell Lee, the Springfield superintendent, who acted as the Harpers Ferry superintendent during Stubblefield's 1827 trial. "Among other things, the rules forbid loitering, gambling, and consuming alcoholic beverages on armory premises, made unexcused absences punishable by immediate dismissal, and held each armorer personally responsible for the damage or destruction of tools consigned to his use" (M. R. Smith 1977:255).

Unaccustomed to the new regulations, armorers protested by harassing Dunn outside the armory gates. Ebenezer Cox was one of the discontented armorers who were released by Symington while the latter acted for Stubblefield as superintendent during the 1829 trials. Cox had asked to be reinstated, but Dunn denied his request. On January 29, 1830, he approached the superintendent's office and shot and killed Dunn at point-blank range (VFP 3 February 1830:3, 17 February 1830:3, 17 March 1830; see the account of the trial [VFP 28 July 1830:2]). Cox became a folk hero among the armorers; whenever future managers tried to impose factory discipline Cox's name was always mentioned to the armory officials (Barry 1988[1903]:25–25; M. R. Smith 1977: 256–257).

George Rust succeeded Dunn as the armory's superintendent in 1830. He was considered a Virginia gentleman who spent most of his time in Loudoun County, attending to the affairs of his estate. Barry describes Rust's tenure as uneventful, although Rust acted to prevent any incitant events, unlike his predecessor (VFP 10 February 1830:3; Barry 1988[1903]:27). One of his most significant actions was to transfer Beckham to the Allegheny Arsenal in exchange for Benjamin Moor. While this action may have seemed relevant to the overall commitment to mechanize the armory, Rust reversed many of the disciplinary actions installed by Dunn and thereby became very popular with the armorers. There were instances during Rust's tenure when armory workers subcontracted their duties to a number of men and boys to do their work but themselves received the pay for the piecework. The Ordnance Department requested an end to this practice, since the "Department is, to have the arms etc. completed in the best workmanlike manner which, it is thought cannot be effective by boys who are unacquainted with the business" (HFNHP microfilms 1835a).

THE DEVELOPMENT OF SURVEILLANCE TECHNOLOGIES AND WORKERS' DISCONTENT

Edward Lucas, a congressional representative from the Harpers Ferry area, succeeded Rust as armory superintendent in 1837 (VFP 19 January 1837:2). During the seven years of his predecessor's administration, the armory had remained in a state of disorganization, and to some extent this state continued into Lucas's tenure. Misappropriated monies were a long-standing problem in the armory, and during the first months of Lucas's superintendency, the paymaster loaned money from the armory's treasury to James Davis, a contractor who made gunstocks. Several years later, over $200 was stilled owed to the armory (HFNHP microfilms 1939a). Apparently, there were few checks and balances to assure proper use of the armory's money. Paymasters were charged with caring for the money and often took it home with them at night in order to keep it safe. As late as 1840, Paymaster Richard Parker requested installation of a vault at the pay office. He took the funds home with him each night or put them in an iron chest at his office, which was not secure (HFNHP microfilms 1840a).

Unlike Stubblefield or Rust, Lucas played a more active and visible role in the armory and moved to town. Although he was unacquainted with arms manufacturing, his participation allowed Master Armorer Benjamin Moor time to improve the mechanization of the armory. During Lucas's tenure, the War Department made strides in reimposing a factory discipline at Harpers Ferry. In June 1840, Chief of Ordnance Talcott informed Lucas that the president of the United States insisted that the armories and arsenals adhere to a 10-hour workday. The directions noted that between the vernal and autumnal equinox, the workday was 6:00 A.M. to 6:00 P.M. with 2 hours for meals. Winter hours were not established at the time the letter was written (HFNHP microfilms 1840b).

When Lucas, a former Jackson supporter and Virginia politician, was faced with fiscal constraints, he quickly released armorers, 70 of whom were affiliated with the Whig Party. Lucas was accused of firing the Whig-supporting armorers in order to help Democrat William Lucas, his brother, get elected (VFP 1 May 1839:3). William McClure, in a sworn affidavit, claimed that Lucas stated that "he considered the enemies of his brother his enemies . . ." (HFNHP microfilms 1841a). When he rehired workers, Lucas employed mostly Democrats, although three Whig supporters were reinstated.

Armorers and citizens increasingly protested Lucas's unjust hiring practices and political favoritism. Lucas allowed a local newspaper editor who supported his political views to live and operate in a government house. A stump orator, Mr. Riddle, was also given one of the best government houses (HFNHP microfilms 1841b).

Lucas also threatened to discharge a workman, Francis C. Melhorn, and others "for visiting the Drug Store of Fontaine Beckham and the store of Messrs. Breitenbaugh and Kirby, prominent Whigs of this place." Lucas confirmed the rumor: "I know my friends and my enemies and am determined to the place of the latter, and you are one of them." On another occasion, Lucas called a group of 5 Whig armorers "Damned Tories and the descendants of Damned Tories. . . ." (HFNHP microfilms 1841c). A committee of 11 armorers was appointed to investigate the charges, only to conclude that the superintendent was impartial (VFP 23 May 1839:1).

On the day of the presidential election, Lucas was near the polls all day, and "his conduct was overbearing and insulting to the Whigs." He even urged on a fight, rather than trying to stop it (HFNHP microfilms 1841c). With the election of William Henry Harrison and the Whig Party in 1840, Lucas's job was in jeopardy. Colonel George Talcott of the Ordnance Department reexpressed his strong feeling that the Harpers Ferry Armory must be separated from political influences. He believed that the armory could not thrive "under a malign influence, that will taint every movement of the Superintendent and place him at the feet of a clique, seeking only their own ends and governed alone by base motives. A politician must serve his party and I think I can foresee the breaking down of the armory in the event of a return to the old order of things" (HFNHP microfilms 1841d). Several of the armory supervisors also believed that the military system would obviate hiring preferences based on political affiliations (see HFNHP photostats 1842).

Many Harpers Ferry citizens wanted Fontaine Beckham to be chosen as the next Harpers Ferry Armory superintendent (VFP 24 December 1840:3). In early 1841, however, a military officer, Major Henry

Craig, acted for Lucas, and on April 15, 1841, he permanently replaced the armory's superintendent (HFNHP microfilms 1841e; VFP 15 April 1841:2, 22 April 1841:2). Craig immediately took action to control the work process. With a military background, he enforced a disciplined factory system and dictated orders for all armorers to follow under his leadership. Hours of work were established; idle, drunk, or disorderly employees were dismissed; workmen were to explain their absences; and abusive or disrespectful language would not be tolerated. A second offense meant dismissal (HFNHP microfilms 1841f). These were very much the same rules that were established at the armory in 1827 by Roswell Lee (while he was acting as superintendent during the Stubblefield trial) and enforced by Thomas Dunn in 1829. A meeting was held by those citizens and armorers who opposed the replacement of the civil superintendency, and the local newspaper wrote editorials against the new system (VFP 17 June 1841:2, 12 August 1841:2, 11 August 1842:1). Armorers petitioned John Tyler, who became president after Harrison's death, to remove the military superintendency and to reappoint Edward Lucas (HFNHP microfilms 1841g).

Colonel George Bomford, Chief of Ordnance, defended the military superintendency, noting that the change was made to improve working conditions and to increase the armorers' production. For instance, a report from the Ordnance Department noted the extremely high cost of production. From March 31, 1841, to September 30, 1841, the Springfield Armory manufactured 10,700 muskets at cost of nearly $20 per musket. At Harpers Ferry, during the same period, armorers manufactured 8650 muskets and 190 Hall's rifles at a cost of more than $22 per musket (VFP 6 January 1842:2). With the military superintendency, no new regulations were established and workers were not ruled by military tactics. Rather, the military system enforced the rules and regulations already existing on the books. Since the armory relied more on machinery, Bomford suggested that adherence to regular work hours was essential to the armory's operations (HFNHP microfilms 1941h).

Armorers also protested Master Armorer Moor's attempt to mechanize the armory. They accused him of being "nothing more than a theorist, with his head crammed full of whims, Yankee notions, and useless machinery, so that he is all most in a state of derangement. . . ." An armorer claimed that before Moor's mechanization program began in the 1830s, only 3 to 4 machinists were needed at the armory; now there were 25–35, all commanding relatively higher wages than the armorers. He also claimed that even with all these innovations, production had not increased (HFNHP microfilms 1841i).

While there were two types of laborers in the factory—day workers and pieceworkers—Craig ordered these occupational differences to be abolished. All armorers and workers were to labor the same amount of hours each day (HFNHP microfilms 1842a). Craig also stationed a guard at the armory gates to regulate and monitor the comings and goings of armorers and visitors, and he installed a clock at the factory (Barry 1988:30; M. R. Smith 1977:271). There had been no public time-keeping device in the armory before that time.

The armorers were outraged by the new military discipline, and the thought of conforming "to the hours for labour indicated by the bell" made them fear becoming "mere machines of labor" (HFNHP micro-films 1842b). In a letter to President Tyler, they wrote of their "feeling that their rights as Freemen have been wrested from them . . ." (HFNHP microfilms 1842c). The pieceworkers led a strike that lasted for a week, only to be told by President Tyler that he admired their craft, but they must work out their labor disagreement with their supervisors at the armory.

In defense of the military system, George Talcott wrote (HFNHP microfilms 1942d):

> The real ground of opposition to the present mode of supervision is well known to be this: The men have been paid high prices, and were in the habit of working four to six hours per day, and being absent whole days or a week, and at the end of a month their pay was generally the same in amount as if no absence had occurred. The factory system required armorers to adhere to fixed hours and the master of the shop accounted for their time spent on labor.

Talcott continued and claimed:

> The armorers may attempt to disguise or hide the truth under a thousand claimers, but this is the real cause of their objection to a Military Superin-tendent. He enforces the Regulators, which lay bare their secret practices. They can control a Civil Superintendent, and have often done it; they have occasionally ousted one, and they have shot one. We say to the Armorers, here are our Regulations, if you will not abide by them, go elsewhere, for we know that twice as many and better workmen can be had at any moment.

Rules and regulations for the workshops were reprinted and posted in the armory buildings (HFNHP microfilms 1842e) and included the following:

> Harpers Ferry Armory Oct 16, 1842
>
> Rules & Regulations for the Workshops US Armory
>
> 1st. Engagements will hereafter be made annually commencing with 1st January.

2nd. Workmen, etc., can be discharged at any time, but except in cases of improper conduct a reasonable notice will be given of the intention of discharge when the interest of the Armory will permit. (See Acts of Congress passed 7th May 1800 & 23rd August 1842)

3rd. The workmen have the right of withdrawing from their engagements, but it is expected that they will give timely notice of their intention. (See Acts of Congress passed 7 May 1800)

4th. Wages are subject to alteration by Commanding Officer, the change going into effect after the date of the Order. (See Acts of Congress passed 7th May 1800)

5th. All persons employed at this Armory will, at the signal for work, repair to their appropriate Stations, and then perform their duties diligently and in an orderly manner; and workmen, etc. must not quit their places of labor without the knowledge and [permission] of the Inspectors or Master workmen except on the calls of nature.

6th. Where prevented by sickness or any urgent business from repairing to their labour, workmen will as soon as possible send word to their inspectors or Master Workmen of the cause of their detention.

7th. No private business must be transacted in the shops—workmen must not lounge about each others benches, nor by idle conversation or other [sic] means distract each others attention from their employment—nor are they to encourage visitors to do so, by holding conversations with them.

8th. Newspapers must not be brought into the shops or place of labour, where seen, the owner or person bringing them in will have to bare [sic] the responsibility.

9th. Meetings & corroborations among the workmen for the purpose of meddling in the affairs of the Armory are improper and will not be tolerated. (See Act of Congress approved July 8, 1815)

10th. Piece workmen will be charged with Files, oil, and Sand paper at the wholesale cost of the articles.

11th. Inspectors and Master workmen will see to the strict observance of the Laws and Regulations, and will report all violations of the same to their knowledge.

Armory Regulations
Harpers Ferry
1842

Throughout the 1840s, armorers continued to protest the new work conditions and factory discipline, to which they were now subject. Facilitating the imposition of work discipline, Symington standardized factory layout and appearance. Symington replaced Hall's Rifle works, since it was in poor condition and had an "inconvenient arrangement." He insisted that the rifle-works be totally rebuilt on a "proper and systematic plan." New buildings in a "factory Gothic" architectural style were constructed (HFNHP microfilms 1845) (Figure 26).

Throughout the redesigning process, Superintendent Symington continually feared worker unrest and noted that Harpers Ferry did not have any "municipal regulation to check riots or disorders nor for

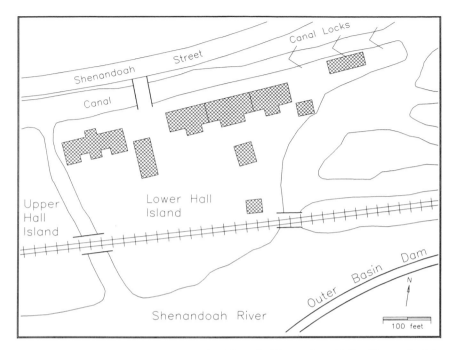

Figure 26. Plan view of the redesign of Hall's Rifle Works, circa 1850s. (Drawn by John W. Ravenhorst)

ascertaining proper police" (HFNHP microfilms 1845). Symington knew that his policies were not liked by the armorers, and he reported that an inspector said in reference to him that "the damned son of a bitch we must run him off too" (HFNHP microfilms 1849a). In order to reassert the military's authority, the Ordnance Department issued new work rules for both workmen and supervisors (HFNHP microfilms 1847):

> Rules for the Government of the Workmen employed in the Armory
>
> 1. The Bell will ring *Ten* minutes as a signal for labor, commencing 5 minutes before the true time, at the termination of which signal, all persons not present for work, will be allowed to work only three fourths of that day. To enable the Smiths, barrel welders, and Tilt hammer men to comply with this rule, the Smiths will be allowed to make up their fires from 10 to 15 minutes and the barrel welders and Tilt hammer men 25 minutes, before the ringing of the Bell.
> 2. No person will be allowed when engaged at work to break off before the ringing of the bell for meals or ceasing labor.
> 3. In case of necessity or emergency when any workman has to leave the Armory on his personal business, he will give notice of the same to his Inspector or Superintendent.

4. During the hours for labor it is expected that no business or occupation whatever of a private nature, or not connected with the operations of the Armory, will call off the attention of any workman from his work, and any conversation among the workmen that may lead them to neglect their work, should not be indulged in. Conversation, or business transactions with visitors or others not connected with the Armory is entirely prohibited.

5. A respectful deportment towards the Inspectors, their Assistants, Master Workmen and others in authority, is due to them and will be observed, and their orders upon all matters touching the business over which they have control will be strictly followed.

6. It is required that the benches, machines, or place of business of each workmen, be kept at all times neat and tidy, the work and tools pertaining to each one, to be disposed of in the closets, drawers and boxes provided for the purpose, and not left upon the floor or benches to litter the shops. Smoking at any time within the shops will not be allowed, nor noisy or boisterous conduct.

7. The shop tender will keep the shops at all times clean, and will suffer no litter to remain upon the floors, under or upon the benches, nor the walls to be defaced or soiled in any way. When strangers visit the shops the shop tenders will if necessary conduct them through seeing that these rules are not transgressed. Any breach of the foregoing rules will be promptly reported by the Inspector or Superintendent to the Master Armorer.

Harpers Ferry Armory
24 December 1847

Duties of the Clerks, Inspectors & Master Workmen in the Armory

1. The general nature of the duties of the Clerks, Inspectors and their Assistants at the National Armories, is defined in the Ordnance Regulations, by which they will be governed in the performance of their duties, and the Master workmen having charge of other branches of business at the Armory, though not pointed out in those Regulations will adhere to the spirit and meaning intended, in the management of the business confided to them respectively.

2. Inspectors and all other Officers are required to see that the *Rules for the Government of the Workmen in the Armory* are observed, and that they promptly report any breach of them to the Master Armorer.

3. Special instructions in relation to work and the operations of the Armory, will necessarily have to be given from time to time through the Master Armorer, to which the attention of the Inspector and other Officers will be given.

4. The particular attention of the Inspectors and other Officers will be required at all times to the following points— To the quality of the work— To promote economy in all of the various operations— To check any waste in the consumption or use of materials— and to encourage the cheerful performance of duty by the workmen employed under them. Their conduct to the workmen will at all times be respectful, never allowing themselves to enter into controversy in the shops, on matters of duty.

5. A point of great importance in the Armory, is the regularity of business in the various operations so that one may not be too much in advance nor too far behind. This evil is sometimes brought about by the protracted or frequent absence of workmen engaged on particular benches, and the attention of the Inspectors is called to it to aid the Master Armorer in preventing its frequent occurrence.

6. The Clerks employed in the different departments are essentially Armory Clerks, and as such are liable to be called on to assist in any department, where there may be a stress of business. Though generally, and as a rule, they will not be required to perform services out of that department they are usually employed in, except in the case named.

Harpers Ferry Armory
24 December 1847

Along with the new factory discipline and new machinery also came lower wages. This action increased tensions at the armory and the community. Congressman Henry Bedinger and many of his constituents from the armory protested to the War Department regarding their new situation. Symington noted that the lower wages were justified with the introduction of new machinery, increased facilities, and enforced regular working hours (HFNHP microfilms 1846a).

With the new machinery, the armorers' labor became increasingly synchronized. Ordnance Department officials reinforced Symington's position and explicitly noted that punctuality and a full day's work were now necessary for the efficient operations of the armory. All workers labored the same number of hours each day. In this system, no one had idle time to "excite envy, to gossip, or hinder another's work" (HFNHP microfilms 1854a). Symington abandoned an earlier work schedule plan that required labor from sunup to sundown all year; he created a 10-hour standardized schedule. He noted that worktime at Harpers Ferry for workers averaged 9 hours and 54 minutes of labor per day throughout the year. This schedule was "not considering the time given to the workmen on Saturdays, nor 10 minutes each day at the signals for commencing work, . . . for morning and afternoon labor the signal bell rings during 10 minutes commencing 5 minutes before the true time and ceasing 5 minutes after it when the workmen are expected to be in their places" (HFNHP microfilms 1848a).

In an attempt to instill work discipline within the armory, Symington requested authority to discharge the older inspectors, who apparently resisted conforming to the new discipline. In a letter to the Ordnance Department, he noted that "the inspectors, holding their places under the old system, have learned to look upon their appointments as for life, and have many of them grown old in their position, and I consider it very desirable to have in their stead younger men, more efficient and active in their habits to secure an accountability and regularity . . ." (HFNHP microfilms 1849b). These reforms reinforced the stormy relationship between armory workers and the new factory system, and Symington expected violent opposition to his plan. Some townspeople stated openly that Symington ". . . ought to be dealt with as Dunn was" (HFNHP microfilms 1849a).

ENCLOSURE AND TOWN PLANNING

Symington continued an earlier surveillance strategy begun by Stubblefield, which was the building of walls to contain activities and the reorganization of space in order to allow activities to be viewed from a central place. In 1827, Brigadier General John Wool was appalled by the general planning, design, and condition of the Harpers Ferry Armory. He wrote that while large sums of money had been spent in Harpers Ferry, the town and facilities had a temporary appearance. There were few substantial buildings, and those constructed of brick were dilapidated. He noted that "energy and division of character should be combined with a knowledge of the business to enable any one to conduct it as successfully and beneficially as the public intent requires to pull down the buildings which are a disgrace to the establishment and improperly located. . . ." Wool requested that proper and permanent housing also be erected for workers, although the rebuilding of the armory would cost the government between $40,000 and $50,000 (HFNHP microfilms 1827b).

Stubblefield reacted to these comments by making some attempts to modernize the facility. One of his first deeds in 1828 was to enclose the Potomac factories with a brick wall (Figure 27). Construction of the wall would help to occlude "several miserable tossling shops erected along the line nearest the work shops" (HFNHP microfilms 1828). The wall was one of the armory's first attempts to control armorers' movements in and out of the gun factory. It restricted the armorers' access not only to the armory but also to private enterprises, such as taverns, during work hours. Apparently there was a footbridge that crossed over the armory canal into the Wager lot, a privately owned parcel that contained taverns and shops. While building the partition wall, Stubblefield reported that "a small footway leading from the armory to the grogshops on the opposite side of the canal was by some mischievous person thrown down." The Wagers wanted the armory to replace the bridge, but Stubblefield refused to oblige their request. Stubblefield

Figure 27. View of the armory looking north showing the armory ruins, John Brown's Fort, and the armory wall, circa 1870. (Courtesy of Harpers Ferry National Historical Park, HF539)

wrote to the Ordnance Department that replacing it "will continue an evil to the armory" (HFNHP microfilms 1829f).

Walls and fences were seen as an important form of enclosure that allowed easy monitoring of workers and private citizens. In 1842, additional fencing was deemed necessary to control the entry of inhabitants into portions of the armory yard. The armory inspection report suggested that such barriers be built "along the portions of the line of our canal where bridges are kept up, and at the two extremities of the line of shops, in order to prevent intrusion of improper persons, within the range of shops" (HFNHP photostats 1842). As previously noted, other supervisory measures were also taken. The superintendent stationed a guard at the armory gates to regulate and monitor the movement of armorers and visitors. The installation of a clock at the factory also allowed for the monitoring of workers' behavior. Armorers were expected to be in a set place at an exact time (Barry 1988:30; M. R. Smith 1977:271).

Symington redesigned other aspects of the town in order to make production more efficient, to facilitate the movement of goods, to isolate behavior, and to monitor the flow of traffic. After several decades of neglect, the armory was considered to be in a poor and unplanned condition. The armory was described as being "cramped for room, not having been constructed upon a plan arranged before hand, but put up building after building as appropriations were obtained." The buildings had been constructed on fill in a location never designed to accommodate so many structures. Buildings jutted out in all directions, lacking any form of functional or architectural uniformity (M. R. Smith 1977:275; also see HFNHP photostats 1835, 1836a,b).

In 1843 Symington noted that the thoroughfare leading to the entrance to the armory, was inefficient, being narrower than necessary for the easy flow of goods, materials, and workers in and out of the armory. Traffic and trash frequently clogged the entrance, and it was "the usual mart where the country people exhibit their products for sale" (HFNHP 1844ab,). As part of Symington's systematic redesign of the armory, he removed the marketplace to an area several hundred feet from the armory's entry way. All market functions within the town were to be contained within this new building. In 1846, the armory constructed a two-story market house just south of the Winchester and Potomac railroad tracks. The first story was for the sale of market produce, sold at regulated times and on specific days. The second-story hall served as a meeting area for "lectures on scientific and moral subjects only" (HFNHP microfilms 1846b). Two years later, Symington declared the market house to be indispensable to the town and to the "country people" (HFNHP microfilms 1848b).

From 1844 through the 1850s, the armory strived to widen Canal Street (the present Potomac Street), which bordered the western end of the armory canal. The area was congested with shanties, barns, and domestic debris, and the neighbors occasionally deposited refuse in the armory canal, "thus occasioning labor and expenses in cleaning out from time to time" (HFNHP microfilms 1844b). Widening the avenue provided a buffer from private utilitarian uses and secured additional space to protect that establishment from danger of any fires along the alley. A wider public road also allowed easier government surveillance along its only major bordering street (Figure 28). Alterations enabled the town to make proper improvements to correct poor drainage in the area, a benefit to both the town and the armory.

Symington proposed two options to secure a buffer for the armory grounds. The first was to purchase all the lots adjacent to the canal, to remove the stables and shanties, to increase the width of the road from 15 feet to 40 feet, and to use the newly acquired houses on the hill for armory supervisors. This circumstance would "have the Armory build-

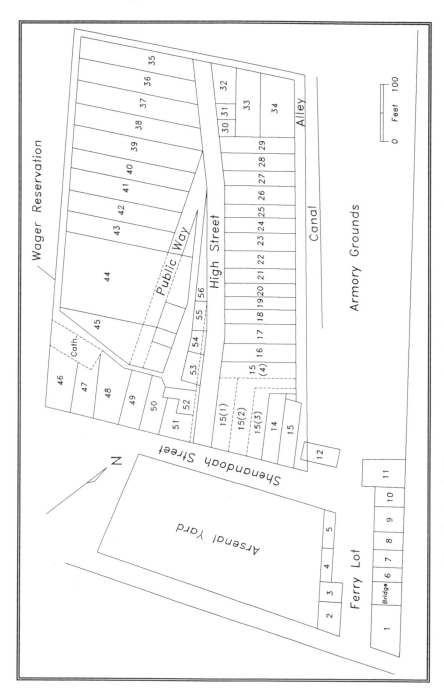

Figure 28. Map of Lower Town showing the Wager reservation lots, ferry lot, armory grounds, and arsenal yard. Symington successfully petitioned to eliminate the narrow corridor at the intersection of Shenandoah and High Streets and widen the alley to 40 feet. (Drawn by John W. Ravenhorst)

ings always under view, and the activity between these dwellings and the avenue neatly cultivated" (HFNHP microfilms 1844b). The second option would include only the acquisition of the lower 25 feet of each lot to increase the road width to 40 feet.

The Ordnance Department opted for the second alternative and negotiated with the lot owners for the acquisition of a 25-foot strip of land to widen the road to 40 feet (VFP 1 December 1847:2). Mr. J. G. Wilson offered to exchange his lot (No. 13 on the 6 acre reservation) for one of the government lots along Shenandoah Street (HFNHP microfilms 1852). Roeder, a local merchant, agreed to sell to the United States 25 feet of land on Lot 15 for $17.00 for the widening project (HFNHP microfilms 1854b). Philip Coons objected to forfeiting any portion of lands. The Ordnance Department insisted that the town of Harpers Ferry (incorporated by an act of the Virginia Assembly passed on March 24, 1851) had the right to condemn this land, which it did (HFNHP microfilms 1855a).

The continuing development of the Lower Town commercial district in the 1840s created a congested atmosphere that included dwellings, stables, and other outbuildings. The armory superintendent's quarters were in need of repair, and their location near the Wager 6-acre lot was deemed no longer desirable or suitable for the superintendent. Since the building was so close to the shops, armory officials believed that the building would be better used as an office for the commanding officer, paymaster, or master armorer (HFNHP microfilms 1843).

By 1848, the superintendent's quarters and several other supervisors' quarters were built on Camp Hill, which was one of the highest points in Harpers Ferry and had a commanding view of the armory grounds (see VFP 15 July 1847:2) (Figure 29). The hill also offered better climate and living conditions, especially during sickly seasons. Movements on the armory grounds could be observed from this point, and individuals could be easily located. The presence of these buildings may have kept the public under the perception of constant surveillance (see Foucault 1979:202). A larger two-story brick dwelling for the paymaster replaced Hall's former quarters. Symington wrote that "the grounds are improved and garden made so that a trifling expense will put them in proper order" (HFNHP microfilms 1848c). A class/status differentiation developed through this new landscape organization. The *Spirit of Jefferson* (SoJ 15 January 1850:3) commented that the appropriations' monies could have been better spent on the armory and that the construction of the houses was a form of self-aggrandizement on Symington's part.

Figure 29. View of the armory ruins, Lower Town, and Camp Hill. The armory supervisor's quarters were located atop the hill and commanded a view over Lower Town and the armory grounds. (Courtesy of Harpers Ferry National Historical Park, HF1155)

Between 1845 and 1854, a total of 25 new buildings were erected at Harpers Ferry. As noted earlier, the new armory buildings were of a Gothic architectural style, which contrasted sharply with the almost random planning of the earlier armory buildings. Interchangeable manufacturing was well under way, and armorers who had once considered themselves craftsmen now tended machines, following the rhythmic motions dictated by technology. In 1852, an inspector was delighted with the rebuilt factories and the implementation of the new system of manufacturing: "The system embraces all the various operations and transactions of the Armory, the hours and distribution of labour, the regulation and police of the workshops, the duties and responsibilities of Foremen and workmen, the accountability for public property . . ." (HFNHP photostats 1852). As described in Chapter 2, a flood in that year had afforded an opportunity to test the reassembly of 9000 muskets from disassembled parts, and the inspector later professed delight over the state of interchangeability at the armory (HFNHP photostats 1852):

The completeness of the present System, so far as *uniformity* in *construction* is concerned, is made manifest by the late submersion of 20,000 arms, during the highest flood ever known at the place. In cleaning those arms, 9000 percussion muskets have been stripped, and completely dismantled, their parts being thrown into great masses and after being repaired their parts are reassembled from these lots of 9000 components, having no distinguishing mark—every limb filling and fitting its appropriate place with perfect exactness.

While many lauded the rebuilding of the armory as a modern success, it still lacked the total efficiency found in most contemporary industrial complexes. Manufacturing was not so arranged that each stage in the operation was under one roof. The process required a finished component to be carried from one shop to another or from one room or floor to another in the same shop. An inspector of the armory noted: "The general arrangement of buildings at this Armory is good, but at the musket factory the work would be greatly expedited and more economically executed if the machinery were arranged so that the passage of the arms from one stage of its progress to another should be simultaneous with its transportation along the line of shops" (HFNHP photostats 1859).

OVERTHROW OF THE MILITARY SYSTEM

Townspeople and armorers were disheartened by the new industrial discipline enforced by Superintendent Symington. He was subjected to considerable political pressure as congressional candidates campaigned to end the "military system" at the armory. The candidates came to the shops "canvassing for votes, with total disregard to the rules." Symington continued, "The character of the population here adds greatly to the difficulties of my position. It consists for the most part of mechanics employed in the Armory, or of persons in some way dependent upon them, practically unacquainted with anything beyond the limits of their neighborhood." Armorers were disheartened by the military system and contrasted it with earlier times when "a man's worthlessness was no ban to his employment in the Armory" (HFNHP microfilms 1849b).

Harpers Ferrians were even more upset when Symington removed the very popular Master Armorer Benjamin Moor in November 1849. Symington justified his action by claiming that Moor did not keep up with the latest technologies in arms manufacturing. "Like the techniques he had helped to replace during the 1840s, Moor had become outdated" (M. R. Smith 1977:299; HFNHP microfilms 1849c). Irate about his removal, he entered politics and became a member of the Virginia House of Delegates in 1850. He made antimilitary speeches regarding the control over armory operations, claiming that military oversight threatened republican ideals and individual liberties. Moor's longtime friend Charles James Faulkner was elected to Congress, served as Chairman of the House Committee on Military Affairs, and attacked Symington and the military system at the national armories. Some armorers opposed the return to the civilian system, including Acting Master Armorer James Burton (M. R. Smith 1977:298–300).

Political pressures forced the removal of Symington, and he was replaced by Benjamin Huger as the armory superintendent in 1851. Political pressure to dissolve the military superintendency in the national armories increased as the military superintendency did not bow to political or religious pressures. The Reverend Welty of the Methodist Episcopal Church protested to the president of the United States that he was unable to visit the workshops and discharge his parochial duties. He was kept out of the workshops, in accordance with a rule that had been in effect for some time to avoid interference with the factory work. The Ordnance Department claimed that there were plenty of other opportunities for parochial duties and that there were no similar problems with the other five denominations at Harpers Ferry. "Reverend Mr. Welty was either a tool in the hands of designing knaves or guided by his own ruffiant spirit" (HFNHP microfilms 1853).

Citizens commented in the newspaper that this form of management was "repulsive and tyrannical" (VFP 29 July 1851:2, 19 August 1852:2, 17 February 1853:2). Workers petitioned to restore the civil superintendency, and in 1852 a bill was presented in the United States House of Representatives to substitute civil for military superintendency (VFP 10 February 1853:2, 22 June 1852:2). While Huger's superintendency lasted from 1851 to 1854, his successor, Major John Bell, appointed in 1854, lasted only a few months (VFP 9 March 1954:2).

In 1854, Congress, under the leadership of Charles Faulkner, ordered the removal of the military system, and Henry Clowe, Benjamin Moor's former assistant, became the next superintendent. Moor and Faulkner, among many others, succeeded in their mission in replacing the military control of the armory. Many townspeople felt that Clowe deserved the position, since he had worked at the facility for many years (VFP 10 August 1854:2, 18 January 1855:2, 25 January 1855:2). Clowe removed more men in 4 years than the military superintendents had removed in 13 years. Most of these men possessed important skills necessary for the operations of the armory, but he punished opponents and rewarded allies. It was clearer than ever that politics controlled the operations of the armory. Armorers reverted to their old habits, the payroll increased, and arms manufacturing decreased to its lowest level since 1845. Money had been spent at an irresponsible rate, and often there was little revenue to fund the entire fiscal year (HFNHP microfilms 1855b). With decreased competency under Clowe's superintendency, some small arms were not interchangeable, but were numbered for corresponding barrels. Clowe was scolded: "The perfect uniformity is so desirable that it should never be neglected where it is possible to affect [sic] it, and when we come to make a new model arm I take it for granted that such uniformity will be attained" (HFNHP microfilms 1855c).

Within two years, the public challenged Clowe's character and performance in the position (VFP 17 December 1857:3; M. R. Smith 1977:301–303). A letter to the *Virginia Free Press* (VFP 21 January 1858:2) noted that

> since the change from the military to the civil system, the operations of the armory have been in a prostrate and abject state. —The commerce of the place has languished near unto death. Industry has little or no encouragement. . . . All of the affairs of the armory, for want of a general, just and intelligent discriminating government of these things, have gone on from bad to worse, till good men begin to doubt whether the consequences of the revolution they assisted in producing, deserve to be called a blessing, and are now ready to return to the old system of military supervision as the only safe one, or which can give peace, harmony, stability or success to the armory, and to the village of Harpers Ferry.

An inspector from the Ordnance Department suggested "that measures of economy should be speedily adopted, or that all work should soon cease and the establishment be closed." These poor results left the Secretary of War no choice but to relieve Clowe of his duties in 1858 (HFNHP photostats 1859). The *Virginia Free Press* (VFP 3 December 1857:2) printed a letter that protested "the repeated instances of official corruption and selfish acts of present superintendent H. W. Clowe, all conceived and directed to promote his own personal interests." The paper itself claimed: "The sooner the military system, so much reviled at one time, be restored, the better. Better the armory be abolished, than that one man (Clowe) shall control the freedom of thought and action of those over whom he may have been placed either through mistaken fitness or party reward" (VFP 10 June 1858:2). Faulkner came to Harpers Ferry and spoke at the armory grounds, asking the citizens for "pardon on his knees for ever having placed over them a man who had disgraced the civil superintendency" (VFP 24 February 1859:2). Even though the press (VFP 5 May 1859) criticized Clowe's performance, they used his removal as an attack on Faulkner. It stated that Faulkner had supported Clowe's appointment as superintendent, but had removed him once he failed to serve Faulkner's interests.

In December 1858, Alfred Barbour became the next civilian superintendent (VFP 30 December 1858:2). Since Congress had cut the armory's budget by 38%, production was extremely low, and costs had increased, Barbour cut the payroll from 400 to 250 employees, and all workers received a 10% reduction in wages. Barbour's actions did not go unnoticed, and the *Virginia Free Press* (VFP 31 March 1859:2) warned the new superintendent of violent protest made against his predecessors (the assassination of Thomas Dunn and the public support for the killer). Barbour reported that under Clowe's leadership, time discipline, enforced by the military superintendency, was no longer enforced. He noted that "men have been in the habit of leaving work in the middle of the afternoon [and it is] doubtful whether more than nine hours per diem have been made by many of the men. . . ." Until Barbour's superintendency, inspectors and supervisors received little support to enforce regulations such as time discipline (HFNHP photostats 1859).

After John Brown's Raid, Barbour had to be careful whom he hired in the armory. The community stirred when there were rumors that the Springfield master armorer was going to be hired to fill a vacancy in the Harpers Ferry Armory (VFP 8 November 1859:2). The *Virginia Free Press* published a rebuttal from Barbour, who did not want to excite the community. He denied that he had ever thought of offering the position to a Northerner, since no Northern man would be safe in Harpers Ferry, although he recognized that worthy armorers labored in the North (VFP 10 November 1959:1–2). Instead, a Harpers Ferry master machinist, Armisted Ball, filled the position (*Independent-Democrat* 15 November 1859:2).

In September 20, 1860, Barbour presented his resignation to the president and his cabinet. They refused his resignation after reflecting on the political consequences of their action (VFP 20 September 1860:2). Barbour had the support of the Harpers Ferry community, and he was seen as a stabilizing factor. In January 1861, the Virginia legislature called for a state convention to settle Virginia's status within the Union. Barbour was elected as a member of the secession committee from Jefferson County, and he promised his constituency that he would vote to conserve the Union. The War Department was eager for Barbour to represent Union sentiments at the convention.

While Barbour remained the superintendent of the Harpers Ferry Armory, his attempt to resign from this position several months earlier may have foreshadowed his eventual intentions regarding Virginia's secession. The assembly commenced on February 13 in Richmond with a majority of the delegates (120 out of 152) having the notion of preserving the Union. While Barbour had hoped to be back at his post in Harpers Ferry by March 1, the deliberations extended into April. Delegates, including Barbour, were pressured by lobbyists from South Carolina, Georgia, and Mississippi to vote for secession. Friends and relatives urged Barbour to abandon the Union. In late March, Barbour had asked for the removal of troops in Harpers Ferry, and shortly after he resigned his position as superintendent. Barbour voted one last time on April 4 against secession. After the fall of Fort Sumter and Lincoln's call for troops to suppress the rebellion, the secession ordinance passed on April 17 (M. R. Smith 1977: 313–316).

Barbour arrived at Harpers Ferry in the morning of April 17 after 24 hours of travel. Addressing a growing crowd at the armory gates, announced that he had signed the ordinance of secession and that he had sided with the state that he loved, rather than with the Union. The majority of the crowd greeted his news with cheers, but some yelled "treason." Fistfights erupted (M. R. Smith 1977:318). Barbour became the chief quartermaster to General J. E. Johnston, and he held the office throughout the war (VFP 17 April 1866:2; *Farmers Advocate* 31 March 1928:1).

Lieutenant Roger Jones was left with 50 men to guard the government property. Only 15 volunteers joined his defense of the armory, since most of the town's militia favored secession. At 9:00 A.M. on April 18, 1861, he received news that 360 Virginia militia and four artillery pieces were approaching the poorly protected facility. Jones ordered his men to torch the armory buildings and retreat north to Chambersburg, Pennsylvania. Townspeople quickly extinguished fires in most of the armory buildings, but the main arsenal, which stored 15,000 arms, was lost along with several other buildings (M. R. Smith 1977:319). Apparently, the War Department did not seriously consider immediately repossessing the armory. They wrote, "Sir: The Armory at Harpers Ferry having been forcibly taken possession of on the night of the 18th April, by the Militia of Virginia, the United States will not be responsible for the services of the operatives after that date" (HFNHP microfilms 1861).

While many arms were lost, the Confederate government was able to salvage two sets of machinery, one from the musket factory on the Potomac River and the other from the rifle works on the Shenandoah

River. The former, including over 300 machines, helped to complete the outfitting of the Richmond Armory. The confederates still operated the rifle works during the dismantling through the first week of June. Operations ceased at the rifle works, and over 132 machines were dismantled in two weeks. They were eventually reassembled at Fayetteville, North Carolina (M. R. Smith 1977:319–320).

On June 14, Johnston destroyed the B&O bridge and burned the armory building on the Potomac River. He returned two weeks later and destroyed the rifle works and a wagon bridge over the Shenandoah River. The armory's numerous skilled mechanics and laborers were dispersed throughout the country. Some traveled north to the Springfield Armory, others found employment in the Confederate armories.

There was only a minor attempt to reestablish the federal armory in Harpers Ferry after the war, but the costs of rebuilding water-powered industry at a time when steam-powered manufacture became increasingly popular seemed to make doing so infeasible. The citizens of Harpers Ferry faced the overwhelming task of rebuilding their local economy without the aid of the federal government upon which they had relied so heavily for over 60 years.

"Their Little Gardens"
—*Virginia Free Press*
Landscapes in an Armory Town

THE GARDEN AND THE MACHINE

Whether or not to allow the rise of American industry during the late eighteenth and early nineteenth centuries was one of the most significant issues that faced the new nation, and the development of Harpers Ferry was significantly influenced by this debate. The majority of American citizens believed that society should remain agrarian, since agriculture was perceived to be the only true and legitimate source of wealth. America was seen as a purifying natural paradise, and relationships to the land were seen as simple, harmonious, and responsible. Pro-agrarians, such as Thomas Jefferson and Daniel Webster, feared that the consequences of industry would destroy the moral fiber of society. The proindustrialists countered and diffused the proagrarian sentiment by presenting an industrial system that the agriculturalists could accept. Proindustrialists, such as Alexander Hamilton and Trench Coxe, conceded that industry should be an activity subsidiary to farming. They believed that factories should be located in rural areas and exploit what they perceived as previously untapped labor resources, such as "idle women, children, and older members of the population" (Kasson 1979; Marx 1964; Prude 1983:31–41; Shelton 1986: 28ff). The creation of a nonurban American industry was meant to avoid the ills of European cities. Industrialists created an ideology that rural industry would make unimproved nature productive.

Industrialists deliberately landscaped around factories to further the belief that the machine could coexist harmoniously with nature. Green lawns were common, as was the deliberate planting of trees along pathways and canals. In some cases, the factory agent allowed employees to have flower beds. "While farmers cleared away natural growth to till their fields, industrialists carefully replanted their mill yards to give them a rustic appearance. Factory owners tried to reassure operatives and townspeople that the transition from farm to factory would not be a wrenching one. The continuing presence of trees and flowers and fields would tame the forces of industry, and perhaps ease the qualms of workers" (Zonderman 1992:66).

Harpers Ferry is one such case of industrial development in America's garden. In the early nineteenth century, Harpers Ferry faced and struggled to resolve the conflicts found between the rural idyllic setting and the growth of industry. Early industry, characterized by its pastoral setting, eventually succumbed to the industrial blight found elsewhere. This chapter focuses on the development of Harpers Ferry at various scales, from the townscape to the urban lot. In particular, I examine how the United States Armory and its individual workers and their families reacted to and tried to resolve the friction between the garden and the machine.

EARLY TOWN DEVELOPMENT: PASTORAL SETTINGS AND UNPLANNED DEVELOPMENT

As an industrial town, Harpers Ferry expanded in the early nineteenth century with little planning and contrasted sharply with the town plans found in the Middle Atlantic and New England regions. When the Harpers Ferry Armory began its operations, the government faced a severe shortage of housing for its approximately 100 craftsmen. The work force doubled within a decade, expanding at a far greater rate than dwellings could be built. Unlike Northern industrialists, the government supplied only a fraction of the needed housing for workers and their families. The federal government had a policy that prohibited private construction on public grounds; therefore, special permission needed to be granted for construction on these lands. Opportunities for workers to build their own dwellings were limited, since the Wager family held a monopoly on all the privately owned $6\frac{3}{4}$ acres of town land and the United States government owned the rest of Harpers Ferry. The Wager family refused to sell any portion of their lot, although they did rent and lease subdivisions of their land at extremely high rates. In 1810, Paymaster Annin wrote to the Secretary of War that the second floors of several of the workshops were serving as lodging for some of the workers. There were "several families accommodated with log houses, or huts, which were built by the army in 1799. Other huts have been rebuilt in more convenient situations which now are generally indifferent" (HFNHP photostats 1810; also see Snell 1981a:31).

An 1810 accounting of armory dwellings on armory land lists 33 households inhabiting 14 structures of various sizes. There is no apparent relationship between occupation, dwelling size, and construction materials except in the case of the superintendent and the paymaster, the two highest-ranking officials in the armory. They each occupied, along with their families, their own single-family, two-story brick structure. Another two-story brick structure existed, although this building accommodated eight families. Mechanics and their families occupied several one-story brick structures. Other workmen and their families occupied the remaining structures, which were built of either frame, log, or stone (HFNHP photostats 1810; also see Snell 1981b:32).

In 1811, the government built six additional houses on public lands. Mechanics occupied these which houses, were of three different sizes and probably a variety of floor plans. While the workforce expanded from 1812 to 1815, the War Department prohibited the armory from building dwellings due to financial restrictions imposed by Congress during the War of 1812. Workers continued to use workshops as lodgings, and the paymaster protested these conditions, saying that "some good mechanics have left us, meeting with better accommodations elsewhere, especially in Pittsburgh" (HFNHP microfilms 1813b). Not only did Annin encounter difficulties attracting mechanics to the armory because of poor accommodations, but also the winter months amplified the substandard conditions (HFNHP microfilms 1813b). Federal appropriations for the construction of dwellings became available in 1816, but there was no other funding for the rest of the decade (Snell 1981a:40–41).

In 1821, only 36 armory dwellings were officially known to exist. Superintendent Stubblefield requested additional funds from the Ordnance Department for housing. When the government asked for an accounting of armory dwellings in 1823, Stubblefield notified the Ordnance Department that 87 armory houses existed on government land, not the 36 that were officially recorded. Apparently, when Stubblefield was confronted with a growing workforce, especially between 1808 and 1814, he permitted his employees to construct dwellings on government land. He also allowed those in existing armory dwellings to construct additions and make repairs to their houses. His actions facilitated the construction of 51 new residences for armory workers (HFNHP microfilms 1823). Unlike practices found in the industrializing North, no single architect or plan guided the building of any of these dwellings. The houses varied widely in styles. There was no formal street plan, many of the streets simply following the town's natural topography.

During the 1820s, armorers forced Stubblefield to settle their claims for repairs, additions, and construction. He encouraged the Ordnance Department to pay for the claims in order for the armory to obtain title to the houses on armory land. In the meantime, armorers constructed 25 more houses on government land with their own funds. Many problems arose with this unchecked system of domestic house building. Armory employees were sometimes left without government housing. Many rents went uncollected, and the superintendent was confronted with the problem of evicting people who no longer worked for the armory, since rents could not be deducted from their paychecks. Mary discharged workers continued to live in government housing; some sold their claims to the houses they occupied. The selling of property claims often perpetuated the problem of nonemployees living on public lands (HFNHP microfilms 1827a,c). Many of the armorers' houses surrounding the factory were in poor condition and deemed uninhabitable (HFNHP microfilms 1827b).

THE GARDENS OF HARPERS FERRY

The town's disrepair and unplanned expansion coexisted with the use of planned vegetation. Creating a built environment that conforms to the existing topography and natural setting are strategies for maintaining a pastoral environment in an urbanizing community. The first several decades of the development of Harpers Ferry were dominated by unplanned housing, unordered factory development, random town development, and the sustenance of a craft ethic. Conversely, landscapes of the town picture a falsely neat and orderly town setting. Many landscapes from the 1800s to the 1830s portray highly picturesque scenes of the manufacturing town and convey the message of the harmonious machine in the American landscape (Figures 30 and 31). Many of these early paintings show people, animals, and pasture as the main subjects, with the industrial complex in the background serving as a secondary focus.

Landscapes and gardens in urbanizing Harpers Ferry were developed for mostly utilitarian purposes, although they also helped to maintain a pastoral setting. Historical evidence of garden plots includes "Mrs. Wager's garden," found on an early nineteenth-century map showing two rows of grapevines (Figure 32). Additional documentation shows that despite the shortage of flat land, gardens thrived in Lower Town. Prior to 1810, the first superintendent, Joseph Perkins, and the first paymaster, Samuel Annin, developed gardens near their homes.

Figure 30. Early-nineteenth-century painting of the armory complex, Potomac River, and surrounding hillsides, including Maryland Heights (*left*) and Loudoun Heights (*right*). (Courtesy of Harpers Ferry National Historical Park, HF628)

Figure 31. View of Harpers Ferry, circa 1834–1836. (Courtesy of Harpers Ferry National Historical Park, HF23)

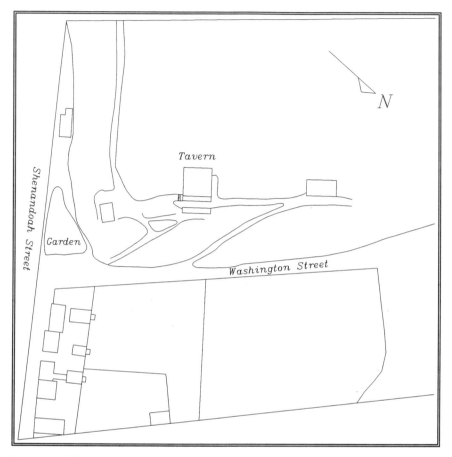

Figure 32. Sketch map of several buildings in Lower Town Harpers Ferry at about 1803, showing the location of Mrs. Wager's garden. (Drawn by John W. Ravenhorst)

Joseph Perkins and his family lived by the ferry landing, adjacent to the armory grounds, in a refurbished warehouse. A 1796 account of his kitchen garden exists. Superintendent Perkins asked one of his employees named Cox to attend to his garden, which was overrun by weeds. Barry (1988[1903]:16) reported:

> Cox did not relish the job, but gave, however, a grumbling consent. Next morning, Cox commenced weeding and, towards evening, he presented himself to Mr. Perkins with the information that "he had made a clean sweep of it." The master was much gratified and he told Mrs. Perkins to give Cox a dram of whiskey. . . . On visiting his garden the next day, Mr. Perkins

discovered that sure enough, Cox had made a clean sweep. The weeds were all gone, but so were the cabbage, turnips, carrots, and everything else of the vegetable kind.

Annin, who lived south of the arsenal yard near the banks of the Shenandoah River, cultivated an extensive yard that contained a variety of "trees, fruits, etc. . . ." When Annin retired and moved to his son's apothecary shop and domicile on Shenandoah Street in 1815, only a few hundred feet to the northwest, he "converted the lot into a garden" (Snell [quoted in C. Gilbert et al. 1993:3.12]).

Some time between 1814 and 1831, a terraced garden was developed adjacent to a tavern that was being constructed by Harper when he died. The garden was used mostly as vegetable plots and service areas. Three terraces were constructed, the lowest one being built with a retaining wall that ranged from 7 to 10 feet high. The wall created a "public walk" between the garden and the house. Openings in the wall that were accessible from the "public walk" held a springhouse, a smokehouse, and a root cellar (C. Gilbert et al. 1993:3.24–3.25).

From 1819 until 1840, John Hall, an inventor and manufacturer, resided on some of the highest grounds in Harpers Ferry that overlooked Hall's Rifle Works and the armory grounds. There, he improved his house and lands by landscaping and plantings. In the words of John Hall's son (quoted in Huntington 1972:80):

> He has enclosed nearly two acres of land, divided it by good fences into gardens and yards, cleared it of rocks and bushes with which it was entirely covered, levelled the inequalities and arranged the declivities, made soil by hauling fertile earth from a distance, and placed the whole in the highest state of cultivation. My father has also planted more than one hundred trees, producing the choicest fruits of the climate; nearly an equal number of grape vines of the most valuable kinds known in America and Europe, all of which are in a very flourishing condition, and many ornamental trees such as locust, etc. In addition to these there is a great variety of the most rare and beautiful flowers, and shrubbery—asparagus & strawberry beds etc. the principal expense for which is the outlay, and which will be serviceable for years to come.

Local newspapers provide additional evidence regarding the utilitarian use of yard spaces by the armorers and their families. Advertisements in the *Virginia Free Press* offered the "choicest kinds of the different varieties [of seeds]" (VFP 7 May 1846:3). Since most armorers and their families lived close to the rivers, these gardens were susceptible to flooding. After a flood in 1843, the newspaper (VFP 21 September 1843:2) noted, "Their little gardens, upon which many of them depend for winter supplies, have been razed, and their losses in various ways have been quite heavy." Superintendent Major John Symington recommended in 1844 that the government purchase an island in the Potomac River, adjacent to the armory, so that armorers and their families could cultivate it. Symington purchased 1947 panels of fencing to enclose armory dwelling gardens (see C. Gilbert et al. 1993:3.40 and endnote 68).

ARCHAEOBOTANICAL ANALYSIS FOR EARLY HARPERS FERRY

Archaeobotanical research complements the historical data on landscapes in Harpers Ferry. This specialized research requires strong interdisciplinary cooperation in order to create a historic context that allows for interpreting the archaeobotanical data. The domestic sites studied include the house of the master armorer, who was manager of the facility's operations, and an armory workers' house, inhabited by households whose heads were laborers and craftsmen. Three types of archaeobotanical analyses (macroflora, pollen, and phytolith) were performed for these domestic landscapes. Analyses of macroflorae (i.e., seeds) have played an important role in reconstructing historical vegetation patterns derived from fruit and some vegetable seeds. Pollen remains provide evidence of a wide spectrum of flora from planned vegetation, such as fruits, vegetables, and flowers, to various types of weeds. Phytolith data contribute complementary information, the strongest research potential of which is the identification of grasses. Grass phytoliths include festucoid (wet, cool habitat), panicoid (wet, warm habitat), and chloridoid (dry, warm habitat).

Pollen and macrofloral analyses by Linda Scott Cummings (1993, 1994) along with Kathryn Puseman (Cummings and Puseman 1994), and phytolith analyses by Irwin Rovner (1993, 1994a,b) from two armory dwellings, follow a growing tradition of archaeobotanical research for the reconstruction and interpretation of historic landscapes. Their work has successfully demonstrated the nature of changing urban land use during the development of the town's industry. The archaeobotanical information from these sites reveals trends that show how armory workers used the area surrounding their domestic structures. These data provide evidence about how these workers reacted to the growing tensions faced by the residents of Harpers Ferry when the pastoral manufacturing setting was besieged by the new order of industrialization.

Master Armorer's House: Pre-1832

In the first quarter of the nineteenth century, there was no formal plan for armory house designs, and the town was irregular in layout and impermanent in nature. This lack of planning was also true of the arrangement of domestic buildings and dependencies on domestic lots. This pattern also prevailed for both the master armorer's lot and the armory workers' house, these structures having been individually built without any oversight from the armory. While the town developed without any master plan, archaeobotanical evidence indicates that a particular house lot occupied by the master armorer's household was kept formal with vegetation. General written descriptions and sketches, drawings, engravings, and other graphic representations portray the town in a natural environment with the machine coexisting harmoniously in the garden. It appears that vegetation planted around the master armorer's house in the form of grasses and planned gardens allowed residents to subscribe to this ideology.

The master armorer's house was constructed by 1815 when Joseph Annin, son of the armory paymaster, constructed his brick apothecary shop and dwelling on Shenandoah Street. During this era, the topography generally sloped from Shenandoah Street to the Shenandoah River. The backyards had an average yard elevation of 263–264 feet above mean sea level and lay about 5 feet below current grade. Historical documents indicate the presence of a small garden behind the domicile. By at least 1821, Master Armorer Armisted Beckham and his household inhabited the dwelling until his transfer in 1830. Beckham was part of the "Junto" described in Chapter 2 that rejected new industrial methods and demanded that the armory remain in craft production.

Analyses from the soil layers dating from the 1820s through 1832 around the master armorer's house indicate the presence of weeds, edible plants, grasses, and formal vegetation. Aggressive weeds that occupy disturbed soils, such as knotweed or smartweed (cf. *Polygonum*), and buffalo bur (*Solanum rostratum*) seeds occur in small quantities. Elderberry (*Sambucus*), often considered a weed but also used as a food, is also present in the yard. Low-spine Asteraceae pollen, which is indicative of ragweed and sumpweed, as well as clover (cf. *Trifolium*), is also proportionately low. Cultivated moss rose (*Portulaca*) and pink family (Caryophyllaceae), a form of cultivated flower, is identified close to the master armorer's house. Other identifiable pollens include mustard (*Brassica*) pollen, probably grown for its seeds and greens, corn (*Zea mays*) pollen, and a single fragment of popped corn (Cummings 1993:7.1–7.46). A substantial number of grasses (Poaceae) are identi-

fied in the phytolith record, indicating an attempt by the master armorer to formalize the backyards. Grasses were intentionally planted,
and indigenous vegetation was kept to a minimum. Grasses dominated
the new landscape, providing an appearance of formality. Chloridoid-
class short-cell phytoliths are present only in the pre-1830s deposits.
Festucoid class phytoliths are also relatively high (Rovner 1993:9.1–
9.10). Generally, it appears that the pre-1830s master armorer's yard
was well groomed in most places with grasses, although some weed intruders existed. An ornamental and utilitarian garden coexisted in the
yard space adjacent to the master armorer's house.

An Armory Worker's Landscape: Pre-1842

The armory workers' house, also located on Shenandoah Street and
several hundred feet north of the master armorer's house, stands as a
two-story-plus attic stone structure. The building was originally constructed in the 1820s and measured 19 feet by 15.5 feet. The dwelling
is also listed as having several associated outbuildings, including a log
house, bake oven, smokehouse, privy, stable, and fence (Bumgardner
1991:10–11; Snell 1980:28–29). During the 1830s or 1840s, a 17.5 by 19
foot addition was constructed on the north side of the building. The
original topography stood about 3–4 feet lower than the present elevation (Shackel and YoungRavenhorst 1994:3.1–3.17). The structure remained in the hands of the armory throughout the 1820s and 1830s.
Unfortunately, armory rental records that date to this era were destroyed in the Library of Congress several decades ago. Armory workers, however, probably lived in the structure during this era.

Archaeobotanical samples were taken from throughout the yard.
Grasses were planted in front of the house, although their presence
fluctuated greatly in the 1820s and 1830s. Caryophyllaceae pollen
(which includes various herbaceous flowering plants such as pinks,
Dianthus, carnations, Sweet William, and bachelor buttons, as well as
native plants) is also identified along with rose family (Rosaceae) pollen. In the 1830s, the proportion of low-spine Asteraceae pollen increases dramatically along with ragweed (*Ambrosia*) and perhaps
cocklebur (*Xanthium*) or marsh elder (*Iva*). High-spine Asteraceae pollen is also present, either in the form of weeds or possibly as cultivated
flowers. The presence of a probable tomato (*Lycopersicon*) seed and the
appearance of charcoal, bone fragments, cloth, eggshell, fish scale, and
mollusk shell fragments from flotation samples indicates that the area
became a receptacle for household debris. Weeds, such as goosefoot
(*Chenopodium*) and carpetweed (*Mollugo*), are also identified. A low

frequency of grass phytoliths exists (Rovner 1994b:9.1–9.10; Cummings and Puseman 1994:8.1–8.31).

The west yard appears to have been kept well weeded and supported a dense population of grasses and possibly a garden. Corn (*Zea mays*) pollen exists, and kitchen debris, such as eggshells, bone, fish scales, and the like, is nonexistent in all the flotation samples (Cummings and Puseman 1994:8.1–8.31).

DISCIPLINARY TECHNOLOGY AND THE REORGANIZATION OF HARPERS FERRY

While early Harpers Ferry existed in a pastoral setting, the factory and town began to modernize in the 1830s. Master Armorer Benjamin Moor slowly made improvements to mechanize the armory. Time-saving machinery, in use at Harpers Ferry's sister armory in Springfield, Massachusetts, for over a decade, was finally introduced. Moor also developed the Model 1840 musket, the first musket constructed of interchangeable parts. Its production was short-lived, and it was produced mostly at the Springfield Armory. The Ordnance Department replaced it with the Model 1842 musket devised by Thomas Warner, the master armorer at Springfield. Its contribution is very significant to the mass production of interchangeable parts for weapons, and it appears that the newer model used many of Moor's basic designs (M. R. Smith 1977:260–261, 280–281). Armorers were slowly losing their independence as craftsmen and pieceworkers as they became increasingly tied to the rhythms of industry.

The government played an increasingly controlling role in dictating the workers' domestic conditions by modernizing housing. In the 1830s, the Ordnance Department prohibited the private construction of any new dwellings on government land. The pre-1830 dwelling construction and floor plan development varied with the needs of individual workers and their families. From the 1830s, the government advertised for contractors to build armory dwellings according to a standard specification of house dimensions and construction materials, much like industrialists were doing in other regions (e.g., see Bond 1987). The new Harpers Ferry structures each had two stories with a stone foundation and brick wall. The main structure measured 22 by 28 feet. Each of the two floors contained one fireplace and consisted of three rooms; two measured 11 by 12 feet, and one was 16 by 22 feet.

There was an attached 12 by 18 foot one-story brick kitchen (Snell 1981a:108–114) (Figure 33).

In 1841, military officers replaced civilian supervisors in an attempt to take control of the work process. The military superintendent reinforced existing strategies that would facilitate the imposition of work discipline, including the division of labor and the enforcement of regular daily work hours. Symington redesigned aspects of the town in order to make production more efficient, facilitate the movement of goods, isolate behavior, and monitor the flow of traffic (M. R. Smith 1977:275; HFNHP photostats 1835, 1836a). Symington redesigned the town and imposed a grid over the earlier street pattern (Figure 34). New buildings were erected in an orderly fashion, and the superintendent implemented a new manufacturing system. Thus was born a "mechanics of power" that trained or forced individuals to perform tasks. Interchangeable manufacturing was well under way by the 1850s at Harpers Ferry and as described in Chapter 3, craftsmen tended machines following the rhythmic motions dictated by machinery (HFNHP microfilms 1845).

TRANSFORMING THE GARDEN INTO AN INDUSTRIAL CENTER

The landscape surrounding the armory changed dramatically during the transition to a modern industrial complex. Da Costa Nunes suggests that during this transition in the 1830s, a turning point in industrial development in the United States as a whole, urban areas began to swell: "[A]fter 1830, the visual harmony of the middle landscape frequently [found in pictures of industrial settings] no longer existed for some of the larger factories [elsewhere in the United States], where the environment was gradually being transformed and urbanized" (da Costa Nunes 1986:25). In Harpers Ferry, the factory and the industrial infrastructure became the focus of the many images created of the town. Smoke billowing from factories, and trains transporting goods, materials, and people became an important focus of America's perception of urban industrialization. The industrial landscape that initially had pastoral features was transformed into one that emphasized manufacturing and the town's functional needs (Figures 35 and 36). In fact, British traveler (Thomas Cather [quoted in Gilbert 1995:61]) wrote about Harpers Ferry:

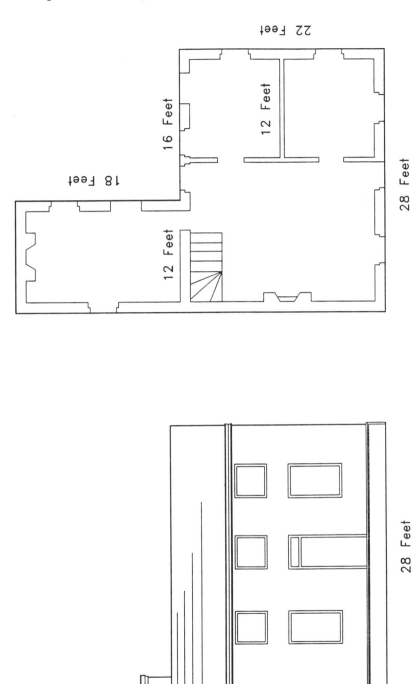

Figure 33. Standardized plan for armory worker's dwellings developed in the early 1830s. (Drawn by John W. Ravenhorst)

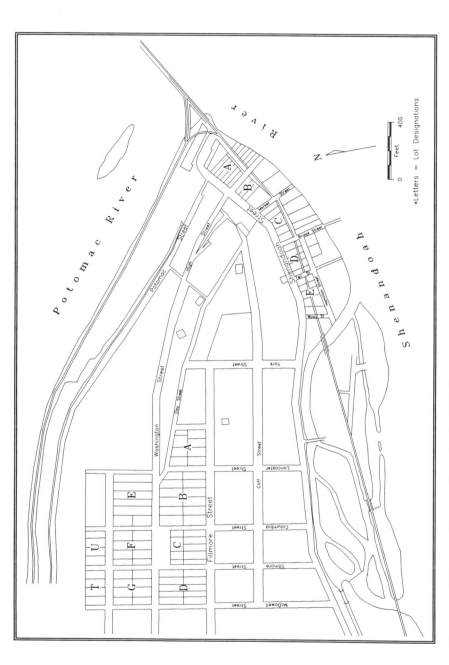

Figure 34. Grid map of Harpers Ferry developed by Superintendent Symington, circa 1840s. (Drawn by John W. Ravenhorst)

Figure 35. View of Lower Town Harpers Ferry from the Maryland shore, showing the elevated bridge across the Potomac River. Sachse Co. Print 1860–1863, based on a drawing by Eidenback, circa 1853. (Courtesy of Harpers Ferry National Historical Park, HF255)

Figure 36. View of Harpers Ferry, 1859. (Courtesy of Harpers Ferry National Historical Park, HF246)

There is a most abominable little village just in the pass between the mountains. Here is the Government Manufactury of Firearms; and the smell of coal smoke and the clanking of hammers obtrude themselves on the senses and prevent one's enjoyment from being unmixed.

While Master Armorer Benjamin Moor dictated general renovations throughout the armory, the government provided general repairs to the master armorer's house. The civilian-operated armory became increasingly concerned with standing water and drainage problems in the Lower Town area. The need for proper drainage may be related to the armory's chronic health and disease problems with stagnant water. Potomac Street was graded and macadamized, and the armory contracted to excavate the lands from Shenandoah Street for better drainage for rainwater runoff. This construction included the grading of lands several hundred feet wide through the "Paymaster's garden." These renovations obliterated a large section of previously undisturbed cultivated lands and destroyed much of the early archaeological record in the lower yards (Myers 1965:2–3; also see Shackel et al. 1993:4.1–4.85). Only the lands adjacent to the buildings escaped this grading. The *Virginia Free Press* (VFP 28 August 1834:3) mentioned the construction of drains to carry water from Shenandoah Street to the Shenandoah River. One of these shale drains was found to lie near the back of the old master armorer's quarters and angle southwest across the yard to Globe Inn Alley (now known as Market Street). Large shale slabs 3–4 feet long capped the drain, which averaged 0.9 feet wide and 0.75 feet high. The drain ran at least 90 feet across the master armorer's back lot (Ford 1993: 12.1–12.33; Shackel et al. 1993: 4.1–4.85).

In 1834, the Winchester and Potomac Railroad cut through many of the domestic lots lining the south side of Shenandoah Street. The railroad encroached upon the master armorer's lot and many of the armory workers' lots and divided them in two. By the late 1850s, the government's main concerns for the armory properties along Shenandoah Street shifted from those that affected general health and hygiene reasons to those that emphasized order and uniformity. As standardization of work and domestic life became prevalent in Harpers Ferry, the armory superintendent expressed concern over irregular landscaping in the backyards. Some areas along Shenandoah Street were as much as 4 feet below the Shenandoah Street grade. As a result, the armory filled and graded these yards, creating a relatively flat and uniform topography. The ground surface was raised by as much as 4 feet behind the master armorer's house and 1.5 feet in front of the armory workers' dwelling. The change in landscape reflects the beginning of an industrial consciousness. Order, regularity, and formality guided the workplace—the built environment—as well as the topography. The generally uniform topography and new architectural standardization reinforced, shaped, and ordered a new industrial culture with which we are very familiar today.

Master Armorer's House: 1832–1852

During this era of general renovations to the armory grounds, Benjamin Moor resided in the master armorer's house. Moor was responsible for the eventual mechanization of the armory, including the development of the first musket constructed of interchangeable parts. In 1834, the United States Government constructed a kitchen and smokehouse on the property inhabited by the master armorer. Three years later, the master armorer's quarters were enlarged from two to two and a half stories (Snell 1981a:170).

The transition to a residential landscape characteristic of the industrial era is noticeable in an examination of the archaeobotanical evidence from the master armorer's house. There is a sharp reduction in grass family (Poaceae) pollen and an increase in ragweed or sumpweed (low-spine Asteraceae) pollen. Probable clover (*Trifolium*), noted in the pre-1830s sample, is all but absent from these later samples. A representation of moss rose or purslane (*Portulaca*) is found along with carpetweed or Indian chickweed (*Mollugo*) and raspberry (*Rubus*) seeds (Cummings 1993:7.1–7.46). Other data indicate a notable dearth of grass phytoliths, although other non-grass categories become especially dense. The strong grass presence in the pre-1830 period disappears, and the presence of a varying mixture of dicotyledonous plants, weeds, forbs, shrubs, and trees increases dramatically (Rovner 1993:6.1–6.13). Generally, the formal vegetation found at the master armorer's house declined.

Armory Workers' House: 1842–1850s

Notable changes in land use also occurred on the grounds surrounding a building that housed armory workers. A two-story east wing addition on the armory workers' building constructed about 1841 measures 20.25 by 17.5 feet. The structure contained the households of various armory workers. Most certainly Augustus Shope and his wife Catherine, who appear on the surviving rent rolls that date to March 1841, occupied the structure. They paid a substantially higher rent than most armorers, probably because of an added east wing that they rented to boarders. From 1844, the structure became a duplex, and two families always occupied the building into the 1850s, one in the original core and the other in the east wing. The heads of both households were employed by the armory (Bumgardner 1991:26–31). By the 1840s, the topography was about 1.5–2.0 feet higher than the 1820s landscape.

Phytolith analyses in the front of the house indicate an increase in the relative presence of grass short cells, both panicoid and festucoid, for a very short time during the early 1840s. Rovner (1994a,b) believes that this anomaly indicates intentional ethnobotanical modification of the landscape. The pollen signature indicates that weeds in the form of sedge or nut grasses (Cyperaceae) were present, and the occurrence of grass pollen increased dramatically. Rose family (Rosaceae) and low-spine Asteraceae pollen are present in small quantities, along with car-petweed (*Mollugo*) and clover (*Trifolium*) seeds, which probably indicate local growth of weeds. Flotation samples show a noticeable in-crease of household debris, including bone, blue porcelain, eggshell, and fish scales. The presence of oogonia of stonewort (*Chara*), a submerged algae found in still, nutrient-poor waters, indicates poor drainage and the presence of a ditch or a low wet spot in the front of the house.

The side yard contains evidence of a garden and provides a signa-ture similar to that of the pre-1842 samples. Corn (*Zea mays*) pollen remains relatively high. Some weeds are found, including daisy family (Asteraceae), mustard family (Brassicaceae), and rose family (Rosaceae). The phytolith content is also very rich during this era. Two types of Asteraceae tissue are noted, signifying the presence of flowery weeds, including garden ornamentals/domesticates such as sunflower. The phytolith signature also exhibits a strong possibility of corn (*Zea mays*) grown in the side yard. No sign of heavy trash deposits, such as kitchen debris, is noticeable (Rovner 1994b:9.1–9.10; Cummings and Puseman 1994:8.1–8.31).

The garden at the armory workers' house was discontinued during the 1850s. Corn (*Zea mays*) and grass short cells disappear from the phytolith signature, although flowers, or flowery weeds, are present. Low-spine Asteraceae pollen increases substantially. Raspberry (*Rubus*) and nightshade family (Solanaceae) seeds as well as bone and fish scale fragments are identified, indicating that the area was used for the deposition of kitchen refuse (Rovner 1994b:9.1–9.10; Cummings and Puseman 1994:8.1–8.31).

By the 1850s, the front yard of the armory workers' house was no longer being used to discard kitchen refuse. Very little charcoal or egg-shell remains are found. Better drainage was created, as indicated by the absence of stonewort (*Chara*) oogonia. Some native or weedy plants grew in this area, including mint family (Lamiaceae), carpetweed

(*Mollugo*), wood sorrel (*Oxalis*), and catchfly (*Silene*). After the 1840s, few pollen and phytolith data exist for the armory workers' house (Rovner 1994b:9.1–9.10; Cummings and Puseman 1994:8.1–8.31). Poor preservation may have been a product of the industrial nature of the landscape. The increased dumping of ash and other high acidic materials and frequent earthmoving in areas that were once groomed and ornamental may have contributed to this decreased frequency.

The 1850s and after the Civil War

In the late 1850s, landscape improvements in the armory yards became necessary. The armory superintendent noted that the grounds between Shenandoah Street and the railroad were extremely irregular and well below street level. Filling and grading were undertaken between 1857 and 1859 to raise the yards behind and adjacent to the master armorer's house to the elevation of Shenandoah Street (Chickering and Jenkins 1994; Shackel et al. 1993). Archaeological excavations have located these filling episodes as well as subsequent landscape changes around the house. Pollen, phytolith, and macroflora evidence does exist for the area surrounding the master armorer's house. Grading and filling appear to have been more frequent at the armory workers' house, and no deposits dating from the late 1850s exist around the house.

During the end of the armory's operation and into the transition to private ownership of former government lands, the degradation of the government holdings continued, including land around the master armorer's house in Lower Town. A greater diversity of pollen types exists because of sustained preservation as well as the escalation of weeds. For instance, low-spine Asteraceae increased in the area surrounding the smokehouse. This evidence suggests increased disturbance, probably due to the transformation of the area into a utilitarian yard for a general store. In these yards, wagons loaded and unloaded coal, gravel, and sand that was sold to local customers. Sedge or nut grasses (Cyperaceae) are found along with cattail/bur-reed (*Typha/Sparganium*). Phytolith data indicate an increase of nongrasses and trash (Cummings 1993:7.1–7.46).

The majority of seeds recovered during the early private ownership of the master armorer's house are weeds, including pigweed (*Amaranthus*), goosefoot (*Chenopodium*), nut grass (*Cyperus*), carpetweed (*Mollugo*), purslane (*Portulaca*), tomatillo/ground cherry (*Physalis*), and buffalo bur (*Solanum rostratum*). Others may represent cultivated plants, including cockscomb (*Amaranthus*), tomatillo/ground cherry

(*Physalis*), and moss rose (*Portulaca*). Seeds from foods include fig (*Ficus*), tomatillo/ground cherry (*Physalis*), and raspberry (*Rubus*). Any or all of these foods could have been grown in a garden, except fig, which grows in more tropical areas and therefore represents a purchased item, although fig shrubs are grown in protected areas of northern Virginia for preserves. These food items are found with many nonfloral remains such as charcoal, coal, eggshell, hair, and fish scales (Cummings 1993:7.1–7.46). Because of this mixing of food-related seeds with kitchen trash deposits, it appears that the backyards were increasingly used for waste disposal.

MEANINGS OF THE BUILT LANDSCAPE

An archaeological and historical analysis of both the topography and the built environment demonstrates the dynamic nature of the landscapes surrounding the master armorer's house and an armory workers' house. From the early nineteenth century, historical occupation and the landscapes were transformed according to the needs and expressions of its occupants and the surrounding community. While some households chose to maintain formalized vegetation in the nineteenth century, others did not. Development, health concerns, commerce, industry, and the persistence of a craft ethos were all influential variables that helped shape, create, and change the landscape. Noticeable differences are apparent in the landscape when comparing the first quarter of the nineteenth century, when armory manufacturing subscribed to a craft ethos, with the second quarter of the nineteenth century, when industrial manufacturing became rooted in the daily routines of workers.

Compared to the Springfield Armory, Harpers Ferry lagged in its efficiency and production output while it sustained relatively higher production costs. Much of the success of early nineteenth-century Northern manufacturing may be attributed to the imposition of factory discipline and the establishment of a corporate paternalism (e.g., see Hanlan 1981; Hareven 1978, 1982). This new ideology served as a mechanism to ensure profit as well as to extend corporate influence into the domestic, religious, and educational realms of the workers' lives. Many communities were deliberately planned by industrial capitalists who standardized the behavior of workers in the home as well as in the factory. The continued reinforcement of discipline trained people in a new work ethic as standardized behavior. This discipline created a more efficient workplace (Aitken 1985; Margolis 1985; Shackel 1993c; Zonderman 1992).

At first glance, the early United States Armory at Harpers Ferry appears to be unstandardized and unplanned, when in fact archaeological analysis demonstrates that this apparent disorganization may have been part of an early industrialist strategy. Archaeobotanical studies of Harpers Ferry (Cummings 1993, 1994; Rovner 1993, 1994a,b; Cummings and Puseman 1994) have allowed new interpretations of the changing cultural environment within the context of industrialization (Shackel 1993a,d, 1994a; Shackel and Winter 1994). While industrialists and agriculturalists of the new republic argued whether this nation should industrialize or become the breadbasket of the world, Harpers Ferry grew as an industrial town at the confluence of the Shenandoah and Potomac rivers, some 60 miles from the major ports of Georgetown and Alexandria. During the early nineteenth century, industrial development in remote areas was justified as making nature productive (Kasson 1979; Marx 1964; Prude 1983; Shelton 1986). Examination of the archaeobotanical remains provides evidence of one strategy that early Harpers Ferry industrialists used to create a compromise that allowed industry and nature to coexist.

Pollen and phytolith data from grounds around armory dwellings indicate that armory officials attempted to provide well-groomed, manicured lawns in this industrial environment. Gardens existed on the Wager lot, and Paymaster Annin kept an orchard, both within a very short distance of the armory grounds. Armory workers kept kitchen gardens, mostly to supplement their diet and for additional income. When floods destroyed the workers' gardens in the 1840s, Superintendent Symington proposed the creation of gardens maintained by the workers and their families on an island within view of the armory complex. Maintaining a quasi-pastoral environment around the armory helped to justify the coexistence of the machine and nature within Harpers Ferry. By the 1830s, when the industrialization process and disciplined manufacturing techniques became established, and the justification of industry's coexistence with nature decreased, the areas surrounding the armory appear to have been less well maintained (Shackel 1993b,d, 1994b). Yards lost their manicured nature as weedy plants dominated the ground's floral composition. Symington's proposal to make gardens on an island was surely a humane gesture to help provide for the workers' families, but it was also one of the last attempts by government officials to encourage or intentionally plant flora on or near the armory grounds.

An archaeological analysis of domestic yard space from this earlier period (pre-1830s) indicates some semblance of a formalized landscape with possible garden plots at the master armorer's house and
the armory workers' house. Archaeobotanical analyses demonstrate
that a well-groomed landscape existed at the master armorer's house
near the heart of the industrial complex, while there was usually man-
aged vegetation growth at the armory workers' house. The yard spaces
mimic the factory's quasi-pastoral surroundings found in the agrarian
countryside. The phytolith analyses of Rovner (1993, 1994a,b) show
that during the early occupation, a formal landscape existed that consisted mostly of grasses. The pollen analyses of Cummings (1993,
1994) and Cummings and Puseman (1994) demonstrate that grasses
and herbaceous plants were common in the 1820s along with cultivated moss rose and corn. Some weeds, in smaller proportions, were
also present. Corn and moss rose may indicate the presence of a utilitarian garden with some formal flora. It appears that during an era
characterized by task-oriented labor and an unplanned town and factory system at Harpers Ferry, the armory employees, both managers
and workers, paid particular attention to both functional and ornamental use of the grounds, thereby creating a quasi-pastoral setting
throughout the major industrial complex. Evidence of a kitchen garden appears at both sites during this era, although trash disposal in
front of the workers' house is prominent.

Modernization coexisted with the degradation of the formal quasi-
pastoral landscape and is visible in the archaeological record. The lands
were graded from Shenandoah Street to the Shenandoah River in order
to create better drainage in the Lower Town area. The prevalent grass
phytoliths disappeared and were replaced by those of weeds, forbs, and
shrubs at the master armorer's house (Rovner 1993, 1994a). Pollen
studies also confirm the relatively low presence of grass (Cummings
1993, 1994). These analyses suggest that during an era characterized
by time-oriented labor and a concern for planning and orderliness, the
quasi-pastoral grounds surrounding the master armorer's house deteriorated, although this pattern was not necessarily the case at the
armory workers' house.

When the military took control of the armory operation in 1841,
some maintenance and grooming took place around the armory workers'
house. A neat and orderly yard existed, and trash was no longer scattered in front of the house. The front yard was raised 1–1.5 feet to meet
the grade of Shenandoah Street. Since the armory owned the lands, the
military supervisors may have taken a new paternalistic interest in the
welfare and living conditions of their employees. This new order found

in the landscape did not last long. As with the master armorer's house, it appears that by the late 1840s, industry took precedence over maintaining the landscape at the armory workers' house. The armory was in the process of standardizing architecture throughout the armory grounds, constructing over 20 new factory buildings, and creating a town plan based on a grid pattern. Industrialists no longer needed to justify the coexistence of the machine in the garden, and many of the natural landscape features appear to have deteriorated.

From the beginning of the industrialization of New England and the Middle Atlantic regions, manufacturers immediately imposed a rigid, disciplined infrastructure on developing industrial centers. By contrast, the unstandardized built environment at Harpers Ferry, such as winding roads and individually built factories and domestic housing, helped to reinforce an ideology that allowed for the coexistence of nature and the machine. While the early armory lacked industrial discipline, it may have been a conscious or unconscious effort by the industrial planners of Harpers Ferry. Unlike New England industries that recruited women and children (Dublin 1977, 1979) and Middle Atlantic industries that employed unskilled labor, immigrants, and poor men (Shelton 1986; Wallace 1978), the Harpers Ferry Armory employed skilled craftsmen. Convincing craftsmen that the new order of industry was justifiable and no threat to their daily routines may have weighed heavily in the decision not to impose rigid factory discipline in the early stages of the armory. With the maintenance of the status quo and the slow imposition of forms of factory discipline, craftsmen were not immediately threatened by a modernizing factory system that would alienate their labor and compromise their livelihood. By being allowed to keep traditional work ethics and undisciplined manufacturing processes, craftsmen may have been convinced that they could coexist with the new manufacturing system and be subject to few or no intrusions made upon their everyday lives.

"Customs and Habits Interwoven with the Very Fibers of Things"

—BENJAMIN MOOR, Master Armorer

Consumerism among Armory Households

CHANGING CONSUMERISM

During the early nineteenth century, American consumption patterns changed dramatically. Industrial behavior became the norm in urban areas, and households no longer relied upon home production and barter for their everyday needs. Instead, they increasingly relied upon monetary exchange for labor and goods for their everyday necessities. Acquiring new and fashionable goods became part of the new Romantic consumer culture. These transformations were felt in the small industrial town of Harpers Ferry. Craftsmen were often forced to substitute their means of production for wage-paying jobs. Goods that were once generated by the family unit were now purchased, since family providers spent an increasing number of hours laboring to the rhythms and motions of machinery.

While many lost their identity by surrendering their means of production, they used wages to purchase their expressions of individuality. Individuals in a consumer society seek self-illusory experiences that they construct from an item's associated meanings. The subscription to Romantic ideals allowed people to believe that they were individuals. Consumers acquired the same mass-produced material and social expressions as others in their social class. Thus, an illusion of individuality was created when, in fact, most people of a given class were becoming more like each other.

In Harpers Ferry, many of the armory households increasingly used consumer goods to demonstrate their acceptance of the new consumer culture and Romantic ideals developing in the early nineteenth century. Other households were more reluctant to participate in these new values; they either partially or totally rejected these new ideals by not participating in consumer values acquired by many urban households located near consumer markets. What follows is a comparison of the archaeological assemblage of two house lots. One site housed successive single families whose male heads of household controlled the daily production of arms at the armory. The other site was occupied by several households with heads who were craftsmen, pieceworkers, and laborers at the facility. The different social and economic backgrounds of the households that inhabited the two sites contributed to very distinct material culture expressions. The separate households reacted in diverse ways to the introduction of a new industrial culture. While the successive households at one site apparently accepted the items of a new consumer culture, those at the other site displayed patterns that adhered to consumption practices that were popular several generations earlier.

MASTER ARMORER BECKHAM AND HIS HOUSEHOLD

The master armorer's house was built in 1812 when Samuel Annin, the armory paymaster and senior administrative officer, petitioned the Secretary of War to grant his son, Dr. Joseph Annin, permission to erect a brick dwelling and apothecary shop on government land. The petition was necessary because the construction of privately owned buildings on armory property was forbidden by government policy. Since the Wagers owned the 6-acre reserve, the only privately owned land in Harpers Ferry, they controlled the numbers and types of business that could be established in Harpers Ferry. Annin argued that the apothecary shop would greatly benefit the armory workers, since there was none in the town (Snell 1981a:44, 155). Permission was granted, and Dr. Annin constructed on Shenandoah Street a two-story brick building that originally measured 33 × 23 feet. Samuel Annin resigned from his armory position in 1815 because of failing health and then resided with his son. Joseph continued to operate his apothecary shop until at least 1818. An 1816 letter from Samuel Annin indicated that his son's house had a garden, although the back lot was only 33 feet wide (the width of the house) by 14 feet deep (Snell 1959b:4–5) (Figure 37).

Dr. Annin left town, and the master armorer took possession of the house no later than 1821. Annin had never been compensated for the house that he built on public lands, and he demanded compensation of

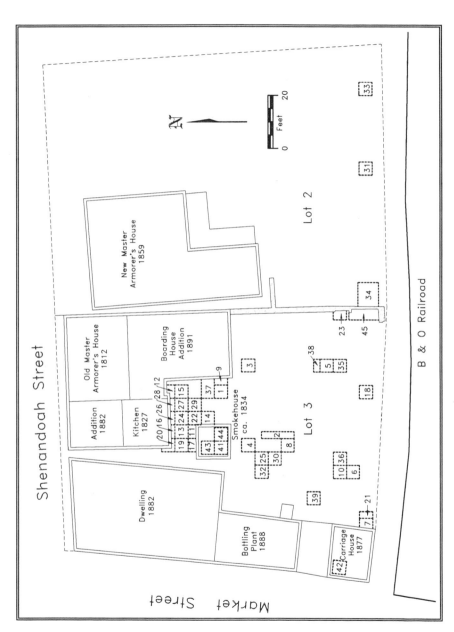

Figure 37. Grid map showing excavation units behind the old master armorer's house. (Drawn by John W. Ravenhorst)

$2500 or he would repossess the house. The government paid Annin the requested amount, and the structure became the permanent residence of the master armorer until the late 1850s (Snell 1959b:7).

The first master armorer to reside in the house, Armistead Beckham, was appointed to that position in 1815 and lived there from at least 1818/1821 to 1830. The 1830 census noted that Beckham's household included his wife, four children, and three slaves (United States Bureau of the Census 1830:164). As brother-in-law of armory Superintendent James Stubblefield, Beckham operated within a powerful oligarchy that exercised control over many of the 1400 residents of Harpers Ferry. Both Stubblefield and Beckham dominated most aspects of Harpers Ferry life between 1815 and 1829. Beckham's and Stubblefield's primary view of the armory was not to manufacture guns efficiently, but rather to provide a source of jobs, patronage, and profit. The Secretary of War became aware of a retail store kept on government land by the firm of Wager, Beckham (one of the other Beckham brothers) and Company. Stubblefield and Armisted Beckham were secret partners in the firm. The secretary scorned these clandestine dealings and advised that they divorce themselves of this enterprise immediately (HFNHP microfilms 1821a). Beckham and Stubblefield often resisted interference from outsiders, since they considered the operation of the armory a local affair. Whether they acceded to the secretary's wishes is unclear.

As New England industries began emphasizing time discipline and interchangeability, Beckham and Stubblefield remained committed to craft-oriented production (M. R. Smith 1977). Generally, few restrictions controlled the armorers' work behavior, and work discipline did not exist. In the late 1810s and early 1820s, Thomas Blanchard, under the direction of the Ordnance Department, tried to introduce various woodworking lathes that could cut nonconcentric forms for gunstocks. Beckham reacted fiercely against the installment of these machines and led a group of workmen who expressed their disapproval of this mechanization (M. R. Smith 1977:137). Blanchard's machinery was not used during Beckham's tenure as master armorer through the 1820s.

Harpers Ferry armorers gained a reputation for their unfriendly reception of outsiders, especially Northerners with innovative ideas or newcomers who adhered to disciplined work habits. One case is that of Nahum W. Patch, a lock filer who came from the Springfield, Massachusetts, Armory in 1822. In 1823, Stubblefield promoted him to inspector. Lock filers began to complain to Master Armorer Beckham that Patch inspected their work too closely for the low wages that they received.

The master armorer temporarily appeased the pieceworkers by raising their rate from 20¢ to 25¢ per finished lock (HFNHP microfilms 1826a).

In 1825, Patch rejected some of the work of Henry Stipes a craft-trained artisan, and claimed the work was substandard. When Patch returned to the armory dinner at his boardinghouse, Henry Stipes greeted him in a deceptively friendly manner. Patch noted that "the instant I came within his reach he struck me with his fist and broke out one of my teeth, and I believe he had something clenched in his hand from the severity of the blow. I was severely injured by his striking and kicking me . . ." (HFNHP microfilms 1826a; also see HFNHP microfilms 1825).

Stubblefield and Beckham discharged both Patch and Stipes for the incident, although Patch protested that Stipes was getting armory work and taking it to an island in the Potomac that was under the jurisdiction of Maryland. The superintendent and master armorer denied Patch's accusation and claimed that Stipes was not on the armory payrolls (HFNHP 1826a,b).

Colonel George Bomford, Chief of Ordnance, ordered Stubblefield to hold a hearing regarding Patch's reinstatement to his position. Stubblefield handpicked the arbitrator, James Stephenson, Master Armorer Beckham's father-in-law. Twenty-two lock filers testified against Patch's character. Patch refused to attend the hearings, since Stephenson was not a magistrate and therefore legal authority. Patch was found guilty, and Stubblefield reinstated Henry Stipes (HFNHP microfilms 1826a; also see M. R. Smith 1977:160).

In retaliation, Patch notified the War Department of Stubblefield's and Beckham's mismanagement of the facilities. For instance, he noted that Samuel Cox, a sickly armorer who had begun his career with the armory at its opening (Barry 1988[1903]:27), periodically spent one to two weeks away from work. He often sent his "two little boys," who were unfamiliar with locksmithing, to "do some of the lock work" during his absence, and they often ruined the product. An armorer, Richard Martin, tried to salvage some of this work, but Patch wrote that they were some of the worst locks he had ever inspected. He also noted that equipment, such as files, was often carelessly mishandled and wasted by the armorers. Some employees, such as foreman George Mallory, remained on the payrolls, not because of their workmanship, but because they owed the superintendent and master armorer money (HFNHP microfilms 1826a). At about the same time, other armorers, such as lock filer Charles Staley, who refused to testify against Patch, lost their positions at the armory. The Ordnance Department received numerous other complaints about the superintendent's improprieties in dealing with the armory (M. R. Smith 1977:161–182). Patch eventually became one of John Hall's most valuable employees, joining the rifle works in 1831. Patch became a highly respected and knowledgeable small arms inspector, and he redesigned various types of breechloaders during his tenure with the armory (Huntington 1972:53).

Stubblefield and Beckham were also concerned about contracting John Hall, a New Englander, to manufacture his breechloading rifle with interchangeable parts. Hall was a threat to the craft-oriented production at the armory. Beckham claimed that Hall was a "visionary theorist" and resented the government's sending him to Harpers Ferry rather than to Springfield (M. R. Smith 1977:156).

Stubblefield stood trial twice, in 1827 and 1829, for mismanagement of the Harpers Ferry Armory. As the latter trial progressed, it became clear that Beckham was the one truly at fault for misusing his supervisory powers. Superintendent Stubblefield resigned his post after the second trial in 1829. Beckham refused to resign, and he was reassigned to the Allegheny Arsenal in Pittsburgh in exchange for Benjamin Moor, a former master armorer at the Springfield Armory (M. R. Smith 1977).

Benjamin Moor, master armorer at Harpers Ferry from 1830 to 1849 and next resident of the master armorer's house, was one of the few dedicated to the facility's industrialization during the first half of his tenure. Moor entered the United States Armory at Springfield as an apprentice in 1797. He completed his training in 1804 and worked at both Harpers Ferry and a private armory in Canton, Massachusetts. He became the master armorer at the Springfield Armory in 1813, and later served at the Allegheny Arsenal until 1830 (M. R. Smith 1977:278). In 1830, at the Harpers Ferry Armory, Moor was confronted with dilapidated buildings, inadequate waterpower, outdated mechanical techniques, and inhospitable behavior toward outsiders. He claimed that "there are customs and habits so interwoven with the very fibers of things as in some respects to be almost hopelessly remitless" (quoted in M. R. Smith 1977:279).

Moor continually petitioned for monies to modernize the factory (HFNHP microfilms 1835b). By the late 1830s, he was devoting an increasing amount of time to mechanical improvements and the development of a new musket design (Model 1840) that relied upon interchangeable parts. Apparently, some armorers embraced an anti-intellectual attitude when faced with the modernization of the factory. Because of Moor's dedication to mechanization, he was labeled a "theorist" by the armorers, making him an outcast among the workers (M. R. Smith 1977:259, 277-278, 284). By the mid-1830s, and definitely by the late 1830s, changes in the labor and mechanical structure of the armory were noticeable. The movement toward standardization and interchangeable parts increased significantly by the 1840s under the direction of Benjamin Moor (M. R. Smith 1977:277–278).

The 1840 census indicates that Moor and his wife had seven children and three slaves (United States Bureau of the Census 1840:241). Moor was dismissed from his duties in 1849, but he was allowed to remain in the master armorer's house until the spring of 1850 (National Archives Record Group 217, V5:411, 415). By the time the 1850 census was taken, Mrs. Moor had died, and Benjamin moved in with his daughter and son-in-law, Philip Stephenson (United States Bureau of the Census 1850:411). Subsequent master armorers and their families resided in the master armorer's house, although each of their tenancies was short, and it is difficult to associate specific archaeological deposits with their occupations.

ARCHAEOLOGY AT THE MASTER ARMORER'S HOUSE

The archaeological assemblage for this analysis was collected from the master armorer's yard. Three goals directed the excavation strategy: (1) to aid architectural historians; (2) to retrieve a representative sample of material remains; and (3) to contribute to the social, economic, and political history of Harpers Ferry.

First, excavations provided information about the physical dimensions of porches and entranceways, structural additions, modifications, fencelines, walkways, and historic grade. The ghosted outlines of porches and doorways initially guided the investigations, while input from architectural historians provided direction for additional excavations. Initial archeological research utilized historical maps, such as fire insurance maps and railroad maps, as well as historical photographs, to locate and define structures and fences. In addition to historical documentation, a geophysical survey located underground anomalies that represented cultural features.

Second, a random sampling retrieved a representative sample of material culture throughout the backyard areas and provided information regarding the general lifeways of nineteenth- and twentieth-century residents of Harpers Ferry. Historical maps do not represent all cultural features that ever existed, either because of the mapkeeper's oversight or prejudice or because of the relatively short existence of the features. A random sample helped locate additional features not represented on maps or defined by geophysical testing.

Third, using archaeological information gathered from architectural and random sample excavations, a large-block excavation was pursued between the master armorer's house/kitchen, and the smokehouse. This area was one of the few places that contained continuously undisturbed deposits from the earliest armory occupation. Excavations provided a diachronic analysis of changing lifeways between the different master armorer households from the early nineteenth century.

Generally, the stratigraphy consisted of distinct occupational layers interspersed with layers of flood silt. Since the site sits in the floodplain, only about 100 feet from the Shenandoah River, the occupational zones were periodically covered and protected by flood silts. Because of the extraordinary amount of deposition, occupational layers dating to the early nineteenth century exist about 6 feet below the current surface. Excellent documentation, such as correspondence between armory personnel and the Ordnance Department, often identifies the periods of flooding that affected the town as well as factory production. The floodwaters left deposits of flood silts. Since many of the flood deposits can be dated, archaeologists can easily date the occupational layers found between the flood deposits, thus making chronological control and a diachronic analysis of material culture an easy task at this site.

The assemblage of Armistead Beckham's household (circa 1815–1832) represents an era in which Harpers Ferry existed as a relatively secluded rural community. Outsiders were seen as intruders, and changes in daily routines or new ideas were disruptive to the existing social order. The community as well as the armory workers planned their daily lives according to the cycles of nature, despite the movement toward industrialization in the rest of the country (M. R. Smith 1977:35). Benjamin Moor's household assemblage (1832–1852) represents a later period when the community was connected to an expanding transportation network and thus experienced increased access to information and new ideas and greater mobility and access to mass-produced goods. Growth and competition among Harpers Ferry businesses also increased. Moor believed strongly in moving the armory toward mass-production techniques, although a large proportion of the armory's labor force adhered to the piecework system through the 1830s. It was not until 1841 that the armory moved to implement a wage-labor system with the military managing the everyday operation of the facility.

A comparison of the household assemblages of the task-oriented master armorer (Beckham) and the factory-system-oriented master armorer (Moor) provides significant insights into interrelationships between industrialization, craft ethics, community-based ties, transportation networks, acceptance of Romantic ideals, and daily domestic life. An assemblage with fewer domestic and ornate artifacts might reflect a household's relative lack of wealth, inability to participate in larger industrial trade networks, adherence to community-based social relations, or resistance to the discipline of industrialization—or a combination of some or all of these factors. An assemblage with a plethora of consumer goods, in contrast, might indicate a household's relatively greater wealth, ability to participate in larger trade networks, or subscription to Romantic ideals—or a combination of some or all of these variables.

Both the Beckham and Moor households had the same types of materials in their archaeologically retrieved assemblages, but the degree of variation within each material type was different in the two households. In a ceramic analysis of the Beckham household assemblage, Michael Lucas (1993a) found refined earthenwares, such as pearlware, whiteware, and creamware, usually used for serving foods in particular place settings, representing 54% (N = 28) of the assemblage. Coarse earthenwares, such as redwares, stonewares, and yellowwares, usually used for storage or cooking, constituted the remainder of the assemblage (N = 24) (Table 1). The proportion of creamware vessels (19%, N = 10) is probably high considering the popularity of pearlwares during this era. In fact, Miller (1990:3) notes that creamwares consisted of less than 10% of all wares sold by English potters during this era. Was this pattern attributable to inaccessibility to consumer goods from the

Table 1. Ceramic Vessels by Type of Ware for the Armistead Beckham and Benjamin Moor Households[a]

Ware type	Beckham Household (circa 1821–1830)		Moor Household (1830–1850)	
	N	%	N	%
Whiteware	—	—	36	26
Pearlware	14	27	66	48
Creamware	10	19	—	—
Porcelain	3	6	—	—
Unidentified refined	1	2	2	1
Refined redware	—	—	4	3
Redware	15	29	16	12
Stoneware	8	15	10	7
Yellowware	1	2	4	3
Total	52	100	138	100

[a]From Lucas (1993a:8.15).

Table 2. Refined Wares by Type of Decoration for the Armistead Beckham
and Benjamin Moor Households[a]

Decorative type	Beckham household (circa 1821–1830)		Moor household (1830–1850)	
	N	%	N	%
Dipped	2	7	5	5
Shell-edged	6	21	34	32
Transfer-printed	1	4	44	42
Painted	7	25	14	13
Enameled	3	11	2	2
Undecorated	9	32	4	4
Other/Unidentified	—	2	2	2
Total	28	100	105	100

[a]From Lucas (1993a:8.16).

eastern seaboard, or did the Beckhams, who were one of the more influential families in the town, intentionally retain a material culture fashionable in the previous generation?

Undecorated ceramics and edged pearlware tablewares were found in large quantities in the Beckham assemblage. Undecorated, refined earthenwares (32%, $N = 9$) comprise the largest category of wares, and painted wares (25%, $N = 7$) are the second largest. The former are mostly associated with creamwares, and the latter mostly consist of a hand-painted "peasant palette" of earth tones, such as browns and greens, although a small proportion are blue Chinese style. The hand-painted ceramics were fashionable for the period, although newer transfer prints were becoming increasingly popular in the 1820s during Beckham's occupation of the site. Unexpectedly, transfer prints (4%, $N = 1$), which were becoming very fashionable during the 1820s, are a very small proportion of the Beckham's dinnerware (Table 2).

Tableware consists mostly of large supper plates, although several serving dishes were also identified. Teawares are also in the Beckham household assemblage. Most notable is the presence of a set of relatively expensive porcelain teacups. Kitchenware vessels consist of bowls, mugs, and pie plates. They represent a total of 23% ($N = 12$) of the household assemblage, with bowls contributing a large proportion to this category. Slip-decorated pie plates are also present. Over one third (34%, $N = 18$) of the assemblage consists of storage wares—coarse-bodied vessels, such as crocks/jars. This pattern suggests that a

Table 3. Vessels by Form and Frequency for the Armistead Beckham and Benjamin Moor Households[a]

Functional category	Vessel form	Beckham household (circa 1821–1830)		Moor household (1830–1850)	
		N	%	N	%
Tableware	Plate				
	10-inch	3	6	5	6
	9-inch	—	—	2	3
	8-inch	—	—	3	4
	8–10-inch	3	6	—	—
	7-inch	—	—	1	1
	4-inch	—	—	1	1
	Diameter ?	5	10	7	9
	Flatware	1	2	11	14
	Unidentified	2	4	—	—
Subtotal		14	28	30	38
Teaware	Cups	6	12	8	10
	Saucers	2	4	6	8
	Other	—	—	4	5
Subtotal		8	15	18	23
Kitchenware	Bowls	7	13	4	5
	Pie plates	4	8	1	1
	Mugs	1	2	2	3
Subtotal		12	23	7	9
Storage ware	Crock/jar	9	17	3	4
	Unidentified storage	9	17	10	13
Subtotal		18	34	13	17
Unidentified forms	Hollow ware	—	—	7	9
	Unidentified	—	—	3	4
Subtotal		—	—	10	13
Total		52	100	77	100

[a]From Lucas (1993a:8.21).

significant amount of the Beckham assemblage was used for food storage (Table 3).

The Moor assemblage, identified by Lucas (1993a), had a larger proportion of transfer-printed pearlwares and whitewares and edged pearlwares (including unidentified wares) (74%, $N = 78$), a significant increase from the Beckham household. Course earthenwares consist of a much smaller proportion than the earlier assemblage (Table 1).

The ceramic decorative types also vary from the earlier deposits. For instance, painted wares in the form of plates account for only 13% ($N = 14$) of the collection. This decrease is significant and reflects the fact that other types of technologies and decorations were becoming more popular among Euro-Americans. Rather than the predominantly peasant palette decorations found among the Beckhams, the painted wares tend to be blue. Other evidence also indicates that the Moors acquired the latest ceramic fashions, such as edge-decorated wares and transfer-printed wares. Transfer-printed wares of various forms (42%, $N = 44$) comprise the largest proportion of decorated wares. Edge-decorated wares (32%, $N = 34$) are the second highest category. These proportions are also significantly higher than those in the earlier context (Table 2).

Tablewares consist of a greater variety of plate sizes than the earlier assemblage, and they range from small plates ("twifflers") to large supper plates and platters. There is also a larger proportion of teacups and associated teaware vessels than the earlier assemblage. Kitchenwares (9%, $N = 7$), such as bowls, mugs, and pie plates, comprise a relatively small proportion of the assemblage. The amount of storage-ware vessels also decreases sharply (Table 3).

Generally, the differences between the two assemblages appear to be slight and may be explained by differential purchasing patterns and access to markets. What is more noticeable is the variation of plate sizes found in both contexts, with a larger proportion of diversity found in the Moor assemblage (Table 3). Variation in tableware forms reinforces the development of a more complex and formal dining ritual and a new discipline associated with eating. The increasing numbers of forms and functions indicate that people increased the number of courses served and formalized the food-serving process. Greater emphasis was placed on the meaning of food serving and consumption. This increasing formalization was spurred by the ritualization associated with the new Romantic ideals (Shackel 1993c; Little and Shackel 1989; also see Lucas and Shackel 1994).

The separations and divisions of life's functions were widespread in an early-nineteenth-century industrial town. For instance, in the armory, the number of individual specialized jobs needed to produce a gun increased by almost 20 times from 1807 to the 1840s. The growing work discipline at the armory corresponds with the greater variety of forms and sizes of ceramics created by English potters that eventually became available on the American market. For instance, in 1814, 24 vessel forms and 69 sizes of printed ceramics were available. As the purchase of sets became popular, the size and complexity of sets also increased. In 1846, 124 vessel forms and 259 sizes were created by the pottery manufacturers (Miller et al. 1994). While the supply of goods was important to create a new form of daily life, it was also necessary to create the demand for these goods. Supply does not create demand, but rather a new ideology regarding consumption, and the creation of separations in daily life was necessary for this consumer revolution to work. The subscription of the middle class to the Romantic ideals during the early nineteenth century facilitated much of this new consumerism. The increased division of labor at the armory, segmenting the work process into many parts, was reinforced on the daily level by the consumption of an increasing number of variety of ceramics that divided and regimented the eating process. The ceramic variation found at the craft-oriented Beckham's assemblage was relatively low during the 1820s, while in the factory-oriented Moor's assemblage, which dates to the 1830s and 1840s, a greater variety of ceramic forms was found. This trend may imply that the Moor household adopted a new, modern attitude and Romantic ethic.

Along with the increased division of labor, the greater reliance on mass-produced goods, and the development of the capitalist infrastructure, such as roadways, canals, and railroads, came the reduction of home production. A comparison between Master Armorer Beckham's and Master Armorer Moor's households provides an example of how greater participation in industrialization standardized the families' diets. With the development of urbanization and the growth of industrialization, traditional home activities were replaced by wage-labor activities. Bowen (1990) uses Maltby (1979, 1982, 1985) and Zeder (1988) to describe the limiting of choice a consumer has when the production of food is removed from the individual's control, especially in urban contexts. Once the individual's participation in a wage-labor system increases, the choice of foods becomes tied directly to the market. During the urbanization process, legal restrictions, based on the need for better sanitary conditions, limited the types and amounts of slaughtering allowed in an area, thus moving the butchering process to peripheral areas, there to be performed by specialists.

Nineteenth-century newspaper advertisements are informative about the types of domestic animals raised in Harpers Ferry. Accounts note that cows often strayed from domestic lots in this area. The presence of cows in an urban context is more likely attributable to the practice of home production of dairy products than to domestic beef production. Hogs were often kept by many Harpers Ferry residents

Table 4. Biomass Percentages and Numbers of Species for the Armistead
Beckham and Benjamin Moor Household Assemblages[a]

	Beckham household (circa 1821–1830)		Moor household (1830–1850)	
Type	Biomass	Number of species	Biomass	Number of species
Domesticates	56.4%	5	52.4%	4
Wild	0.6%	4	0.6%	2
Turkey, wild or domestic	1.0%	1	2.1%	1
Unidentified	41.8%	—	44.9%	—

[a]From Burk (1993:9.1).

and, at times, were permitted to roam free through the town's streets. An 1824 advertisement for food also noted the presence of domestic geese in town (*Harpers Ferry Free Press* 31 March 1824:4).

The analysis of faunal materials from the master armorers' contexts can be linked to increasing ties to wage labor, decreasing consumer choices, and the development of modern discipline. Generally, a comparison between Beckham's and Moor's household faunal assemblages indicates the consumption of a similar ratio of domestic and wild biomass (Table 4). While Beckham's household consumed domestic goose (*Anser anser*), both households also consumed the same types of domestic species (*Gallus gallus* [chicken], *Sus scrofa* [domestic pig], *Bos taurus* [domestic cow], *Ovis aries / Capra hircus* [sheep/goat]) (Tables 5 and 6).

The faunal assemblage was identified by Brett Burk (1993) with assistance from Joanne Bowen. Of the three fish taxa identified for the Beckham assemblage, only two are identifiable to species: herring (family Clupeidae) and American shad (*Alosa sapidissima*). Since herring is not indigenous to the local waters, it had to have been imported.

The bird remains include goose (*Anser* spp.), domestic goose (Anser anser), Canada goose or brant (*Branta* spp.), and dabbling duck (*Anas* spp.); Galliformes (grouse, partridge, or pheasant (Family Phasianidae); turkey (*Meleagris gallopavo*); and chicken (*Gallus gallus*). Turkey appears to have been the most prevalent bird species in the Beckham household diet. Turkey may represent either a domesticated or a wild species. Two species of wild mammals are identified: Eastern gray squirrel (*Sciurius carolinensis*) and Old World rat (*Rattus* spp.).

Three domestic mammals are identified in the assemblage pig (*Sus scrofa*), cow (*Bos taurus*), and sheep/goat (*Ovis aries / Capra hircus*). Pig

Table 5. Summary of the Faunal Assemblage for the Beckham Household (circa 1821–1830)[a]

Taxon	N	Percent	MNI	Percent	Meat weight (lb)	Total meat wt. (lb)	Percent	Weight (g)	Percent	Biomass (kg)	Percent
Class Reptilia (reptiles)	1	0.1	0/0	—	0.0/0.0	—	—	0.3	—	0.00	—
Class Aves (birds)	143	14.0	0/0	—	0.0/0.0	—	—	33.3	1.8	0.13	1.9
Anser spp. (goose)	3	0.3	1/0	5.0	0.0/0.0	—	—	5.0	0.3	0.02	0.3
cf. Anser spp. (goose)	1	0.1	0/0	—	0.0/0.0	—	—	0.2	—	0.00	—
Anser anser (dom. goose)	1	0.1	1/0	5.0	6.0/6.0	6.0	0.7	1.0	0.1	0.01	0.1
cf. Branta spp. (goose or brant)	1	0.1	1/0	5.0	0.0/0.0	—	—	0.9	—	0.01	0.1
Anas spp. (dabbling duck)	1	0.1	1/0	5.0	0.0/0.0	—	—	0.9	—	0.01	0.1
Family Phasianidae	5	0.5	1/1	10.0	0.0/0.0	—	—	2.7	0.1	0.01	0.2
Meleagris gallopavo (turkey)	6	0.6	3/0	15.0	7.5/7.5	22.5	2.6	15.0	0.8	0.06	0.9
cf. Meleagris gallopavo (turkey)	1	0.1	0/0	—	0.0/0.0	—	—	1.7	0.1	0.01	0.1
Gallus gallus (chicken)	11	1.1	1/1	10.0	2.5/1.0	3.5	0.4	9.8	0.5	0.04	0.6
Class Mammalia (mammals)	567	55.5	0/0	—	0.0/0.0	—	—	353.0	18.6	1.20	18.3
Class Mammalia I (large mammals)	12	1.2	0/0	—	0.0/0.0	—	—	181.6	9.5	0.66	10.0
Class Mammalia II (med. mammals)	112	11.0	0/0	—	0.0/0.0	—	—	173.9	9.1	0.64	9.7
Class Mammalia III (sm. mammals)	3	0.3	0/0	—	0.0/0.0	—	—	0.3	—	0.00	—
Sciurus carolinensis (squirrel)	1	0.1	1/0	5.0	1.0/1.0	1.0	0.1	0.2	—	0.00	—
Rattus spp. (Old World rat)	1	0.1	1/0	5.0	0.0/0.0	—	—	0.1	—	0.00	—
Order Artiodactyla II	3	0.3	0/0	—	0.0/0.0	—	—	25.7	1.4	0.11	1.7
Sus scrofa (dom. pig)	137	13.4	3/1	20.0	100.0/50.0	350.0	40.3	671.9	35.3	2.14	32.6
cf. Sus scrofa (dom. pig)	2	0.2	0/0	—	0.0/0.0	—	—	0.9	—	0.01	0.1
Bos taurus (dom. cow)	3	0.3	1/1	10.0	400.0/50.0	450.0	51.8	151.9	8.0	0.56	8.5
cf. Bos taurus (dom. cow)	5	0.5	0/0	—	0.0/0.0	—	—	265.6	14.0	0.93	14.1
Ovis aries/Capra hircus (sheep/goat)	2	0.2	1/0	5.0	35.0/15.0	35.0	4.0	5.8	0.3	0.03	0.5
Totals	1022	100	20	100	—/—	868	100	1901.7	100	6.58	100

[a]From Burk (1993:9.13). Columns: (N) number of bones identified to that taxon; (MNI) Minimum Number of Individuals (adults/immature specimens); (Meat Weight) meat weight of a representative whole animal (adult/immature); (Total meat weight) derived by multiplying the MNI of adult and immature animals by the Meat Weight of each and adding the two totals; (Weight) weight of the actual archaeological bones; (Biomass) skeletal weight.

Table 6. Summary of the Faunal Assemblage for the Moor Household (1830–1850)[a]

Taxon	N	Percent	MNI	Percent	Meat weight (lb)	Total meat wt. (lb)	Percent	Weight (g)	Percent	Biomass (kg)	Percent
Class Osteichthyes (bony fish)	1	0.1	0/0	—	0.0/0.0	—	—	0.1	—	—	—
Class Aves (birds)	145	19.3	0/0	—	0.0/0.0	—	—	30.1	2.9	0.12	3.0
Family Phasianidae	3	0.4	0/1	5.9	0.0/0.0	—	—	1.4	0.1	0.01	0.2
Meleagris gallopavo (turkey)	5	0.7	1/0	5.9	7.5/7.5	7.5	0.9	20.2	1.9	0.08	2.1
Gallus gallus (chicken)	14	1.9	2/2	23.5	2.5/1.0	7.0	0.9	7.8	0.7	0.03	0.9
Class Mammalia (mammals)	385	51.3	0/0	—	0.0/0.0	—	—	226.9	21.5	0.81	20.8
Class Mammalia I (large mammals)	4	0.5	0/0	—	0.0/0.0	—	—	25.8	2.4	0.11	2.9
Class Mammalia II (med. mammals)	70	9.3	0/0	—	0.0/0.0	—	—	181.8	17.2	0.66	17.0
Class Mammalia III (sm. mammals)	6	0.8	0/0	—	0.0/0.0	—	—	3.7	0.4	0.02	0.5
Didelphis virginiana (opossum)	2	0.3	1/0	5.9	8.0/8.0	8.0	1.0	3.9	0.4	0.02	0.5
Sylvilagus floridanus (cottontail)	1	0.1	1/0	5.9	2.0/2.0	2.0	0.2	0.3	—	—	0.1
Rattus spp. (Old World rat)	4	0.5	2/0	11.8	0.0/0.0	—	—	0.5	0.1	—	0.1
Felis domesticus (dom. cat)	1	0.1	1/0	5.9	0.0/0.0	—	—	0.6	0.1	—	0.1
Order Artiodactyla I	1	0.1	0/0	—	0.0/0.0	—	—	1.9	0.2	0.01	0.3
Sus scrofa (dom. pig)	93	12.4	3/0	17.6	100.0/50.0	300.0	37.1	298.2	28.3	1.03	26.5
cf. Sus scrofa (dom. pig)	1	0.1	0/0	—	0.0/0.0	—	—	12.5	1.2	0.06	1.5
Bos taurus (dom. cow)	9	1.2	1/1	11.8	400.0/50.0	450.0	55.6	99.4	9.4	0.38	9.9
cf. Bos taurus (dom. cow)	4	0.5	0/0	—	0.0/0.0	—	—	135.0	12.8	0.51	13.0
Ovis aries / Capra hircus (sheep/goat)	1	0.1	1/0	5.9	35.0/15.0	35.0	4.3	4.3	0.4	0.02	0.6
Totals	750	100	13/4	100		809.5	100	1054.4	100	3.89	100

[a]From Burk (1993:9.18). Columns: (N) number of bones identified to that taxon; (MNI) Minimum Number of Individuals (adults/immature specimens); (Meat Weight) meat weight of a representative whole animal (adult/immature); (Total meat weight) derived by multiplying the MNI of adult and immature animals by the Meat Weight of each and adding the two totals; (Weight) weight of the actual archaeological bones; (Biomass) skeletal weight.

is the most prevalent, consisting of 32.7% of the biomass. Most of the pig elements are present, including skull, teeth, and feet. Innominates (pelves), scapulae (shoulder blades), and humeri (upper forelimbs) are missing. The lack of these elements in the assemblage may indicate that the Beckham family purchased the pig from a butcher with these parts always missing or that the butcher received these parts as payment for his butchering at the site. The latter would likely be true in this case, since a large proportion of inedible elements is found, such as skull and teeth fragments.

The cow bones comprise 22.6% of the Beckham assemblage's biomass. The elements are primarily from the back, pelvis, and feet. The lack of cow skull elements implies that the beef was probably purchased at the market instead of raised and butchered at home. Keeping a cow for dairy purposes is feasible in many urban contexts. Only two bones are identified as sheep/goat, a lumbar vertebra and a left tibia, and they consist of only 0.5% of the total biomass. Although wild species make up only 1.8% of the total biomass for this context, the various wild bird species identified indicate that the Beckham's household exploited wild resources.

During the Moor occupation of the master armorer's house, imported consumer goods and foodstuffs increased dramatically in town. One of the contemporary newspaper advertisements that note the enlarged consumer demand for imported meats and fish read as follows (VFP 18 April 1839:3):

> The subscriber will visit Harpers Ferry this day (Thursday) with a supply of fresh fish and spring oysters. As he intends making weekly trips from below, those in want of a good fresh article, will be enabled to supply themselves on such terms as cannot fail to give satisfaction. —John Gibson.

Rail facilitated the transport of fresh food products. While previous advertisements often announced, for example, preserved fish, fresh fish from ocean ports became increasingly available. The town also became a collection point for country produce to be sold at the Harpers Ferry market or to eastern cities.

Burk (1994) identified fish remains from the Moor household that include imported herring (family Clupeidae) and local catfish (family Ictaluridae). The former is probably one of the preserved imported fish mentioned above. Bird species found include turkey (*Meleagris gallopavo*), chicken (*Gallus gallus*), and family Phasianidae (which could include grouse, partridge, pheasant, chicken, or turkey). Immature bird bones, which are difficult to categorize, comprise the largest sample in the latter category. Turkey, which can be either wild or domestic, has the largest biomass among birds (2.1%) and the third highest biomass following pig and cow (Table 6).

Four domestic mammal species include domestic cat (*Felis domesticus*), pig (*Sus scrofa*), cow (*Bos taurus*), and sheep/goat (*Ovis aries / Capra hircus*). Pig represents the highest biomass (28.0%), followed by cow (22.9%). Only one sheep/goat bone is identified, and it is an ankle element. Much like Beckham's assemblage, a proportionately large number of pig skull, teeth, and feet elements are identified, thus implying that pigs were raised and butchered at the site.

Three species of wild mammals are present and opossum (*Didelphis virginiana*), Eastern cottontail (*Sylvilagus floridanus*), and Old World rat (*Rattus* spp.). Opossum and cottontail may be food remains, although they represent a small amount of meat ($N = 2$ and $N = 1$, respectively).

The major difference between the Beckham and Moor assemblages is the decreased in the variety of wild species consumed. While Beckham's household probably consumed squirrel (*Sciurus carolinensis*), goose (*Anser* spp.), Canada goose or brant (*Branta* spp.), and dabbling duck (*Anas* spp.), Moor's household assemblage of wild species is limited to opossum (*Didelphis virginiana*) and cottontail (*Sylvilagus floridanus*). The decreasing variety of faunal materials is probably related to the limited choice that laborers had when the community became increasingly dependent upon the market system. As the economy of Harpers Ferry slowly changed from craft to industry, and workers became increasingly dependent upon wage labor for their existence, they also became dependent upon other industrial networks for their daily survival. A decrease in the diversity of faunal consumption ensured a greater chance for a standardized diet, standardizing the behavior of individuals, decreasing the self-sufficiency of the laborers, and increasing their reliance on larger industrial systems. This transformation aided in the success of industrialism.

In terms of meat weight as it contributed to diet, pork accounted for 32.7% of overall biomass from the Beckham context, and beef accounted for 22.6% of the biomass. For the Moor household, beef is about the same at 22.9% of the biomass, but pork to 28% of the total biomass. The decrease of pork, which was most probably home-grown, is an expected change found in a modern industrial culture that relied more heavily upon market goods.

ARMORY WORKERS' HOUSEHOLDS DURING THE ERA OF PIECEWORK AND TASK ORIENTATION

William Smallwood constructed an armory worker's dwelling in the 1820s. He and his family may have resided in the structure for at least a short time, although these are no historical data that place the Smallwood family, or any other specific armory worker's family, in the building before 1841. Since the structure was located on armory land, it is probable that armory workers and their families inhabited the structure from the 1820s until the outbreak of the Civil War. Archaeological deposits around the building, such as armorer's tools and gun parts, suggest that armory workers were in the house prior to 1841 (see Chapter 6). The original core of the house dating to the 1820s measures 15.5 feet by 19 feet. An addition constructed in the 1830s measures 17.5 ft by 19 ft. An east wing added circa 1841 measures 20.25 feet by 17.5 feet (Figure 38).

In 1832, Smallwood purchased a large tract of land in Bolivar Heights for $2400, and he probably moved to this area (Bumgardner 1991:15). This sum seems rather large for an armory worker, and there is little evidence to indicate how the Smallwood family obtained the capital to buy the property. Whatever the case, it appears that the Smallwood family was financially secure, especially after William became active in local politics. The *Virginia Free Press* (VFP 5 July 1832:3) listed Smallwood as a candidate for alderman in the town of Bolivar. Smallwood was also listed as a Harpers Ferry representative at a Democratic convention held in Martinsburg (VFP 7 March 1839:2, VFP 4 April 1839:1). In 1852, Smallwood was again involved in local politics as a candidate for district commissioner (VFP 13 March 1852:3; also see Bumgardner 1991).

While no rent rolls exist for the period prior to 1841, there is a good likelihood, on the basis of the archaeological evidence and general rental trends in the town, that armorers occupied the dwelling for a significant portion of this era. Since most of the armory workers converted to the piecework system in the 1820s and 1830s, and the dwelling was relatively small, there is a good likelihood that pieceworkers, rather than supervisors, inhabited the structure. The archaeological record provides some information on consumer behavior related to workers and their families.

The earliest surviving rent rolls date to March 1841, and they place armorer Augustus Shope and his wife Catherine in the armory workers'

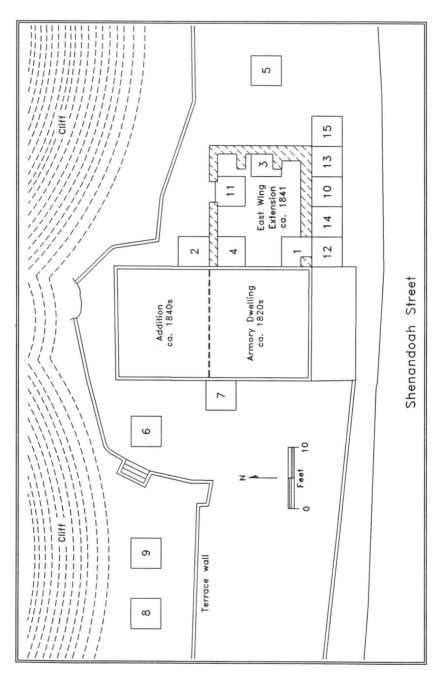

Figure 38. Grid map showing excavation units around the armory workers' house. (Drawn by John W. Ravenhorst)

dwelling. Shope's exact ties to the armory are unclear. However, Augustus attended an armory dinner, and he served on a committee to investigate the controversial hiring and firing practices of Superintendent Lucas. The rent rolls listed the Shopes as paying a relatively high rent for their Shenandoah Street residence. Archeological evidence indicates that an east wing was constructed on the dwelling in the early 1840s. As suggested earlier, the higher rent may be related to the construction of this east wing, which Catherine Shope probably used to run a boarding house. The Shopes occupied the structure until Augustus's death in February 1844 (Bumgardner 1991:24–25). Catherine probably moved her boarding house to Michael Melhorn's former residence, where she could accommodate 10 or 12 boarders (VFP 14 March 1844:3). Melhorn probably moved into the Shope's former residence between April and September 1844 (Bumgardner 1991:25).

The armory workers' dwelling served as a duplex after Melhorn moved out. The rent rolls show that the John Berlin and the James Y. O'Laughlin families shared the structure in December 1844 (Bumgardner 1991:26). John Berlin worked at the armory from 1836 until its destruction in 1861 as a "jobber" through at least 1840 and later as "assistant jobbing smith." He resided in part of the duplex from 1844 to 1849 (Bumgardner 1991:26, 27). Berlin was apparently married twice, first to either Mary Wrinkle or Mary Emis in 1843 (VFP 26 October 1843) and later to Elizabeth Deck in 1851 (Bumgardner 1991:27). It remains uncertain whether either of the marriages produced any children.

Historical data on the family of James Y. and Pleasant O'Laughlin are sparse. It is known, however, that they resided in the structure from 1844 to 1846 (Bumgardner 1991:28). After the O'Laughlins moved out of the duplex, William H. Wentzle, an armorer, and his family replaced them, living adjacent to the Berlin family. William and Mary Wentzle and their two children lived in the dwelling from 1846 to 1849 (Bumgardner 1991:29). William was an officer in the local Sons of Temperance division (Bumgardner 1991:30).

John W. Roderick and Armistead Ball and their families replaced the O'Laughlins and Berlins in 1849 as residents of the dwelling. Very little information exists on armorer Roderick and his family. It is known, however, that along with his wife Artridge and their son John, they lived in the armory workers' dwelling until 1849 (Bumgardner 1991:30).

Armistead Ball married Hannah Hayman in 1839 (VFP 31 October 1839:3). By 1850, Armistead and Hannah, along with their two children, George, 10, and Randolph, 2, lived in the building (Bumgardner

1991:32). Armistead Ball was evidently a valuable employee at the armory. He was considered a fine mechanic, being promoted to master machinist in 1849 and to master armorer by 1859 (M. R. Smith 1977:247, 248). Ball became fairly active in community events, special interest groups, and Harpers Ferry politics. His involvement in local meetings included topics ranging from the organization of a Lyceum and Polemic Society, set up as a forum for public lectures, to a relief fund for peoples of Ireland, to the organization of a complimentary dinner held in Harpers Ferry (VFP 30 November 1843:2, 25 February 1847:1, 24 March 1853:2). Ball also became involved with the temperance movement (VFP 31 August 1843:3) and local politics. He represented the Harpers Ferry precinct in a Democratic meeting held in Charles Town (VFP 19 February 1852:2). He also became a candidate for the District 8 magistracy in 1852 (VFP 27 May 1852:2). The Ball family lived in the armory dwelling until 1852. Because armory records were destroyed, it remains impossible to determine the residents of the armory dwelling from 1853 to 1861.

CRAFT VERSUS INDUSTRY AMONG ARMORY WORKERS AND THEIR HOUSEHOLDS: THE ARCHEOLOGICAL EVIDENCE

Three goals directed the excavation strategy at the armory worker's house: (1) to aid architectural historians; (2) to provide a diachronic analysis of the changing physical and cultural landscape; and (3) to contribute to the interpretation of nineteenth-century domestic life among armory workers in Harpers Ferry.

First, excavations provide specific information about the general dimensions and construction techniques of the existing structure. The remains of the east wing foundation initially guided investigations to determine the articulation between this feature and the existing structure. Excavation units were also placed adjacent to the dwelling in order to discern the different building phases and additions to the original house. Input from architects and historians provided direction to discern information pertaining to building construction sequences.

Second, excavations contribute to the analysis of the changing cultural landscape surrounding the structure. Initial archeological research utilized historical maps, such as those developed by the government in the antebellum era, as well as fire insurance maps and railroad maps. Archeology can reveal the presence of previously undocumented features such as entranceways, structural additions, fencelines, walkways, location of outbuildings, and the historical grade. Pollen and phytolith analyses enhanced the interpretation of the adjacent yard by determining the presence, extent, and duration of vegetative growth.

Third, using the initial data provided for the architectural and cultural landscape questions, a block excavation was conducted just south of the east wing extension. This area contained continuously undisturbed deposits from the earliest armory occupation through the turn of the twentieth century. This locality yielded a large quantity of domestic and work-related objects from an armory worker's occupation and contributes significantly to the interpretation of early-nineteenth-century social and economic relations in Harpers Ferry. Archeological data help to reveal the acceptance rate of new consumer goods and cultural ideas by armory workers in the first half of the nineteenth century.

Generally, most of the earliest deposits existed 3.5–4 feet below the present surface. Flood deposits were not as noticeable at this site as they were at the master armorer's house. Clear distinctive zones of occupation exist within the site, and archaeologists can easily delineate occupational eras. Stratigraphic zones are also discernible due to the large quantities of construction debris deposited throughout the site when additions to the original dwelling were constructed.

Most of the material deposits from the site were found in front of and on the side of the house (excavation units 10, 12, 13, 14, and 15) (Figure 38). Since the house abuts steep, rocky cliffs, no early contexts could be identified in the small backyard. Bedrock was only a few inches from the surface in many places. The earliest historical layers, located in the front and side of the house, contained 151 vessels.

Archeological evidence from an armory workers' household reveals very different patterns from those found at the master armorer's domestic assemblage. This information shows the complex and changing interrelationship between the armory's factory production and its relationship to domestic life. Dramatic differences are noticeable when the early (1820s–1841) and later (1841–1852) armory workers' household dining assemblaged are compared. Like the master armorer's assemblage, the armory workers' ceramic assemblage changed in relationship to the increased division of labor found at the armory, but in a very different way.

Lucas (1994a) performed the ceramic analysis for this assemblage, and he notes that in the earlier armory workers' assemblage, pearlware dominates the assemblage (60.9%, $N = 92$), while creamwares are relatively low (6.0%, $N = 9$). Coarse redware (16.6%, $N = 25$) and porcelains (12.6%, $N = 19$) constitute a relatively large portion of the ceramic forms.

Table 7. Ceramic Vessels by Type of Ware for the Pieceworkers' and Wage Laborers' Households[a]

Ware type	Pieceworkers' household (circa 1821–1841)		Wage laborers' household (1841–1852)	
	N	Percent	N	Percent
Pearlware	92	60.9	83	61.9
Creamware	9	6.0	15	11.2
Whiteware	1	0.7	2	1.5
Porcelain	19	12.6	9	6.7
Refined redware	1	0.7	0	0.0
Coarse redware	25	16.6	22	16.4
Stoneware	4	2.6	3	2.2
Total	151	100	134	100

[a]From Lucas (1994a:5.11).

Enameled porcelain is the most popular porcelain. Stoneware constitutes a relatively small portion of the assemblage (2.6%, $N = 4$) (Table 7).

Transfer-printed ceramics dominate the refined earthenware assemblage with over one third of the vessels (38.8%, $N = 47$). Shell-edged (14.0%, $N = 17$) and painted earthenwares (23.1%, $N = 28$) together comprise about the same amount. Other decoration types, dipped, sponged, and molded, make up a smaller amount of the entire assemblage (6.6%, $N = 8$). Undecorated wares, which are mostly creamwares, also constitute of a small proportion of the assemblage (5.8%, $N = 7$) (Table 8). This pattern of a high proportion of fashionable transfer prints and a very low amount of—no longer popular—creamwares indicates that the pre-1841 armory households subscribed to contemporary household fads found in other east coast cities.

Tableware forms comprise about one third of the total assemblage, with the majority consisting of plates (22.5%, $N = 34$) of a variety of sizes (see Table 10). Shell-edged (44.1%, $N = 15$) and transfer-printed plates (35.3%, $N = 12$) are abundant in this early context. Only a small proportion are undecorated (8.8%, $N = 3$) (Table 9). Bowls (17.4%, $N = 8$) are found in moderate proportions of the assemblage (Table 10).

More teaware is found in this assemblage than any of the other functional groups identified (43.0%, $N = 65$) (Table 10). A relatively large proportion of the teaware is porcelain[*] (24.2%, $N = 16$), and this

[*]Porcelain is used in association with white earthenware decoration types because porcelain outweighs earthenwares in monetary or aesthetic value no matter what the decoration type on the earthenwares.

Table 8. Refined Ceramics by Type of Decoration for the Pieceworkers' and Wage Laborers' Households[a]

Decoration type	Pieceworkers' household (1821–1841)		Wage laborers' household (1821–1841)	
	N	Percent	N	Percent
Shell-edged	17	14.0	23	21.1
Transfer-printed	47	38.8	30	27.5
Painted	28	23.1	29	26.6
Enameled	14	11.6	5	4.6
Dipped	7	5.8	5	4.6
Sponged	0	0.0	1	0.9
Molded	1	0.8	2	1.8
Undecorated	7	5.8	14	12.8
Other/Unidentified	—	—	—	—
Total	121	100	109	100

[a]From Lucas (1994a:5.11).

Table 9. Plates by Type of Decoration for the Pieceworkers' and Wage Laborers' Households[a]

Decoration type	Pieceworkers' household (1821–1841)		Wage laborers' household (1841–1852)	
	N	Percent	N	Percent
Shell	15	44.1	23	65.7
Transfer	12	35.3	4	11.4
Undecorated	3	8.8	7	20.0
Porcelain	2	5.9	1	2.9
Molded	1	2.9	—	—
Other	1	2.9	—	—
Total	34	100	35	100

[a]From Lucas (1994a:5.12).

proportion is higher than in most other contemporary assemblages found in Harpers Ferry (Table 11). Painted (31.8%, $N = 21$) and transfer-printed (40.9%, $N = 27$) cups and saucers, however, comprise the largest proportion of teaware. Seven matching vessels are present, all teawares. The majority are transfer-printed, 71.4% ($N = 5$). The largest set of matching vessels is the transfer-printed gilded set.

Storage and kitchenware is the smallest functional category. The most abundant form present is the crock (68.4%, $N = 13$), followed by baking dishes (26.3%, $N = 5$) (Table 10).

Table 10. Ceramics by Vessel Form for the Pieceworkers' and Wage Laborers' Households[a]

Functional category	Form	Pieceworkers' household (1821–1841)			Wage laborers' household (1841–1852)		
		N	%F	%T	N	%F	%T
Tableware	Plate						
	10-inch	2	4.3	1.3	2	4.7	1.5
	9-inch	5	10.9	3.3	1	2.3	0.7
	8-inch	3	6.5	2.0	1	2.3	0.7
	7-inch	3	6.5	2.0	2	4.7	1.5
	6-inch	1	2.2	0.7	—	—	—
	3–5-inch	—	—	—	3	7.0	2.2
	Unidentified diam.	20	43.5	13.2	26	60.5	19.4
	Plate total	34	73.9	22.5	35	81.4	26.0
	Platter	1	2.2	0.7	2	4.7	1.5
	Flatware	2	4.3	1.3	2	4.7	1.5
	Tureen	—	—	—	—	—	—
	Baker	—	—	—	—	—	—
	Pitcher	1	2.2	0.7	—	—	—
	Bowl						
	6-inch	4	8.7	2.6	2	4.7	1.5
	5-inch	—	—	—	1	2.3	0.7
	Unidentified diam.	4	8.7	2.6	1	2.3	0.7
	Bowl total	8	17.4	5.2	4	9.3	2.9
Subtotal		46	100	30.4	43	100	31.9
Teaware	Tea cup	28	43.1	18.5	21	42.0	15.7
	Saucer	34	52.3	22.5	27	54.0	20.1
	Teapot	2	3.1	1.3	—	—	—
	Creamer	1	1.5	0.7	2	4.0	1.5
Subtotal		65	100	43.0	50	100	37.3
Storage ware	Crock	13	68.4	8.6	9	50.0	6.7
	Bowl	—	—	—	—	—	—
	Jug	1	5.3	0.7	2	11.1	1.5
	Bottle	—	—	—	—	—	—
	Baking dish	5	26.3	3.3	7	38.9	5.2
Subtotal		19	100	12.6	18	100	13.4
Other/ unidentified	Flower pot	—	—	—	1	4.3	0.7
	Hollow ware	17	81.0	11.3	16	69.6	11.9
	Flatware	1	4.8	0.7	—	—	—
	Other	—	—	—	—	—	—
	Lid	—	—	—	—	—	—
	Unknown	3	14.3	2.0	6	26.1	4.5
Subtotal		21	100	14.0	23	100	17.1
Total		151		100	134		100

[a]From Lucas (1994a:5.13). Percentages are of functional category (%F) and total assemblage (%T).

Table 11. Teaware by Type of Decoration for the Pieceworkers' and Wage Laborers' Households[a]

Decoration type	Pieceworkers' household (1821–1841)		Wage laborers' household (1841–1852)	
	N	Percent	N	Percent
Painted	21	31.8	26	52.0
Transfer	27	40.9	18	36.0
Undecorated	1	1.5	2	4.0
Porcelain	16	24.2	4	8.0
Lustre	1	1.5	—	—
Total	66	100	50	100

[a]From Lucas (1994a:5.14).

In the later (1841–1852) armory workers' assemblage, pearlware (61.9%, $N = 83$) dominates the assemblage, with lesser proportions of coarse redware (16.4%, $N = 22$) and stoneware (2.2%, $N = 3$). The proportion of creamware is much higher than that in the earlier assemblage. The assemblage contains a lower proportion of porcelain than the earlier assemblage, although enameled porcelain is the most popular type identified (Table 7).

Lucas (1994a) notes that the later assemblage also contains a relatively large proportion of shell-edgedwares (21.1%, $N = 23$). This proportion is higher than that in the earlier assemblage, and it is an anomaly, especially since shell-edge lost its general popularity in the United States during this era (see Miller 1980, 1991). The assemblage also contains a significant proportion of transfer-printed wares (27.5%, $N = 30$), although much less than the earlier occupation. It also includes a larger proportion of undecorated creamware vessels than the earlier assemblage (see Table 8).

Tableware is the largest functional group, with the great majority being plates (81.4%, $N = 35$) of various sizes (Table 10). The assemblage contains a larger proportion of shell-edged plates (65.7%, $N = 23$), but a much smaller proportion of transfer-printed wares (11.4%, $N = 4$). Undecorated wares (20%, $N = 7$) are more than double the proportion of the earlier context (8.8%, $N = 3$) (Table 9).

The overall percentage of teaware consists of over one third of the assemblage (37.3%, $N = 50$) (Table 10). It contains many fewer porcelain teawares (8.0%, $N = 4$), but a large proportion of painted teawares (52.0%, $N = 26$). Transfer-printed teawares (36.0%, $N = 18$) are also predominant in the assemblage (Table 11). Five matching vessels are present in this context of which three are painted. Storage and kitchen-ware is the smallest functional category, with crocks constituting the largest amount (50%, $N = 9$), followed by baking dishes (38.9%, $N = 7$) (Table 10).

While the master armorer's household subscribed to Romantic ideals and purchased the most fashionable consumer goods by the 1840s, this phenomenon was just the opposite in the armory workers' assemblage. Vessel analysis by Lucas (1994a) reveals a significant difference between the pre-1841 assemblage and the post-1841 assemblage at the armory workers' house. The earlier context, inhabited by a relatively wealthy family for at least part of the occupation and later by armory workers, contains relatively higher-quality ceramics. Porcelains and fashionable transfer prints dominate the plate assemblage, and the majority of tea sets were transfer-printed wares. The later context, occupied by workers and their families, does not follow this pattern of armorers' purchasing the most fashionable wares, even though they had greater access to larger markets. The post-1841 assemblage contains materials that would have been outdated by several decades. These materials include creamware plates and a relatively large proportion of hand-painted teawares.

It is particularly interesting that the earlier assemblage contains three two-pronged forks and two knives, while the later assemblage contained only one knife. According to Kasson (1990:189) (see Lucas 1994a), the two-pronged fork is associated with left-hand eating. At about 1830, three-and four-pronged forks were introduced. Associated with this new material good was the practice of transferring the fork to the right hand after cutting a piece of food. Even though keeping the fork in the left, hand is a holdover from European customs, none of the residents can be traced to this continent. Apparently, the dwelling residents purchased the most fashionable dinnerwares but retained the material culture of a recently outdated eating ceremony, i.e., "left-handed" eating. The retention of unfashionable goods and the continued use of old cultural traditions may be seen by outsiders as a sign of vulgarity when, in fact, it may have been a standard cultural norm found among armorers who did not accept, or would not adopt, the new modern norms associated with industrialization.

The high percentage of porcelains found in the armory workers' pre-1841 household may indicate that they were emulating Harpers Ferry's higher social groups, while they continued to use other unfashionable dining equipment. The use of outdated consumer goods may be explained as culture lag. This interpretation can only partially explain this phenomenon, however, and the larger context of the armorers' new relationship to industrial work needs to be examined.

The diachronic faunal analysis by Burk (1994) from the armory workers' households provides additional contrasting data between the two assemblages at the armory workers' house. The fish found at the pre-1841 assemblage consists of bony fish (class Osteichthyes) and sucker (family Catostomidae). Sucker fish are prevalent in the Potomac and Shenandoah rivers surrounding Harpers Ferry.

Turkey (*Meleagris gallopavo*) and chicken (*Gallus gallus*) are the only two bird species identified in the earlier context. Residents probably raised chickens on the site for both meat and eggs. Chickens may also have been purchased at the market, and the turkey remains probably represent wild fauna. Fragments of grouse, partridge, or pheasant (family Phasianidae) are recognizable birds (Table 12).

The three wild mammal species identified are Eastern gray squirrel (*Sciurius carolinensis*), Old World rat (*Rattus* spp.), and white-tailed deer (*Odocoileus virginianus*). While the squirrel bones show no evidence of butchering, it is possible that they were consumed by the armory workers' household. The presence of a deer molar may indicate that the fauna was butchered on site or that the head was used as a part of soup.

Cow (*Bos taurus*) makes up the largest biomass portion (22.5%), followed by pig (*Sus scrofa*) (11.6%) and sheep/goat (*Ovis aries*/*Capra hircus*) (6.5%) (Table 12). These domestic species, including chicken, account for 40.7% of the biomass for the pre-1841 assemblage. While the presence of wild or domestic turkey is certain, squirrel, deer, and sucker bones also indicate the consumption of local fauna.

The most noticeable butchering trend in the earlier armory workers' household is the difference between pig and cow. About 65% of the cow bones and 4% of the pig bones show indications of butchering. Almost all the cow bones and two thirds of the pig bones are sawn, and one third of the pig bones show axe or cleaver marks. These different patterns imply that the meat came from different sources. The majority of the cow was cut in premeasured segments and distributed in somewhat equal proportions according to cuts of meat. Since pigs were commonly kept by many households in town, and pig butchering was often done with a cleaver or an axe, it may be speculated that the pigs represent species butchered domestically (Burk 1994).

The later armory workers' household assemblage (1841–1852) had only one identified fish, the sucker (family Catostomidae). Sucker fish, as noted above, are a common food retrieved from the Potomac and Shenandoah rivers. The presence of only a few fish remains is probably

Table 12. Summary of the Faunal Assemblage for the Pieceworkers' Households (1821–1841)ᵃ

Taxon	N	Percent	MNI	Percent	Meat weight (lb)	Total meat wt. (lb)	Percent	Weight (g)	Percent	Biomass (kg)	Percent
Class Osteichthyes (bony fish)	5	0.6	0/0	—	0.0/0.0	—	—	0.9	—	0.01	—
Family Catostomidae (sucker)	2	0.2	1/0	5.9	0.0/0.0	—	—	0.7	—	0.01	0.1
Class Aves (birds)	89	11.0	0/0	—	0.0/0.0	—	—	53.8	1.1	0.20	1.2
Class Aves/Mammalia III (birds/mammals)	1	0.1	0/0	—	0.0/0.0	—	—	2.5	—	0.01	0.1
Family Phasianidae	1	0.1	0/0	—	0.0/0.0	—	—	0.6	—	0.00	—
cf. Family Phasianidae	2	0.2	0/0	—	0.0/0.0	—	—	2.8	0.1	0.01	0.1
cf. Meleagris gallopavo (turkey)	1	0.1	1/0	5.9	7.5/7.5	7.5	0.7	3.6	0.1	0.02	0.1
Gallus gallus (chicken)	3	0.4	2/1	17.6	2.5/1.0	6.0	0.6	3.9	0.1	0.02	0.1
cf. Gallus gallus	2	0.2	0/0	—	0.0/0.0	—	—	1.1	—	0.01	—
Class Mammalia (mammals)	398	49.1	0/0	—	0.0/0.0	—	—	706.4	13.9	2.24	13.7
Class Mammalia I (large mammals)	84	10.4	0/0	—	0.0/0.0	—	—	1652.9	32.5	4.82	29.5
cf. Class Mammalia I	1	0.1	0/0	—	0.0/0.0	—	—	20.1	0.4	0.09	0.6
Class Mammalia II (medium mammals)	85	10.5	0/0	—	0.0/0.0	—	—	422.2	8.3	1.41	8.6
Class Mammalia III (small mammals)	14	1.7	0/0	—	0.0/0.0	—	—	21.8	0.4	0.10	0.6
cf. Sciurus carolinensis (squirrel)	2	0.2	1/0	5.9	1.0/1.0	1.0	0.1	0.9	—	0.01	—
Rattus spp. (Old World rat)	6	0.7	1/0	5.9	0.0/0.0	—	—	0.8	—	0.01	—
Order Artiodactyla I	10	1.2	0/0	—	0.0/0.0	—	—	162.6	3.2	0.60	3.7
Order Artiodactyla II	4	0.5	0/0	—	0.0/0.0	—	—	31.2	0.6	0.14	0.8
Sus scrofa (domestic pig)	67	8.3	3/1	23.5	100.0/50.0	350.0	34.3	525.6	10.3	1.72	10.5
cf. Sus scrofa	3	0.4	0/0	—	0.0/0.0	—	—	42.0	0.8	0.18	1.1
cf. Odocoileus virginianus (deer)	1	0.1	1/0	5.9	100.0/100.0	100.0	9.8	1.0	—	0.01	—
Bos taurus (domestic cow)	9	1.1	1/1	11.8	400.0/50.0	450.0	44.1	557.9	11.0	1.81	11.1
cf. Bos taurus	8	1.0	0/0	—	0.0/0.0	—	—	576.2	11.3	1.87	11.4
Ovis aries / Capra hircus (sheep/goat)	8	1.0	3/0	17.6	35.0/15.0	105.0	10.3	211.4	4.2	0.76	4.6
cf. Ovis aries / Capra hircus	4	0.5	0/0	0.0	0.0/0.0	—	—	78.3	1.5	0.31	1.9
Totals	810	100	17	100		1019.5	100	5081.2	100	16.34	100

ᵃFrom Burk (1994:7.16). Columns: (N) number of bones identified to that taxon; (MNI) Minimum Number of Individuals (adults/immature specimens); (Meat weight) meat weight of a representative whole animal (adult/immature); (Total meat weight) derived by multiplying the MNI of adult and immature animals by the Meat Weight of each and adding the two totals; (Weight) weight of the actual archaeological bones; (Biomass) skeletal weight.

due to the low resistance to taphonomic stresses (Colley 1990; Limp 1979; Reitz 1986). The assemblage was collected from a yard scatter, and the excavation located no major features, such as privies or trash pits, that would have protected the fragile bones of fish.

Turkey (*Meleagris gallopavo*) and chicken (*Gallus gallus*) are both present in the post-1841 assemblage. Chickens may have been purchased at the market or more likely, kept in a household henyard for both eggs and meat. The turkey was probably caught in the wild. Fragments of bird (class Aves), and grouse, partridge, or pheasant (family Phasianidae) are also present (Table 13).

Identified wild species include Eastern cottontail (*Sylvilagus floridanus*), rodent (order Rodentia), and Old World rat (*Rattus* spp.). While the cottontail bone may have been food for human consumption, the rodent and Old World rat bones are probably commensal species. Domestic cat (*Felis domesticus*) and cat (family Felidae) bones are also present.

The domestic triad pig (*Sus scrofa*), cow (*Bos taurus*), and sheep/goat (*Ovis aries / Capra hircus*), along with two galliformes (turkey and chicken), constitute the largest proportion of identifiable biomass (26.4%) in the post-1841 assemblage. The cottontail is the only certain wild taxon, although the turkey remains may also represent a wild species. Evidence of butchering is relatively equal between pig (10.4%) and cow (12.5%). Generally, there is an increase of sawed bones relative to chopped and hacked bones in this assemblage. This pattern reflects the development of more efficient methods of butchering, and it indicates the growing reliance on market-produced meat as opposed to homegrown and home-butchered meats (Burk 1994).

With the development of urbanization and the growth of industrialization, traditional home activities were replaced by wage-labor activities. Once the individual's participation in a wage-labor system increased, the choice of foods became tied directly to the market. During the urbanization process, legal restrictions, based on the need for better sanitary conditions, limited the types and amounts of slaughtering allowed in an area, thus moving the butchering process to peripheral areas to be performed by specialists (Bowen 1990). An examination of the armory workers' faunal assemblages indicates that this trend was not adhered to in the case of the armory workers' household. Food production at home appears to have increased slightly, as pig remained important in the post-1841 diet. Food procurement strategies did not shift away from raising pig at home, and there was increase of importing beef from regional and national markets. This sustained home production may be a product of the armory workers' growing poverty

Table 13. Summary of the Faunal Assemblage for the Wage Laborers' Households (1841–1852)[a]

Taxon	N	Percent	MNI	Percent	Meat weight (lb)	Total meat wt. (lb)	Percent	Weight (g)	Percent	Biomass (kg)	Percent
Class Osteichthyes (bony fish)	2	0.3	0/0	—	0.0/0.0	—	—	0.2	—	0.00	—
Family Catostomidae (sucker)	1	0.2	1/0	5.6	0.0/0.0	—	—	0.2	—	0.00	—
Class Aves (birds)	74	11.2	0/0	—	0.0/0.0	—	—	62.4	2.5	0.23	2.7
Family Phasianidae	3	0.5	0/0	0.0	0.0/0.0	—	—	1.5	0.1	0.01	0.1
Meleagris gallopavo (turkey)	2	0.3	1/0	5.6	7.5/7.5	7.5	0.8	9.7	0.4	0.04	0.5
cf. Meleagris gallopavo	1	0.2	0/0	—	0.0/0.0	—	—	1.4	0.1	0.01	0.1
Gallus gallus (chicken)	5	0.8	2/0	11.1	2.5/1.0	5.0	0.5	6.9	0.3	0.03	0.4
Class Mammalia (mammals)	341	51.7	0/0	—	0.0/0.0	—	—	573.1	23.4	1.86	22.2
Class Mammalia I (large mammals)	46	7.0	0/0	—	0.0/0.0	—	—	723.0	29.5	2.29	27.4
Class Mammalia II (medium mammals)	74	11.2	0/0	—	0.0/0.0	—	—	414.7	16.9	1.39	16.6
Class Mammalia III (small mammals)	33	5.0	0/0	—	0.0/0.0	—	—	36.8	1.5	0.16	1.9
Sylvilagus floridanus (cottontail)	1	0.2	1/0	5.6	2.0/2.0	2.0	0.2	0.9	—	0.01	0.1
Order Rodentia (rodent)	1	0.2	0/0	—	0.0/0.0	—	—	0.2	—	0.00	—
Rattus spp. (Old World rat)	8	1.2	4/0	22.2	0.0/0.0	—	—	2.6	0.1	0.01	0.2
cf. Family Felidae (domestic cat)	1	0.2	0/0	—	0.0/0.0	—	—	2.8	0.1	0.02	0.2
cf. Felis domesticus	2	0.3	1/0	5.6	0.0/0.0	—	—	8.9	0.4	0.04	0.5
Order Artiodactyla I	2	0.3	0/0	—	0.0/0.0	—	—	21.1	0.9	0.10	1.1
Order Artiodactyla II	1	0.2	0/0	—	0.0/0.0	—	—	8.4	0.3	0.04	0.5
Sus scrofa (domestic pig)	43	6.5	5/0	27.8	100.0/50.0	500.0	50.0	257.4	10.5	0.90	10.8
cf. Sus scrofa	5	0.8	0/0	—	0.0/0.0	—	—	40.1	1.6	0.17	2.0
Bos taurus (domestic cow)	5	0.8	1/1	11.1	400.0/50.0	450.0	45.0	153.8	6.3	0.57	6.8
cf. Bos taurus	3	0.5	0/0	—	0.0/0.0	—	—	87.8	3.6	0.34	4.1
Ovis aries/Capra hircus (sheep/goat)	6	0.9	1/0	5.6	35.0/15.0	35.0	3.5	33.7	1.4	0.15	1.7
Totals	660	100	18	100		999.5	100	2447.6	100	8.36	100

[a]From Burk (1994:7.13). Columns: (N) number of bones identified to that taxon; (MNI) Minimum Number of Individuals (adults/immature specimens); (Meat Weight) meat weight of a representative whole animal (adult/immature); (Total meat weight) derived by multiplying the MNI of adult and immature animals by the Meat Weight of each and adding the two totals; (Weight) weight of the actual archaeological bones; (Biomass) skeletal weight.

created by the introduction of the new wage-labor system. Throughout the armory's existence, wages continually dropped (Lucas and Shackel 1994). The failure of armorers and their households to acquire products associated with the industrial infrastructure may also be explained as the armorers' desire to be relatively independent of the new industrial order. Self-sufficiency in food production, while others were increasingly relying on the market economy even in small quantities, was one means that the armorers had to demonstrate their control over their own daily lives.

CONSUMERISM AND REACTIONS TO INDUSTRIAL CULTURE

Studies that outline consumption often describe changes in consumer behavior, but scholars pay little attention to why people desired, purchased, and used material goods (McCracken 1988). Changing consumption patterns need to be explained as more than the pursuit of commodities as an "irresistible drug" (McKendrick et al. 1982:10); rather, these patterns need to be explored in the social circumstances in which they were created within a consumer society. Historical context as well as group dynamics need to be examined. The explanation by Colin Campbell (1987), placing the growth of consumer culture in the context of new Romantic ideals, seems logical (see Chapter 1).

This analysis of Lower Town Harpers Ferry addresses research questions about the relationship between people and a new modernizing behavior that is associated with industrializing society. To understand how these people survived and interacted with each other on a daily basis, it is essential to link the material correlates and the growth of an industrial town to issues related to the new ideology of industrial capitalism.

Harpers Ferry became increasingly industrialized through the nineteenth century and was greatly affected by the introduction of the canal and the railroad. What cannot be gathered from the historical records is how this movement toward an industrial environment affected the daily lives of the inhabitants of Harpers Ferry. What remains in the archaeological record are the domestic assemblages of the households of managers and workers with extremely different outlooks on work discipline. This analysis presents a picture of domestic life in the early industrial era. Through the analysis of some of the material assemblages left behind by these households, we can see the degree to which the private lives of the master armorers and armory workers reflect their views on changing industrial and consumer society, and reveal their relative acceptance or rejection of consumer goods and behaviors transported from eastern mercantile centers.

Women played an influential role in creating and reinforcing new consumer and industrial ideals at home. With the rise of nineteenth-century industrialism, many lower-class women found jobs in mills in the Northeastern and Middle Atlantic states, although these opportunities were limited in Harpers Ferry. As industrialization moved traditional professions and crafts from the house to the factory, women became excluded from traditional fields. Traditional goods could be purchased, and middle-class women focused on such Romantic ideals as caring for the children and the home and preparing the workers for the workday. Boundaries and roles became increasingly codified, and the home developed as a separate sphere from the rest of society. The emphasis on public order was replaced by a stress on private discipline and self-control. Etiquette and social rules provided restricting guidelines for behavior (Mintz and Kellogg 1988; Strasser 1982:5; Wall 1994).

While the roles of middle-class women transformed from home production to household management, women had to adapt to and reinforce the new schedules of time discipline. They trained a new generation of children in the cultural behaviors and attitudes of society. New consumption patterns of household goods from the master armorer's house demonstrate how industrialism increasingly influenced the consumer choices of Moor's family. These patterns also indicate how the Moors chose to reinforce industrial behavior in their household, although they seem to encourage some home production. In contrast, in the case of the armory workers' post-1841 households, they chose not to accept the new consumer goods readily available from the market. Instead, they acquired goods that were fashionable one or two generations earlier. Home production did not decrease in favor of market goods.

Buying matched sets, or at least purchasing a variety of sizes of similar wares, and buying precut portions of meat at the marketplace, requires an expenditure on the consumer's part. But what motivated the individual to pursue new purchasing patterns? Emulation, social separation, consciously or unconsciously participating in a new industrial culture, and subscribing to the new Romantic ideal are all variables that need to be considered when explaining material culture patterning in a consumer society. The earliest contexts in this study, both the Beckhams and the pre-1841 occupants at the armory workers' house, show signs of residents buying into the consumer culture. As the workers in the armory were being deskilled in the 1820s and 1830s and made into pieceworkers for their eventual entry into the wage-labor system, they acquired a new domestic material culture associated with industrialization. The new materials, along with new behaviors, helped to train households for their inevitable confrontation with or absorption into industrial culture.

Some households continued to subscribe to the Romantic ideal by buying into the new consumer culture, as did the master armorer. Others, like the post-1841 armory workers' household, acquired a material culture that was fashionable generations earlier. The deskilling of workers and the embracing of the material world associated with wage labor were not acceptable to some employees. While there were relatively few explicit protests, such as strikes, at Harpers Ferry, workers did rebel by slowing production, by damaging equipment, and by frequent absenteeism. In the domestic sphere, some families chose alternative goods for the types of material culture they acquired. These goods were not the goods that were often purchased by those conforming to the ideology of mass production and mass consumption. Consumers, those in charge of the domestic sphere of family life, and by the end of the second quarter of the nineteenth century, were often middle-class women who were making choices about what types of goods they should purchase. These decisions demonstrated their commitment or their lack of commitment to the new consumer culture and the Romantic ideal. Acquiring out-of-date materials that were fashionable generations earlier may possibly show consumers' discontent for the new modern culture. These households also apparently raised more livestock for daily consumption, even when the town's marketplace expanded. They could have longed for the good old days, when the heads of household still had some control over their means of production and their daily lives. They lived out this dream with a material culture that was fashionable during these earlier years when they felt they had more control over their destiny.

"Oh! Let Oppression's Hand Be Stay'd"

—Virginia Free Press

The Transformation from Craft to Wage Labor

EARLY ARMS PRODUCTION

Arms production at the Harpers Ferry Armory began with craftsmen who were knowledgeable in the production of the whole gun. The transformation from craft production to wage laborers in a production line creating interchangeable parts came with great difficulty at the armory; as a result, it was not fully implemented until the 1840s. While it appears that some armorers accepted their fate in return for wages, others felt that their livelihood was at stake, especially when their wages decreased with the introduction of new machinery. However, the craftsman was not immediately transformed into a wage earner at Harpers Ferry. Rather, an intermediate form of production was created—piecework. The piece-worker comprised a significant proportion of the armory's labor force in the 1820s and 1830s. The pieceworker was no longer considered a true craftsman, since he specialized in the production of only one part. The pieceworker, however, did have some control over his production; he was able to dictate his work hours as well as his rate of production. His presence represented the last vestiges of the freedoms that were synonymous with craft production.

Historically, it has always been assumed that piecework occurred solely within the armory grounds. Workers were allowed the freedom to come and go as they pleased as long as they met monthly quotas. There is no documentation to hint that armorers could have done some of their work in their own homes. It has always been implied that all parts of the arms-manufacturing process occurred within the factories. Excavation of an armory workers' assemblage, dating to the time that piecework predominated, the 1820s and 1830s, indicates the possibility that armorers had greater freedom in determining where to do their work than had previously been thought.

DIVISION OF LABOR AND CRAFT PRODUCTION

Through the first decades of the armory's existence at Harpers Ferry, workers and supervisors considered themselves craftsmen. The craft ethos is evident in the appointment of a new superintendent in 1807. James Stubblefield, whose experience did not exceed that of a craftsman from a small country shop, qualified for the superintendency by demonstrating to the ordnance department that he could successfully fabricate and assemble an entire gun (Barry 1988[1903]:20).

Once in charge of the operations, Superintendent Stubblefield insisted that he needed to increase the number of apprenticeships as a means of expanding the armory. Under the established system at the armory, workers served "from the time they are bound until of age." They received $12 per month and were given board and clothing. Education was supposed to be part of the apprenticeship, although the armory sometimes neglected this obligation. When apprentices were skilled enough to file a lock, they were given a quota of 17 locks per month; they received full price for any locks completed over this allotment. At the expiration of the apprenticeship, the armory provided them with a new suit of clothes and a position at the armory (HFNHP microfilms 1807, 1820). Apprenticeships ranged from 5 to 7 years. At the end of the apprenticeship, the worker had the option of staying with the armory or becoming a journeyman gunsmith. About 30 boys served apprenticeships between 1800 and 1813 (M. R. Smith 1977:63), although labor relations were far from amicable. James Stubblefield advertised rewards, ranging from 1¢ to $10, for at least three runaway apprentices (VFP 30 November 1810:3, 9 August 1811:3, 13 March 1812, 27 March 1812:4, 3 April 1812).

While apprenticeships continued into the 1810s, the ending of this institution was marked by the beginning of the piece-rate accounting procedures. This new work condition ended a fundamental craft practice. No longer was an armorer committed to teaching a helper the trade and making the helper proficient in all aspects of the trade no longer existed. No obligations, such as clothing, educating, or feeding, existed between the armorer and helper beyond payment for finished products. This new system hindered the development of the general and overall expertise of the armorer. Armorers, though, often hired their sons, thereby teaching them skills that would allow them to become full-fledged armorers (M. R. Smith 1977:64).

It had been thought that between 1799 and 1801, armorers crafted and assembled the entire gun. An 1800 advertisement in the *Virginia Free Press* (VFP 28 October 1800, 3 December 1800) challenges this assumption. It noted that along with a few thousand bushels of coal, Paymaster Annin requested a few thousand black walnut gunstocks of good quality for the United States Armory Factory at Harpers Ferry. By the time the armory was in full operation in 1802, the facility had adopted traditional European craft practices. While the armorer was adept at producing the entire gun, a form of division of labor existed whereby artisans made a particular part of the gun, i.e., lock, stock, mounting, or barrel. The master armorer's principal duty included coordinating the output of each part and determining work assignments so that an equal number of parts would be made simultaneously. As noted in Chapter 2, in 1807, the manufacturing of the gun at Harpers Ferry consisted of six separate branches: barrel making, lock forging, lock filing, brazing, stocking, and finishing (M. R. Smith 1977:78–79).

Eli Whitney claimed to have used this form of division of labor as early as 1798, and Superintendent Benjamin Prescott of the Springfield Armory in Massachusetts imposed this concept in 1806. In 1807, the production of a lock mechanism in Springfield entailed the use of two artisans. By 1816 the manufacturing process was divided into 21 separate processes. Stubblefield copied many of Springfield's labor innovations, and whatever division of labor existed in the Harpers Ferry Armory in the 1810s occurred prior to the facility's mechanization. By 1815, Stubblefield assumed the role of an absentee superintendent and moved his family to a country plantation. He delegated much of his authority and supervision to Master Armorer Beckham, his brother-in-law. With much of the daily routine under Beckham's control, little significant advancement in the division of labor occurred at the Harpers Ferry Armory for the next 14 years (M. R. Smith 1977:82–84).

CRAFT ETHOS AND FACTORY OPERATIONS

Even with this rudimentary division of labor, the Harpers Ferry Armory lacked the labor discipline found in contemporary industrial society. During the first decades of its existence, the factory opened at sunrise and closed at sunset. Armorers were free to work whenever they chose, as long as they met their monthly piecework quotas (M. R. Smith 1977:66):

Often skilled artisans would achieve their monthly quota in two or three weeks and could devote the remainder of their time to other pursuits such as farming, operating a small business, or making weapons for a private customer in the armory shops. Others preferred to alternate between farming and arms making by allocating five to six hours to each task daily. Harvest time abbreviated the factory schedule even further, although armorers usually compensated for this by great bursts of activity before and after a season.

Generally, a systematic manufacturing schedule did not exist in Harpers Ferry.

As the 1820s approached, the War Department boasted of new and labor-saving devices found in its armories, although most of the innovations occurred at the Springfield facilities. As long as craft-trained artisans remained in key managerial positions at the Harpers Ferry Armory, there was little chance to substitute factory discipline for their craft ethos. While arms made in the United States cost more than those manufactured in France and Britain, the War Department claimed that the United States had more efficient armories and employed more highly skilled workers. The department maintained that at Springfield "new and ingenious methods have been invented for doing different parts of the work which give greater dispatch and greater precision and uniformity than can be attained when the eye of the workman is the sole guide" (HFNHP microfilms 1819c). The Harpers Ferry Armory lacked many of these inventions and ran less efficiently than its sister armory, as its workers vehemently rejected any machinery that threatened their livelihood.

The cost of arms production at the Harpers Ferry Armory outpaced expenditures at the Springfield Armory. Tremendous waste existed within the armory, created by both inferior materials and workers' resistance to any attempt to change their means of production. For instance, in 1815, the Springfield Armory installed a trip-hammer, a water-powered device that produced up to 400 heavy blows a minute. The process created a much sounder seam for gun barrels in about half the time needed to hand-weld one. The process also cut the cost of labor by about 20¢ per barrel. Stubblefield wrote several times during the 1810s and 1820s that he wanted to install trip-hammers in the Harpers Ferry facility, but in 1830 armorers continued to hand-weld barrels. M. R. Smith (1977:114–115) notes that the failure rate of trip-hammered barrels in Springfield averaged 10%, while the failure rate of the Harpers Ferry hand-welded barrels averaged 25%. About half of these barrels failed during boring, while the remainder burst during proof.

In an attempt to lower the cost of production at the Virginia facility, Stubblefield presented a plan to the War Department, although his strategy lacked any form of industrial discipline. Instead, it emphasized a philosophy that adhered to a piecework system. He insisted that armorers who were increasingly participating in the piecework system should purchase their materials, tools, and coal from a storekeeper. The government would supply the shops and machinery. This new structure, he believed, would decrease waste and lower the cost of production (HFNHP microfilms 1821b). Stubblefield also proposed a 10–12$\frac{1}{2}$% reduction of wages, since the cost of supporting a family had generally decreased in Harpers Ferry (HFNHP microfilms 1821c). An 1822 tour of inspection from the War Department reinforced Stubblefield's ideas. The report claimed that workers should be compensated for their particular work on a piece (HFNHP microfilms 1822a).

Nevertheless, the armories were susceptible to problems resulting from delays in appropriations from Washington. Armory workers were not always paid on time; in one instance in 1816, their pay was delayed for 7 months. There are many instances of armory workers selling promissory notes to merchants for 6% up to 20% throughout the existence of the armory operations. Wage payments were sometimes so overdue that some merchants refused to accept any more promissory notes. This situation in 1816 eventually led the Springfield superintendent to sell off arms in order to raise cash and supplement the needed cash for the armorers (Deyrup 1948:103; Whittlesey 1920:n.p.; Zonderman 1992:175).

Because of the financial strain often imposed upon armorers delayed payments, the armorers continually resisted accountability for their products and tools. Superintendent Lucas wrote that it was the practice of workmen to become possessive of their government-issued tools: "Sort of a fee simple inheritance—and instead of the operators of the Armory being under the control of the officers, were to some extent controlled by the workmen" (HFNHP microfilms 1839b). Lucas declared that he had stopped this practice and claimed that the tools belonged to the government, stayed with the job, and were reissued.

Generally, workers were accountable for their losses. The armory established an accountability system whereby materials were assigned to workers. The cost of the materials was deducted from the person's salary if a piece was rejected or lost (HFNHP photostats 1832).

An 1832 report by Lieutenant Colonel Wolcott found good workmanship at Harpers Ferry, but the armory "lacked many useful machines adapted at Springfield and the private armories which go far towards producing a uniformity of work that is scarcely attainable by manual labor" (HFNHP photostats 1832). Wolcott also noted that while the general condition of the establishment was fair, many of the buildings were too narrow for efficient operations. Some of the waterwheels were inside buildings, occupying needed space and producing moisture "that is supposed to be unfavorable to health" (HFNHP photostats 1832).

Throughout the 1830s, a uniform factory discipline was not enforced, and many armorers were still paid by the piece. It was during Rust's administration that Master Armorer Moor installed the trip-hammer, although it was not until 1840 that trip-hammers completely replaced hand welding at Harpers Ferry. While Moor made strides to mechanize the armory, operations at the facility were lax compared to our modern industrial standards. The shops were often noted as places of business where armorers socialized, performed outside contract work, and labored at their own pace (HFNHP microfilms 1849a; HFNHP photostats 1836b). In 1836, the Secretary of War received a letter from another inspector noting that the workers left their jobs at 1:00 P.M. on Saturdays, a regular custom at the facility. He seemed unconcerned about the practice, "since workers are paid by the piece" (HFNHP microfilms 1836).

HOME PRODUCTION AT THE ARMORY WORKERS' HOUSE

The armory worker's house was originally constructed in the 1820s along with a bake oven, smokehouse, privy, and stable (Figure 39). While it is uncertain whether its original owner actually inhabited the building, armory workers and their families probably occupied the building for most of the first half of the nineteenth century. While armory records from 1841 to 1852 indicate the specific households that rented the structure, armory records dating before and after this era have been destroyed, thus making identification of specific families in the structure difficult. Since a significant proportion of armory workers were piece-rate workers in the 1820s and 1830s, and the dwelling was relatively small, there is a good probability that pieceworkers, rather than supervisors, inhabited the structure. Even though the archaeological evidence consists of one house lot, it does provide an example of changing relations between work and domestic life at the armory.

Piecework production occurred mainly within the boundaries of the armory grounds. No historical documentation accounts for the produc-

Figure 39. An early 1960s photograph of the armory workers' house. (Courtesy of Harpers Ferry National Historical Park)

tion of arms at the domestic dwellings of armory workers. Archaeological evidence from the armory workers' house supplies some evidence of home production, probably in the form of piecework. The earliest archaeological context at the house dates from the 1820s until 1841. The later date is easily defined, due to the presence of distinctive archaeological features, such as the documented construction of the east wing of the house.

Excavations adjacent to the armory dwelling discovered part of a .52 or .54 caliber gun barrel, a gunlock of which the lock plate measures nearly 6 inches, a side screw for securing the lock to the stock, and a

Figure 40. Model 1819 gun lock found in the pre-1841 context. (Photograph by Cari YoungRavenhorst)

large wood screw for attaching the butt plate to a gun stock. These items are probably from a U.S. Rifle Model 1819 (see Brown 1968:65). Also found is a middle barrel band, a nearly complete socket bayonet from a U.S. Flintlock Musket Model 1816 (Reilly 1970:2-3), and two ramrods (Larsen 1994b:6.6) (Figures 40 and 41).

Several different tool assemblages are in this context. One is a stonemason's toolkit that includes a wedge and single feather from a stonemason's toolkit, and a possible thumb latch or feather. These tools were found in heavy shale debris and may be related to the removal of shale for the construction of the 1841 east wing addition. Tools directly related to armory production include a wood chisel, probably for the modification or construction of stocks. Three different types of files— flat, half-round, and triangular—relate to metalworking. Also identi- fied was a combination tool. Combination tools varied in form and shape, depending upon the model that they serviced. Huntington (1972:251–255) describes the constant modifications made to the com- bination tool during the 1830s. This combination tool probably serviced a pre-1840 model (Figures 42 and 43).

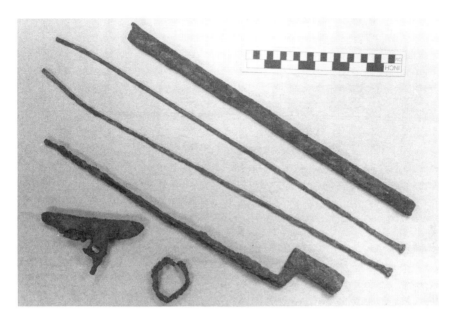

Figure 41. Middle barrel band, Model 1819 gun lock, Model 1816 socket bayonet, ramrods, and a .52 or .54 caliber gun barrel. (Photograph by Cari YoungRavenhorst)

The tools identified in association with the various craft-made arms parts (all muskets prior to the 1840s) provide an interesting scenario. The assemblage dates to the era of craft and piecework manufacturing prior to the imposition of manufacturing discipline. The armory workers who occupied the structure prior to the 1840s apparently engaged in the manufacturing of weapons at their domicile. The tools probably came from the armory, and the discarded gun parts were produced by the armorer to supplement his family's income, or they may have been part of the armory's piecework production. In either case, the gun parts are all from guns that were primarily produced in the United States Armory during the era dominated by piecework. As noted previously, there is no documentation at present stating that some types of piecework were performed by armorers at their house. The presence of gun parts and wood and metal filing tools at an armorer's dwelling suggests that some may have been. Prefactory discipline at the United States Armory may have encouraged, or at least it did not discourage, armory workers from laboring in their homes.

Figure 42. Wood chisel (*bottom*), metalworking files (*1st–5th, top*), and masonry tools (*6th, 7th, top*) related to the pre-1841 context. (Photograph by Cari YoungRavenhorst)

LABOR AND THE MILITARY SYSTEM

When the military assumed control over arms production at the armories, two types of labor existed in the factory—day workers and pieceworkers. As noted, many of those who labored in the piecework system worked until their quotas were met. The differences in time required by the different types of workers to complete tasks and meet quotas were noticeable into the 1840s. In 1842, Master Armorer Benjamin Moor noted that some of the armory employees "work as much as 10, some as much as 11, some not more than 8, and some not more than six; the Barrel welders, between 8 and 9 hours" (HFNHP photostats 1842). Although Moor believed in the mechanization of the armory, it seems that he failed to understand the implications of a modern factory discipline. When asked how many hours an armorer should work, he replied, "I think 8 hours for the Barrel forgers, in addition to time for repair and tools &c, and about 9 for the Grinders, about 8 to 10 for the other forgers; from 9 to 10 for the filers; and for the machine tenders from 10 to 12 hours" (HFNHP photostats 1842). Henry K. Craig, the

Figure 43. Combination tool used by armory workers. (Photograph by Cari Young-Ravenhorst)

first military superintendent, ordered these occupational differences to be abolished and all armory workers to labor the same number of hours each day (HFNHP microfilms 1842a).

In response to Craig's actions, the pieceworkers and many of the day hands at the musket factory marched to the rifle works on March 21, 1842, and gathered additional support from their fellow armorers. They returned and assembled in the arsenal yard, where some made speeches denouncing the military system, and they discussed the recently enforced regulations that required all workmen to conform to a new time discipline reinforced by the bell. They then quietly departed

to the Free Church to deliberate their course of action (HFNHP microfilms 1842b). While they were on strike for more than a week, no disor-
der or violence occurred, although citizens rallied in public gatherings
in support of the armorers (HFNHP microfilms 1842f; VFP 31 March
1842:2). An unsigned letter to President Tyler from the armorers protested the actions taken under the military system. It stated that "the
armorers of the Harper's Ferry Armory, feeling that their rights as
Freemen have been wrested from them . . ." (HFNHP microfilms
1842c).

The *Virginia Free Press* (VFP 31 March 1842:3) published on
March 31st "The Armorers Appeal!," a poem regarding the "late TURN
OUT against oppression":

> God of mercy, king of kings,
> Supreme Ruler of all things,
> To thee we fly on fond Hope's wings,
>   Oh, guard our little band!
> We ask thy counsel, beg thy aid,
> Oh! let oppression's hand be stay'd,
> And let us not foul slaves be made,
>   In Freedom's native land.
> We love our country and her laws,
> We're even foremost in her cause,
> That country we now ask to pause,
>   And leave us Liberty.
> We do not ask for sordid gain,
> But Freemen's rights we dare maintain,
> And hope we shall not sue in vain,
>   For slaves we cannot be.
> By our wrongs ad by our pains,
> By the free blood in our veins,
> We swear we will never wear the chains
>   Of servile slavery.
> By our sires and by our sons,
> By our wives and little ones,
> Whilst in our veins life's current runs,
>   We wil [sic], we must be free.
> He who dares to slink away,
> And who a traitor's part would play,
> Let him the "orders" still obey,
>   And wear the collar too.
> Firm, naked one and all,
> We will march at freedom's call,
> Resolved, that we will stand or fall,
>   As freemen ought to do.

A large number of armorers chartered a Chesapeake and Ohio
canal boat and proceeded to bring their grievance to President Tyler.

The president greeted the armorers courteously and shook hands with each of them. Tyler told the armorers that he greatly appreciated their work, considering "the workmen as the bone and sinew of the land and its main dependence in war and in peace . . ." but "they must go home and hammer out their own salvation" (Barry 1988[1903]:31–32). Tyler also promised that their grievances concerning the military system would be addressed. Upon their return to Harpers Ferry, the workers were granted amnesty by the Secretary of War and returned to their jobs on April 1 (HFNHP microfilms 1842f; VFP 7 April 1842:2). The House of Representatives created a committee to investigate the armorers' protest, and the committee ruled in favor of the military system (VFP 1 December 1842:2). Both houses of Congress adopted a bill providing for a military superintendency (VFP 25 August 1842:2).

Rules and regulations for the workshops were reprinted and posted in the armory workshops (see Chapter 3). For instance, rule 5 stated: "All persons employed at this Armory will, at the signal for work, repair to their appropriate Stations, and then perform their duties diligently and in an orderly manner" (HFNHP microfilms 1842e). This rule implied that all workers were to be accounted for and therefore must labor within the factory at their assigned work station. Rule 10 stated: "Piece workmen will be charged with Files, oil, and Sand paper at the wholesale cost of the articles" (HFNHP microfilms 1842e). This regulation implies that piecework still existed within the armory, and these workers were made accountable for their means of production.

Standardized hours of production became synonymous with the military superintendency. Symington, who succeeded Craig as armory superintendent, wrote: "It is important at Establishments like this where almost every branch of the business is done by the aid of machinery, that the workmen employed whether at piece or day work, conform to the same working hours, and I doubt very much if an industrious man at piecework finds the time too long" (HFNHP microfilms 1848a). Pieceworkers resented adhering to fixed hours, and each believed that he "should enjoy the privilege of laboring as few or as many hours and during such parts of the day that might best suit his interests and convenience" (HFNHP photostats 1852).

The archaeological context from the armory workers' dwelling provides data that reflect changes between the relationship of production and domestic life. With the formality of the workplace and the imposition of time discipline and accountability of laborers, tools, and products, the armory worker increasingly lost control over a portion of his life. This new work discipline, as noted above, was not easily accepted by most armorers. The change to this new manufacturing discipline and its effects on the daily activities of armory workers are noticeable at the household level.

MILITARY DISCIPLINE AND DOMESTIC LIFE AT THE ARMORY WORKERS' HOUSE

An archaeological context that dates from 1841 through 1852 from the armory workers' house described above contributes some clues to the effects of the new work discipline on domestic relations. The historical record indicates that in the early 1840s, at least, an assistant jobbing smith, who may have done some piecework, lived in the structure. By the late 1840s, a mechanic and his family occupied the structure. Since the mechanic needed to be bound to the rhythm of industry and was an essential component of the industry's mechanization and operations, therefore, he did not operate under the piecework system and could not spend any of his work time anywhere else except at the factory.

The archaeological record indicates a substantial decrease in the number of arms parts found in the domestic assemblage at the armory workers' house. One arms part, a mainspring from a gunlock, was the only arms item found in this assemblage. Four different types of tools were found, including a wedge and three different types of files (a flat file tang, a half-round file, and the tang from a triangular file) (see Larsen 1994b:6.5).

The changing patterns in the domestic assemblage of the armory workers' dwelling are indicative of the changes found in the armory as a whole. The new military system greatly impacted the worker as well as his household's domestic relations. The new work reforms eradicated any vestiges of craft production remaining in the armory. Many of the armory workshops were stripped of their outdated machinery starting in 1838, and the machinery was replaced with new machinery that created interchangeable parts for the mass production of guns. While Moor's Model 1840 was never produced in Harpers Ferry, the United States Percussion Musket, Model 1842, replaced the traditional Model 1816 flintlock at the Harpers Ferry Armory in 1845. Much of the handwork and craftsmanship necessary to complete a musket was no longer needed (M. R. Smith 1977:284). Every part and every person became accountable in the production of firearms. Hours of operation were established, and workers were to maintain a 10-hour workday (M. R. Smith 1977:271).

Only one arms part and a few tools were found in the post-1841 assemblage from the armory workers' domicile. This pattern is probably reflective of the increasing control that the military superintendency had over the production process and the ownership of tools. A clearer division was made between the work process and domestic life. Any means that an armory worker had to supplement his income through greater production in the piecework process was thus taken away. Workers were confined to the factory for a 10-hour workday, which was probably a longer time than they were accustomed to.

CHANGING DOMESTIC RELATIONS

Production at Harpers Ferry was initially based upon a European craft tradition. Apprenticeship allowed one to work as a journeyman. With time and experience, one could then become a master craftsman. By the 1810s, armorers were no longer responsible for knowing the production of the whole gun. Rather, they became specialists and were paid by the piece and were thereby allowed them to retain a form of individual freedom. They were free to come and go at their convenience.

Historian Merritt Roe Smith (1977) produced a history of arms manufacturing at Harpers Ferry. He, and others before him (see Barry 1988[1903]:30–36), note the fundamental changes experienced within the armory during the 1840s. Administration during the armory's first decades has been characterized as overly reflective of local allegiances and too undisciplined (M. R. Smith 1977:266). Production costs were considerably higher at Harpers Ferry, while the quality of arms was considered well below that of arms from the Springfield Armory.

This investigation describes the social and political contexts in which armory tools and weapons were found at the domestic site once occupied by armory workers and their families. Craft orientation dominated armory production until the military assumed control of its manufacturing process in 1841. Prior to this time, a relatively high quantity of files (flat, round, and triangular) and weapon parts were found in association with each other in the pre-1841 domestic assemblage, even though Superintendent Rust claimed to have put an end to armorers' possessing government tools. The tools found at the dwelling may be a product of home production since some workers were paid by the piece.

Only a few files and one arms' part were found in the later armory assemblage. This sparseness of gun-related materials in the later assemblage may be evidence of stricter manufacturing regulations,

including the implementation of factory discipline and the abandon-
ment of the piecework process. Some home production may have continued, but in smaller amounts. M. R. Smith (1977:270) notes that
armorers sometimes illegally resold government tools to the public
prior to 1841. This practice may have continued to some degree after
the administrative changes, and it may have been a way for the armorers to hold onto their familiar traditions and resist the orders of the
new military superintendency.

Landscape architects (C. Gilbert et al. 1993; Joseph et al. 1993) and
historians (see Snell 1981a,b) have made significant contributions to
our understanding of the changing physical history of Harpers Ferry
and of the development of new technology and social unrest (M. R.
Smith 1977). They have paid little attention to the social and domestic
relations of armory workers' everyday life in an armory town. This
archeological investigation of an urban house lot provides data on the
transformation of domestic relations in an industrializing town. The
change from piecework to wage labor truly affected the domestic context of armory workers' households as well as their relationship with
the rest of the community.

"Home . . . ! Refuge from Sadness"

—LYDIA H. SIGOURNEY

THE NEW DISCIPLINE OF THE INDUSTRIAL ERA

Early Harpers Ferry was based on a precapitalist and noncommercial economic order, which may be characterized as a household mode of production. With growing industrialization, however, there were increased pressures to conform to the new economic system. Industrialization encouraged punctuality and moral behavior. Family members who were not directly involved in arms production or the domestic activities of the household were encouraged to join the manufacturing process. A newspaper editorial in the *Virginia Free Press* noted that "great portions of the idleness and consequent laxity of morals which now exist, among children [and those] unemployed, might be obviated" [if they worked in newly developed factories at Harpers Ferry] (VFP 9 October 1834:3). The transition from a household mode of production to a market economy created great social tensions in society (Kulikoff 1989:125–132; 1992). While the home became perceived as a "sanctuary" during the industrial era, many tensions developed as a result of changing domestic and work relations. For instance, education and religion were traditionally perceived as a family responsibility. The formal introduction of the institutions of public schools and churches into Harpers Ferry as distinct entities outside the family marks some of the most obvious tensions between the new superstructure of capitalism and the town's traditional lifeways.

HARPERS FERRY AND THE DEVELOPMENT OF PUBLIC SCHOOLS

The education of the mass population was not a major concern of the leading Harpers Ferry families, especially since most of their children received formal education at academies or boarding schools in other areas. Armory workers' children received their schooling from their parents, and they learned the ways of their parents, including their crafts and trades. They did not receive much news of the outside world, nor were they exposed to the changing cultural values associated with Romantic consumerism and puritan ethics that most citizens of urban east coast cities were participating in during the early nineteenth century.

In many cases, outsiders were the ones who tried to establish educational facilities for Harpers Ferry residents. The first documented attempts at schooling occurred in 1818 when Superintendent Stubblefield tried to acquire the services of a teacher, Reverend George Snider. Whether Snider made it to Harpers Ferry or not is unknown (HFNHP microfilms 1818b). Soon after John Hall's arrival in town in 1818, he was appalled by the lack of educational facilities at Harpers Ferry, especially when compared to his former New England residence. Hall believed that a proper education taught at a formal institution would instill in students the habits of good order and punctuality, which would also benefit the national interest (HFNHP microfilms 1822b). Apparently, most of the families at Harpers Ferry were unaccustomed to practicing and teaching this new order of behavior.

In 1822, John Hall tried to formalize schooling for the armorers' children and he requested financial help from the War Department. Hall believed that a school financed by the government for one year would thereafter support itself. The plan met resistance from Superintendent Stubblefield, Master Armorer Beckham, and a few of the armorers (HFNHP microfilms 1842c). The source of the money concerned Stubblefield, claimed that housing should be a priority and rents from armory dwellings should be used for the repair and the upkeep of dwellings rather than for education (HFNHP microfilms 1822d). The War Department sided with Stubblefield's plea and affirmed that the department was not authorized to apply rents to any nonarmory purposes. The armory needed an Act of Congress to use rent funds to support schools or ministers (HFNHP microfilms 1822e).

Schools were eventually created, but with little public support. Enrollment was low, although Hall reported in 1822 that it had increased from its initial 40 students to about 100. These enrollments were still disappointingly low for Hall, as families still saw it as being their role to educate their children. Epidemics in the early 1820s also aggravated the situation, as workers missed many days of work, thereby reducing their earnings. Many workmen could not afford the tuition (HFNHP microfilms 1822c, 1824a).

By the late 1820s, Roswell Lee, superintendent of the Springfield Armory, who sometimes acted as the Harpers Ferry superintendent, wrote that Harpers Ferry was in dire need of a formal school. Townspeople began to raise money for completing the "church and school house." The building was to be two stories and 60 feet by 40 feet in floor plan. The first floor was to accommodate a church and the second floor was to be divided into three apartments for schools—one for a "Lancasterian school," one for "higher branches," and one for a "female seminary." Lee also noted that the upper, third story "will be one of the most splendid Masonic Halls in this part of the country" (HFNHP microfilms 1827d). It seems that the building was never constructed, since in 1829 the school system was still perceived as deplorable. John Hall once again urged the Secretary of War to find some way, preferably through special Congressional funding, to finance a school system. Good teachers rarely stayed a year, and those who remained earned barely enough to pay their board (HFNHP microfilms 1829g).

After Superintendent Dunn replaced Stubblefield in 1829, he reiterated many of Hall's concerns about the educational system. Appalled by the number of Xs on the receipts for payment on the payrolls, he wrote: ". . . there is no community within my knowledge of the same extent, where so many illiterate human beings have been raised as this place, and nearly all of whom have been raised in the service of their country, in the manufacture of arms . . ." (HFNHP microfilms 1829h).

Apparently, Dunn and later superintendents made some effort to increase the town's educational facilities. Master Armorer Moor established a library society for use by the workers, although by the late 1840s it no longer existed (VFP 7 November 1831, 18 October 1832, VFP 17 October 1833). Along with the redevelopment of the work facilities and the work process within the armory, greater attention was paid to the town's educational system by armory officials. New morals, values, and time discipline were no doubt part of the everyday curriculum. Schools were increasingly perceived as a necessary training ground to promote a modern discipline in order to exist in a growing industrial society. By 1848, there were four schoolhouses built by the United States on public lands. Under Superintendent Symington's recommendations, school districts were designed, and Harpers Ferry residents elected a school commissioner (HFNHP microfilms 1848d; VFP 13 August 1847, 8 July 1848:3; also see P. R. Smith 1959b).

HARPERS FERRY AND THE DEVELOPMENT OF CHURCHES

    In the early nineteenth century, evangelical Christianity was perceived by the emerging bourgeoisie as a means to stabilize social order. Revivalism functioned to promote concord and conformity. Implicit within the doctrine of individual salvation was the consensual notion that "economic conditions were a matter of fate, rather than for struggle" (Shelton 1986:129–131). The evangelical promise of salvation was necessary for the new industrial worker who faced brutal and impoverished conditions. The notion of salvation for the workers and judgment and hellfire for the exploiting owners may have helped to subvert the anguish that many workers felt. Church services also supported the ideals of orderliness, productivity, and punctuality, as clergy claimed that they were necessary for spiritual redemption. Churches were not formally established in Harpers Ferry for several decades after the armory's founding, and armory officials often complained about the lack of suitable public space for worship. Workmen and their families often met in a workshop for Sunday services (HFNHP microfilms 1810b). The Methodist-Episcopal church was established in Harpers Ferry in 1825. From 1830 through 1851, five additional churches were established: Catholic (1830), Presbyterian (1841), Methodist Protestant (1843), Lutheran (1850), and Episcopalian (1851) (P. R. Smith 1958a,b, 1959a,c,d; Snell 1959c). These churches were usually in financial trouble throughout the antebellum period, mostly due to low attendance. M. R. Smith (1977:331) claims that since these churches had limited influence during the antebellum era, formal instruction in moral behavior and discipline reached few people. Any education on these matters primarily received at home, although the increasing number of churches, especially after the 1840s, hints that general attendance increased. In an attempt to reach individuals, preachers would enter the workshops and approach workers. As noted earlier, the preacher's behavior may have been acceptable at one time, but by the 1850s, this action was no longer condoned, as it interfered with production. (HFNHP microfilms 1853).

Overview of Public Schools and Churches in Harpers Ferry

    Churches and public schools were generally absent in the first several decades of the development of Harpers Ferry. Parents probably felt that it was their duty and traditional role to educate their offspring.

They therefore neglected to support the establishment of any formal institution that would replace them in this traditional role. One reason for the slow adaption and formalization of these institutions was the lack of contact with the outside world. Harpers Ferry is situated at the confluence of the Potomac and Shenandoah rivers in what was an agrarian hinterland region. Frederick, which was a small farming community, stands 20 miles to its east; Hagerstown, about 25 miles to the north; Washington DC over 60 miles to the south. Stagecoach, horseback, and foot were the only means of reaching these other communities until the mid 1830s. While interaction did occur between these other towns, it was relatively infrequent. "This cloistered condition fostered a cultural milieu much more akin to the elemental and primitive folkways of the back country than to the increasingly specialized urban life of the East" (M. R. Smith 1977:329). It was not until the Chesapeake and Ohio Canal and the Baltimore & Ohio Railroad reached the Maryland shores of the Potomac opposite Harpers Ferry in the mid-1830s that transportation and communication were facilitated. The travel of ideas and of people became frequent and relatively inexpensive. With the development of military supervision in the armory after 1841, some of the ideals fostered in the schools and church were being achieved in the factory, M. R. Smith (1977:330) notes that both churches and schools

> idealized political, economic, and social order. By emphasizing the harmony
> of godliness, progress, and democracy and inveighing against strikes, idle-
> ness, and other forms of deviant behavior, they implanted a sense of disci-
> pline, conformity, and adaptability among populations which helped ease
> the transition to an urban-industrial age.

With relatively low church and school attendance in Harpers Ferry, however, there was only minimal success in implementing these new modern ideals in the community. Throughout the 1850s, until the destruction of the armory in 1861, workers generally were unwilling to be controlled by a new work discipline and corruption often was rampant among supervisors. The new morals, values, and disciplines prescribed by many nineteenth-century institutions appear to have aided in the creation of a division of labor, but these ideals had only minimal affects in controlling the behavior of the entire workforce.

DESKILLING

The responsibility for schooling and religious education was increasingly being removed from the household at the same time that labor was also being separated from the home. Outside the home, individuals tended to work for entrepreneurs who owned the means of production and dictated the work process, circumstances that led to the deskilling of workers. Deskilling was accomplished by segmenting the labor process and reducing the level of skill needed to perform a task and constrain the workers' autonomy. The skill was transferred from worker to machinery, thereby giving the owner increasing control over the work process and the workers (Braverman 1974; Marglin 1974; Noble 1986).

Deskilling workers has traditionally been interpreted as a way to increase the efficiency of the factory system and reduce the costs of production. Some scholars challenge this interpretation and search for other meanings in this industrial process. When capitalists introduced new technologies to the work process, they chose to impose a new form of life, which workers either complied with or resisted (Nasseney and Abel 1993:254). Therefore, the deskilling of craftsmen at Harpers Ferry was not just a way to increase production, nor was it only a product of technological efficiency.

The deskilling process preceded the drive to build large machine-centered factories (Laurie 1989). The process of deskilling prior to wage labor is evident in the historical and archaeological record in Harpers Ferry. While machinery was introduced during the earliest years of the armory, craft-oriented practices remained an integral part of the production process. Even though the factory system was not implemented, deskilling occurred with the introduction of the piecework system. Rather than making the entire gun, the individual became responsible for making only part of the weapon. In the first decade of the armory's existence, the manufacturing process was divided into at least six parts. While armorers were trained to make the entire gun, it was the master armorer's function to assign work to individuals so that production would not bottleneck. During the 1810s, the work process was divided even further. With this new implementation of increased division of labor, armorers were no longer responsible for knowing how to manufacture the entire gun. Rather, many of the workers were subjected to a piece-rate manufacturing system; they became experts in manufacturing one part, or a portion of a part, to be used in a gun (see Chapter 3).

With the establishment of piecework, armorers lost their skills and became interchangeable within the larger manufacturing process. Armorers continually petitioned the Ordnance Department for increased wages during the establishment of piecework. In one instance in 1819, the department responded to Stubblefield, who had asked for a raise for workers. Wadsworth noted that the superintendent was to set the wages, using his best judgment. Then he added: "I can see no reason for a general increase of wages at the present time, but rather the reverse, owing to the general want of money among every class of society, which must have the effect soon of producing a reduction of prices in labor, as well as everything else" (HFNHP microfilms 1819d).

Stubblefield recommended a general reduction in wages in April 1821. A deflation of prices existed in the early 1820s, and Stubblefield may have tried to anticipate a call for across-the-board wage cuts at the facility. His offer to reduce wages may have been an attempt to curtail the harshness of a more severe pay cut. Apparently, Stubblefield knew what was coming, because in May 1821, Colonel Bomford of the Ordnance Department ordered a reduction of wages of 15% at both armories due to the "cheapness of subsistence, and the reduced price of labor generally, throughout the country" (HFNHP microfilms 1821c,d). Even though the value of goods dropped in the 1820s, the armory superintendents persistently recommended wage increases through the 1820s (Zonderman 1992:180).

Apparently, armory workers simultaneously resisted and accommodated the new division of labor and wage cuts. Armorers rarely exceeded their monthly quotas under the piecework system. Workers probably conspired among themselves and set their own agenda. Even with new machinery, production did not increase. In fact, records from the armory show a decrease in production in the 1840s, when new "labor saving" machinery and strict division of labor was introduced (see M. R. Smith 1977, 1985:82). Increased production would mean lower wages per piece if the armory workers produced more. Interviews with armory workers note that many pieceworkers labored for fewer hours than the average factory/mill worker of the era (see the Appendix). Armory workers did produce the products that they were required to manufacture, but on their own terms. Under the piecework system, workers had the means to restrict output and limit capitalist exploitation (e.g., see Clawson 1980:168ff; Hounshell 1982; James Scott 1990).

Evidence of an armory worker controlling his output is also visible in the archaeological record at Harpers Ferry. As noted in Chapter 6 at a workers' domestic site, large quantities of armorer's tools—including a variety of metal and wood files—were found throughout the site. Gun parts, such as lock, barrel, butt plate, and ramrod, were also discovered. It appears that the armory worker did not necessarily spend all his time laboring in the factory, but sometimes worked at home. When work was performed at home, without the oversight of the supervisor, the armorer had some control over his means of production and could work at his own convenience. Other skilled family members, such as young armory workers-to-be, may have helped their fathers reach their quotas while learning a skill. This scenario is only one of many possible stories that can be associated with this assemblage, but what is certain is that some form of labor occurred at the domestic site of an armory worker and the individual had some control over his production.

In 1842, George Talcott wrote of the armory: "In one branch of labor, every man finishes his work by ten o'clock in the morning. In others, they complete it in the first half of the day. A very limited number work over five hours, and probably not so long as seven hours a day when engaged in 'piece-work.' " (HFNHP microfilms 1842d). A board of examiners also confirmed that "no class of workmen have averaged ten hours per day. Those employed in the finishing shops have, perhaps, averaged between nine and ten hours; those employed in forging at the hill shops, between seven and eight; while the workmen at the water-shops average from four to seven hours per day." The board recommended that barrel-welders and bayonet forgers work seven-hour days and all the other armory workers, including pieceworkers and hourly wage workers, work a ten-hour day (Benét 1878:395; Lowrie and Franklin 1834:543 Zonderman 1992:255–256).

"Mechanization did narrow the skills of the armorers but it did not eliminate them all together" (Zonderman 1992:256). By the 1840s, the Harpers Ferry Armory employed both machine tenders and skilled machinists and pattern-makers. An entirely unskilled workforce was never obtained. Some machinery required workers to tend complex machinery and then meticulously to hand-work parts easily to fit with other parts. Working on parts after they were machined was common with most machine operations. Armories faced a paradoxical situation. They built new machinery to deskill the labor force, but in turn they had to hire highly skilled machinists who could build, repair, and retool the machinery (Zonderman 1992:256).

Deskilling workers and reducing wages often led to workers discontent. After a wage reduction in the 1840s, Superintendent Symington wrote that there was some unrest in the facilities, even on the part of some who were not employed at the armory. He justified the reduction because of the introduction of new machinery, increased wage labor, and the lack of the need for skilled craftsmen (HFNHP microfilms 1846a).

After 1842, there was no more of the evidence of piecework that once existed in an armory workers' domestic assemblage at Harpers Ferry. It is rare to find any part of an armorer's toolkit or gun parts in armorers' household deposits after 1841. Piecework had been discontinued and wage labor had become the standard mode of production throughout the armory. Arms production and workers' behaviors were under the close supervision of inspectors in the factory.

Discontent, either with working conditions or with the lowering of wages, was often met with various forms of protest at the armory, although none of these challenges can be associated with specific events. For instance, the armory's "bell shop," also known as a polishing and finishing shop, was destroyed in an 1824 fire. There was considerable loss of tools and machinery, and operations were impeded until the equipment was replaced. Superintendent Stubblefield suspected arson. While the origin of the fire is unknown, workers often built fires in the armory yard for cooking. A stray spark may have caused the fire, or the fire may have been an attempt by the craft-oriented armorers to sabotage the operations (HFNHP microfilms 1824b). There were other destructive occurrences throughout the history of the armory, although it is unclear whether they were intentional (HFNHP microfilms 1832). Labor relations between supervisors and workers worsened in the late 1830s and early 1840s as workers were increasingly being deskilled. The implicit paternalism demonstrated by the armory's supervisors, which protected workers' rights, faded significantly after Stubblefield and Beckham left the armory, in 1829 and 1830, respectively.

With the superintendency of Rust in the late 1830s, political factionalism and favoritism became a major concern that divided the allegiances of many of the workers and supervisors. No longer were outsiders necessarily distrusted, but biases were based on political affiliations. With this increased internal factionalism and increased labor unrest, the government saw the need to print a warning in the *Virginia Free Press* (VFP 1 June 1837:3). The notice was a warning to persons "trespassing and committing depredations upon U.S. lands at & near Harpers Ferry & upon the mountain, such as cutting timber, taking wood and lumber, stripping planks from houses & bridges, breaking into shops and houses, tearing down doors & windows, breaking glass, putting stones in pumps, pilfering tools, oil, steel, from public grounds and shops" (VFP 1 June 1837:3). Discontent was also displayed when the armory workers walked off their jobs in March 1842. They soon realized that their cause would not be supported by the federal government or the president of the United States.

LANDSCAPE

While wage-labor practices were enforced and discontent grew throughout the armory, the government intentionally reconceptualized and redesigned the armory. The early armory was well-groomed and planted with grasses in the early 1800s. By the 1830s, this image faded. The armory was no longer seen as operating within nature; rather, the armory took on the entity of an independent industry that could dominate nature. The armory grounds became generally unkempt for the most part, and weeds and gravel fill dominated parts of the landscape. At about this same time, the government paid greater attention to workers' housing at Harpers Ferry. In the early nineteenth century, armory workers and their families could construct their own dwellings, according to their own needs, on armory grounds. By the 1830s, the government dictated the size and shape of newly constructed houses to be inhabited by armory workers.

The early town plan followed the natural topography of the area. During the 1840s, a grid pattern was imposed over the town and some streets were widened. This action allowed for the easy flow of materials and people, as well as facilitating the surveillance of individuals. The development of supervisors' housing above the armory grounds separated these families from the workers' families. It also allowed supervisors to keep watch over activities on the grounds when necessary. Walls were built around the factory, with the result that movement into and out of the armory grounds was limited to controlled access points. Armory buildings were also redesigned in the open-floored Gothic style throughout the facility to improve efficiency of production. The flow of goods within the factory became more orderly, and new machinery dictated the rhythm and movement of workers. Armory workers lost many of their freedoms at the gun factory, and at the same time domestic relations changed at a rapid pace. Roles at the home and in the household took on new forms that were unfamiliar to the craftsmen, the pieceworkers, and their households.

DOMESTICITY AND CHANGING SOCIAL RELATIONS

During the nineteenth century, an integrated family economy faded as a wage economy emerged. Town landscapes also changed as commercial and industrial zones became entities distinct from domestic sites. A dichotomy of men's and women's spheres developed. The main responsibility of men was to care for the economic welfare of the household, while the main role of women was to maintain the household, nurture children, and teach their offspring values (Bender 1978; Ryan 1981; Wall 1994:4–7). This division of roles became explicit during the

early nineteenth century. Alexis Tocqueville visited America from 1830
through 1831 and wrote (quoted in Wall 1994:8):

> The Americans have applied to the sexes the great principle of political econ-
> omy which governs the manufacturers of our age, by carefully dividing the
> duties of man from those of women in order that the great work of society
> may be better carried on. . . . In no country has such constant care been
> taken as in America to trace two clearly distinct lines of action for the two
> sexes and to make them keep pace with the other, but in two pathways that
> are always different. American women never manage the outward concerns
> of the family or conduct a business or take a part in political life.

Housework during America's industrialization received an increasing amount of attention (e.g., see Cowan 1983; Mathews 1987; Ogden
1986; Strasser 1982). There was a change in housework, as well as a
change in the housewife's image, with the rise of industrial capitalism.
Home was often perceived as a sanctuary from the toils of everyday
labor. For instance, Lydia H. Sigourney wrote in 1850: "Home, holy
word! Refuge from sadness, and despair. . . . Home, —blessed spot!. . . .
Blessed Bride, —thou art about to enter this sanctuary, and to become
a priestess at its alter" (Sigourney 1989[1850]:113). Home became perceived as a refuge from the rest of society (Boydston 1990:99). Cowan
(1983) cautions that industrialization affected the home as well as the
workplace at about the same rate, although the experiences were quite
different. The home was not necessarily a realm distinct from and separate from the workplace.

While society industrialized, labor was reorganized, and new technologies replaced older ones in the household. "What is most striking
about the early industrial period is, not how different housework was
becoming from paid labor, but rather how closely the reorganization of
the two forms of work were replicating each other" (Boydston
1990:101). The changes in the household were directly linked to the
changes in modern society. As the rest of the industrializing world
became engulfed with time-consciousness, the household had also to
operate within those constraints.

Women negotiated their family's position within society. In charge
of refinement within the home, they became responsible for promoting
their homes among friends and acquaintances (Wall 1994:147–158).
Part of this promotion was involved in the ritualization process of the
meal. The setting of specific mealtimes helped to ritualize middle-class
life, and as women increasingly influenced the domestic sphere, their
role in this ritualization process also increased dramatically (Wall
1994:111). When held on a regular and timely basis, and when all family members participated, the ritualization process associated with the

meal taught "punctuality, order, neatness, temperance, self-denial, kindness, generosity, and hospitality" (Sedgwick 1837:28 [quoted in Wall 1994:112]). As Wall (1994:147) notes, however, "The sensory stimulus of the food was the primary focus of family . . . meals. . . . The dishes simply provided a frame for the important item, the food itself." During the 19th century, middle-class, urban women began to ritualize family meals, and the dishes became a vehicle to present the meal. They were physical symbols that were manipulated as part of the ritual.

Ceramics became more elaborately designed, and the number and types of dishes increased. By the 1820s, women further institutionalized the meal's ritualization. The number of courses increased, and they became more specialized in the types of foods served. Ceramic decorations allowed for greater symbolic representation and they could express the sanctuary of the home (DeCunzo 1995:121; Klein 1901:79; Wall 1994).

Much of the domestic materials found archaeologically at Harpers Ferry is probably a by-product of women's increasing participation in consumer choices and Romantic ideals. How these women decided to manipulate their choices and express their families' positions vis-à-vis the outside world through these newly acquired Romantic ideals differed for each household.

One of the earliest archaeological assemblages dating to the 1820s and 1830s is associated with Master Armorer Beckham's household. The material remains appear not to be diverse, and few ceramic types and designs were incorporated into the family's daily dining activities. Creamwares and undecorated ceramic waves were predominant in the assemblage. Wild foods were also a relatively larger part of the Beckham's daily diet compared to later household assemblages.

On the other hand, at another contemporary site once inhabited by armory workers, one household bought into the ideology of a consumer society and the Romantic ethic. A much larger diversity of mass-produced material goods was found, including various types of transfer-printed ceramics. The armory worker's household diet appears to have been more diverse than the master armorer's household, and the former purchased meats from a central marketplace.

Another household assemblage dating from the 1830s through the 1840s was associated with Master Armorer Moor. The Moor household was caught up in the new industrialization and consumerism, purchasing the most fashionable products. The ceramic assemblage is diverse, with a variety of transfer-printed ceramics of various forms. The family increasingly purchased goods from the town's marketplace and probably adhered to a Romantic consumer ethic.

A contemporary armory worker's family had a very different material world. Rather than buying into the new industrial culture, they had an assemblage very similar to the Beckham household, approximately two decades earlier. This unconforming pattern is not common in contemporary sites throughout the United States (Miller 1991). There was a profusion of nostalgic architecture and home furnishings in the United States in the 1840s. This nostalgia probably also carried through to other forms of a household's material world. With concern about the upheavals in domestic life, purchasing a ceramic assemblage that was fashionable several decades earlier may have also been a nostalgic effort to re-create the "good old days."

The new industrial order and the infiltration of the Romantic ethic into nineteenth-century industrial and everyday life is linked to the changing social, political, and economic spheres associated with public industry and private life in Harpers Ferry. The discipline associated with factory work was not eagerly accepted by armory workers, and the armory's industry developed in what appeared to be a haphazard fashion. The armory's development was marred by corruption, misappropriation of monies and labor, and political favoritism. Armory workers insisted that they protect their craft, and they opposed many forms of time discipline and supervisors' control that became the norm in many New England and Middle Atlantic factories. Early armory supervisors in Harpers Ferry accommodated many of the worker's demands, much to the dismay of War Department and Ordnance Department officials.

The eventual deskilling of armory workers was a slow process that led to piecework and eventually to the wage-labor system. As long as the proponents of the craft system remained in control of the armory's supervision, little could be done to influence workers' production. In order to regulate the work process, the government took an increasing role in overseeing and controlling the needs of the workers. Deskilling workers, creating a grid-pattern town plan, and dictating the style and shape of workers' housing were all important steps to controlling work and domestic behavior. Some households accepted these changes, subscribed to the Romantic ethic, and purchased some of the most fashionable goods of the time. Other armory workers' families chose not to participate in this consumer behavior, but rather obtained material goods that were fashionable several generations earlier. While the home was perceived as a "refuge from sadness," it was also a place where people played out their responses to these new social pressures.

As the home and the workplace became separate and distinct entities, they also became very similar. They were places where disciplined behavior and new moral ethics were created, nurtured, and reinforced—or rejected.

Appendix

Interviews with Armory Workers, 1842

Following are transcribed 1842 interviews with armory workers regarding the Harpers Ferry Armory. Interviewees include Benjamin Moor, Master Armorer; Adam Rhulman, Inspector of Finished Arms; William Moor, Inspector of Forged Work; Philip Hoffman, Inspector of Barrels and Rods; Henry Miller, Inspector of Bayonets & Filed Mounting, Zadoc Butt, Inspector of Filed Lock Work and Components; George Zorger, Inspector of Finished Lock Work; and John H. King, Inspector and Director at the Rifle Works.

MR. BENJAMIN MOOR, the Master Armorer, being called, answered the following questions, viz:

Q: What employment do you hold at this Armory—and how long have you held it?

A: I am Master Armorer, and have held that office since July, 1830.

Q: How long have you been engaged in the gun-making business?

A: I think since 1796.

Q: Have you been employed at other establishments, and what ones?

A: Yes, at Springfield, Richmond, VA., At Canton, Mass. At Hartford, Conn. State Arsenal (and have been employed as U.S. Inspector of Contract Arms in 1810 & 1811) at Pittsfield, Mass., and as Foreman & Master Armorer at Alleghany [sic] Arsenal.

Q: How many hours labour do the operatives generally perform, per day, at this Armory?

A: Some work as much as 10, some as much as 11, some not more than 8, and some not more than six; the Barrel welders, between 8 and 9 hours.

Q: How many hours per day are allotted for similar work at private establishments, and what wages are allowed to workmen there of various kinds?

A: I understand Mr. North to say last summer that' their best hands made $2 per day, at making Carbines.

Q: Can workmen at this place labour as many hours as at the Establishment at the Eastward? and if not what is the cause?

A: I do not think men can labour here in the summer as long as at the North, on such work as Forging, &c, on account of the heat of the climate.

Q: How does the cost of living here compare with that at Springfield?

A: I cannot speak positively, but from what I learned at Springfield, I am of the opinion that a man with a family of four or five children can live for about $52.00 per year or $1 per week less at that place than here. In this Estimate, I have not considered the superior advantages and cheapness of education at Springfield, nor the greater cost of medical attendance & medicines here.

Q: How is the welfare of the workers affected, generally, by the Government owning the Dwelling Houses?

A: I think the condition of many of the workmen would be improved if they had an opportunity of purchasing small lots of land, and erecting Dwelling Houses thereon, in the neighborhood.

Q: Are the Inspectors competent and faithful in the discharge of their duties?

A: Generally speaking, I think they are; circumstances have existed which have prevented that rigid performance of duty which ought to have been exercised. One of the Inspectors, although a good judge of work, I think he is not as exact as he ought to be.

Q: Have you reason to suppose that any one of them pass or approve work which they think or know ought to be condemned, under an improper influence of the workmen?

A: I cannot say, but I think one of the Inspectors has for some reason or other been too remiss in his inspections, and in keeping accounts.

Q: How many hours per day ought men at this Armory to work?

A: I think 8 hours for the Barrel forgers, in addition to time for repair of tools &c, and about 9 for the Grinders; about from 8 to 10 for the other forgers; from 9 to 10 for the filers; and for the machine tenders from 10 to 12 hours.

Q: Do the workmen for their own convenience or advantage run the Machinery, further than ought to be done? If so what is the cause for such an increase of velocity, and what is the effect on the Machinery and the Armory interests generally?

A: They sometimes do for the purpose of executing their work more expeditiously; the effects are injury to the Machines, the Tools, and even to the buildings; to obviate in some measure these evils, we want a Governor for the water wheel which moves our principal machinery.

Q: Do the Inspectors make any examination of the machinery and Shops, during working hours? Can any change in the present system of the control of labour and Machinery be introduced, advantageous to the Government?

A: They do pay attention to those matters, but greater vigilence [sic] is required. I do not think any change in the system could be advantageously introduced. This kind of work or exertion seems to restore the faculties of Inspectors, which become obscured by close attention to those offices, and they also are enabled to see the work in the incipient operations, and correct any errors in the performance.

Q: How are the accounts, with the Piece workers, kept? and has it been strictly attended to?

A: The accounts are kept by the Inspectors, the rule is to charge the components, when given out, and to credit them when returned, and has generally been faithfully attended to by the Inspectors, with, perhaps, the exception of one or two.

Q: Have not workmen turned in work without strictly accounting for what they had drawn out and when? And how can the evil be remidied [sic]?

A: Yes, I have known some, and suspected other instances. The practice is decidedly injurious to the interest of the United States. The last instance was in October 1841, and has been corrected; it was the first one which was known with certainty.

Q: Is your machinery now as complete and perfect as it should be, for performing the greatest quantity of work, with accuracy and economy?

A: No.

Q: What saving will probably be effected by the contemplated change and addition of machinery on the present cost of work?

A: I think we will be able to save between 10 or 15% in some of the branches and possibly more—We will also attain greater perfection in the work.

Q: Is there great loss in Gun-Barrels and other work—What is the cause? and how can it be avoided?

A: The loss on Gun-Barrels is very great, it sometimes amounts to 30 or 40%; it has been down, I think, as low as about 25%. The principal cause is, I think, to be attributed to the quality of the Iron, say 4/6 or 5/6 of the whole loss. Something is to be attributed to workmanship. I think defects in the material and workmanship may be obviated by twisting the Barrels after welding, and submitting them to a second welding or hammering, under a welding heat.

Q: What number of arms do you now make annually? What addition to your present power, shops and Machinery (supposing the last to have been improved) will be necessary, and in what time can these be made to enable you to fabricate Twenty Five Thousand stand? And would it be practicable or expedient to exceed that number without a considerable extension of your power, shops and Machinery?

A: We have not averaged for some years past, more than 9000 muskets; if you had no more than ordinary repairs and improvements, we could make from 10 to 12 thousand—To fabricate 25,000, certain improvements in our Dam, and enlargement of the inlet of the Canal, a new Barrel Shop, an increase of Shop room, an addition of some kind for Barrel Boring, and some addition to our cutting Machines. As a new

Barrel—forging shop ought to be provided, for even our present operations, I think the addition of $13,000 would make it answer for the fabrication of 25,000 muskets. If we could commence preparations immediately, the work could be completed within the present year— With our natural means, we could manufacture 5000 more.

Q: Are any instances known to you of partiality or preferment of persons employed, by the Superintendent or subordinate officers, in consequence of *political* opinions, and how have, or how can, their recurrence best be obviated?

A: I think such things have occurred, and I think such things have been and will be obviated by the present system, that is, having the Armory under control of an Officer of the Ordnance Department.

Q: What are the rates of rent for public buildings here, compared with private dwellings of the same description, and are there enough of the Public buildings for the accomodation [sic] of the Armory workmen?

A: They are considerably lower, say as 40 to 70%, in some instances; but generally the difference is somewhat lower. The number of private dwellings is very limited. There are not a sufficient number of Government houses for the Armorers.

Q: What is your opinion as to the degree of skill of the workmen at this Armory, compared with those at Springfield and other establishments for manufacturing arms at the Eastward?

A: With regard to Springfield, I do not think there is any great difference in the aggregate. In some branches, the workmen here are equal to those at Springfield, and in some branches the workmen there may be a little superior to those her—say for instance in Stocking.

Q: Is the public interest in any way affected by the Winchester and Potomac Railroad? and How?

A: It is affected in several ways—it endangers the public buildings by the sparks from the Engines—several fires have already been caused thereby. It has deprived many of the Houses of conveniences they formerly possessed, either by taking up the ground, or by rendering such erections subject to great risk by fire. The communication between one of the dwellings and the shops has been obstructed by the Road.

Q: Is there a heavy or unreasonable loss and wear of Files? and how can they be avoided?

A: I think without being definite, the consumption of files is too great. To effect a remedy, I think the best course would be by a strict examination, by myself and Inspectors, to ascertain the smallest number and size of files that would answer for the execution of given work, then credit the value of those files, by adding it to the piece price, and charge the workmen with all the files delivered to them, requiring them to return the old ones.

Q: From your official position and knowledge and skill as a mechanic and Machinist, do you know of any other subject connected with this establishment, in which a change or improvement could be made, to promote the public interest or to advance the quantity or quality of work?

A: Yes—In the first place, we want an enlargement of our Boring Shop, as well for the promotion of the health of the workmen as for the quantity and quality of the work. It is too narrow for the free passage through the shop and too low for the due admission of light and air, and for the proper arrangement of the Pullies and Drums. 2ndly, The erection of a large Forging shop for Lock Work, mounting, &c, in a situation where machinery can be conveniently introduced—This kind of work is now done in the lower stories of two buildings, which are too low and too narrow for such work, besides being subject to have the second story rendered inconvenient and uncomfortable to workmen, by the smoke from below. If we could introduce machinery into our Forging shop this could by its means, make a saving on many of the components of 2/5 or 2/7. 3rdly, A new Barrel forging shop, Rolling and Slitting Mill & a Forge and Puddling Furnace. I think that in order to obtain, for the Rifle Works on the Shenandoah, the greatest power, which that River affords, and which is much needed at that Establishment, the Government ought to own the Mill-Seat at the head of the Shenandoah Company works, known as Strider's Mills. The Barrel Forging Shop which I have adverted to will cost about $24,293.06. The Forging Shop will cost about $17,065.15. Enlarging the Boring Mill will cost $5,107.03.

February 25, 1842
ADAM RHULMAN, being called, answered as follows:

Q: What employment do you hold at this Armory, and how long have you held it?

A: I have been Inspector of Finished Arms, Eleven years and upward, and am in that Office now.

Q: Have you been employed at other Establishments and at what ones?

A: I have—since I have worked for myself, I worked at John Roger's factory, in Philadelphia. It was conducted by Brook Evans. The former had the contract for Arms.

Q: How many hours labour do the operatives generally perform at this Armory?

A: They are various—some would average 12 hours per day—some have not work enough to keep them employed 10 hours per day—I think the workmen under me are disposed to be industrious and would willingly work their 10 hours per day.

Q: How many hours per day are allotted for labour for similar work at private establishments? And what wages are allotted to workmen there, or the various kinds?

A: The day workers worked from sunrise to sunset through the year—in the summer 3/4 of an hour being allowed for breakfast, and in the winter they breakfast before going to work. One hour was allotted for

Dinner through the year. Those employed by the day received $1.75 per day, generally, some were paid as high as $2, and the labourer received $1. This was in 1821 to 1823.

Q: Can workmen at this place labour as many hours as at the Establishments at the Eastward, and if not, what is the cause?

A: I do not think men can labour here as many hours per day in the summer as further north—they do not seem to last so long—the climate is debilitating, more so, I think, than it is in Greenville, S. C. where I worked at the manufacture of Arms.

Q: Do workmen attempt to impose bad work on the Inspectors? And do the Inspectors ever meet with improper behavior from the workmen, in consequence of their strict performance of duty?

A: I believe there are workmen who attempt to impose bad work on the Inspectors. I have never received, to my face, bad treatment from the workmen, for performing my duty strictly, though I have heard grumbling—Some of the other Inspectors have told me they have received it.

Q: Have you reason to suppose that any of them pass or approve work which they think or know ought to be condemned, under an improper influence of the workmen?

A: I cannot say, though I have had work frequently come to me, which ought not to have passed—but I cannot say what influenced the Inspectors to pass it.

Q: Have or have not interchanges of components in their various stages, been made by the workmen, to the injury of the United States?

A: Yes, I believe it has, certainly to the injury of the United States, in putting work on the United States which ought not to be passed—and the Government may sometimes have been compelled to pay twice for the same part.

Q: What is your opinion as to the degree of skill of the workmen at this Armory, compared with those at Springfield and other establishments for the manufacture of Arms at the Eastward?

A: As far as I have been acquainted, not having been farther East than Philadelphia, I think we have as good workmen here as anywhere in the United States.

Q: Is there a heavy or unreasonable loss & wear of files? and how can they be avoided?

A: I think there is, and the remedy I would propose would be for the Inspectors to issue the files, in small numbers, and keep an account with the men, and when more were wanted, to require that the former issue should be strictly accounted for. In this way, besides saving in the number of files, there would be a saving in the size of files—workmen are fond of working with large files, when smaller and less costly ones would answer. The Inspector would see that the surface worn on the large files was not longer than on smaller ones.

Q: Is there an order against the practice of reading newspapers in the Shops? Is it complied with?

A: There is. In my Shop I have had occasion in but two instances in the same individual, to check the practice; he had no work to perform at the time.

February 25, 1842

MR. WILLIAM MOOR, being called, answered:

Q: What employment do you hold at this Armory and how long have you held it?

A: I have been Inspector of Forged work, for three years and upwards.

Q: How long have you been engaged in the Gun-making business?

A: Ever since I was capable of being an Armorer. I am now 32 years of age.

Q: Have you been employed at other establishments? And what ones?

A: I have worked at the Pittsburg [sic] Arsenal.

Q: How many hours labour do the operatives generally perform per day at this Armory?

A: In my Shop, at Mounting, forging &c, from 12 to 14 hours per day, say 12 1/2 on an average when they pretend to work regularly.

Q: Have you any reason to suppose that any of the Inspectors pass or approve work which they think or know ought to be condemned, under an improper influence of the workmen?

A: I do not.

Q: Do the workmen, after losing time, endeavor to make up their wages by unusual exertion? and if so, what is the effect of such irregularity on the public interest?

A: It is frequently done to the injury of the public interest. The quality of the work is never so good as when done with regularity.

Q: Have or have not interchange of components in their various stages, been made by the workmen to the injury of the United States?

A: Yes, I have known instances—I have detected it myself.

Q: Do workmen attempt to impose bad work on the Inspectors? And do the Inspectors meet with improper behavior on the part of the workmen in consequence of their strict performance of duty?

A: I have frequently.

Q: Are any instances known to you of partiality or preferment of persons employed, by the Superintendent or subordinate officers, in consequence of *political* opinion, and how have, or how can, their recurrence best be obviated?

A: I have not known any.

Q: What are the rates for rents for public buildings here, compared with private dwellings of the same description, and are there enough of the public buildings for the accommodation of the Armory workmen?

A: The rents of public buildings are much lower than of private dwellings, say about at the rate of 60 or 70 to 100.

Q: What is your opinion as to the degree of skill of the workmen at this Armory, compared with those at Springfield, and other Establishments for the manufacturing of Arms, at the Eastward?

A: Judging from the quality of work performed, I should think the skill here equal to that at Springfield or elsewhere as to forged work in my Department.

February 25, 1842

MR. PHILIP HOFFMAN, being called, answered as follows, viz:

Q: What employment do you hold at this Armory and how long have you held it?

A: I am now Inspector of Barrels and Rods, and have been so for about 11 or 12 years. I have been Inspector here since 1818.

Q: How long have you been engaged in the Gun-making business?

A: Ever since the year 1808 at this Armory, during which time I have occasionally been absent on inspection duties, once I was absent about a year on my private business.

Q: How many hours labour do the operatives generally perform per day at this Armory?

A: Some of the piece workers work, I think, about 12 hours, some not more than 4 or 5—there are not a great number of the latter among those under my immediate notice; the Barrel Welders, I do not think, work 10 hours, the Borers work I think more, the Grinders work pretty much as the Borers.

Q: How many hours per day are allotted for labour for similar work at private establishments and what wages are allowed to workmen of the various kinds?

A: I was in Philadelphia about 3 years ago, the men in Mr. Deringer's manufactory work,,I understood, 10 hours per day, and some more, but I do not know how much.

Q: Can workmen at this place labour as many hours as at the Establishments at the Eastward? and if not what is the cause?

A: I should think men could work here as long as at the North, except perhaps in the heat of summer.

Q: How does the cost of living here compare with that at Springfield?

A: In some articles of provisions, &c, the price here is about the same as at Springfield, but in others, such as groceries, clothing and store good generally, I think it greater. My knowledge was obtained 4 years ago.

Q: How is the welfare of the workmen, generally, affected by the Government owning the Dwelling Houses?

A: I think it for the advantage of the workmen, as the rent is now less than the interest on the cost, and if owned by individuals the Armorers would have to pay a higher rent than they do at this time.

Q: Have you reason to suppose that any of the Inspectors pass or approve work which they think or know ought to be condemned, under an improper influence of the workmen?

A: I understood that a few years since an attempt was made, to intimidate one of the Inspectors.

Q: Do the workmen, after losing time, endeavor to make up their wages by unusual exertions? and if so, what is the effect of such irregularity on the public interest?

A: I have known such practices—They are injurious to the public interest, for no man to my mind can make as good work when he executes it hurriedly as when he does it carefully.

Q: Have or have not interchanges of components in their various stages been made by the workmen to the injury of the United States?

A: I cannot say from my personal knowledge, though I have heard of such things, and have no doubt of the facts—such practices are injurious to the interest of the United States.

Q: Do workmen attempt to impose bad work on the Inspectors, and do the Inspectors ever meet with improper behavior from the workmen in consequence of their strict performance of duty?

A: I have known men guilty of such conduct—there are none here under my direction who have been so.

Q: Are any instances known to you of partiality or preferment of persons employed, by the Superintendent or subordinate Officers, in consequence of *political* opinion; and how have, or how can, their recurrance [sic] be obviated?

A: It was reported and generally believed here, I think, that 5 men were discharged on account of their political opinions differing from those of the Superintendent—the reason for their discharge was, that they had complained of the rates of their wages—3 more of the opposite party, who had united in the complaint, were retained.

Q: What is your opinion as to the degree of skill of the workmen at this Armory, compared with those at Springfield and other establishments for manufacturing Arms at the East?

A: I consider them equal as a body of men. We employ boys here, who of course are now not equal to workmen, ultimately however the practice will be beneficial.

Q: Is the public interest in any way affected by the Winchester & Potomac Rail Road?

A: It is very much I think—it has taken away the gardens, and it endangers the houses. I had two stables burnt by sparks from the engines, and my kitchen has been on fire three times—these fires occurred at different times. I live in a Government House; other buildings have been set on fire at various times. Independent of the dangers from fire, the occupants of the houses on the South side of Shenandoah Street experience great inconvenience and annoyance from the road running thru their back yards.

February 25, 1842

MR. HENRY MILLER, being called, answered as follows:

Q: What employment do you hold at this Armory, and how long have you held it?

A: I am now Inspector of Bayonets & Filed Mounting; I have been an Inspector about 17 years.

Q: How long have you been engaged in the Gun-making business?

A: Since 1808.

Q: Can workmen at this place labour as many hours as at the Establishments at the Eastward? And if not what is the cause?

A: I should think they could, except perhaps in the heat of Summer.

Q: Do the workmen after losing time, endeavor to make up their wages by unusual exertions, and if so, what is the effect of such irregularity on the public interest?

A: I believe they do, a good many of them, and I believe the public sustains some loss, though I could not state the amount.

Q: Have or have not the workmen turned in work without strictly accounting for what they had drawn out, and when, and how can the evil be remided [sic]?

A: I have known no instances.

Q: How long do workmen labour in your shop generally per day?

A: I think mine mostly labour from 10 to 12 hours.

Q: Do workmen attempt to impose bad work on the Inspectors? And do the Inspectors ever meet with improper behavior from the workmen, in consequence of their strict performance of duty?

A: It has been the case with myself, formerly, very little recently.

Q: What are the rates for rent of public buildings here, compared with private dwellings of the same description?

A: I suppose they are 30% lower than private Dwelling houses.

Q: What is your opinion as to the degree of skill of the workmen at this Armory, compared with those at Springfield and other establishments for manufacturing Arms at the East?

A: As far as I have seen, I think Arms manufactured here equal those sent from Springfield.

February 25, 1842

MR. ZADOC BUTT, being called, answered as follows:

Q: What employment do you hold at this Armory, and how long have you held it?

A: I am Inspector of Filed lock work and components. I have been such since 3rd June, 1841.

Q: How long have you been engaged in the Gun-making business?

A: Twenty-Six years.

Q: Have you been employed at other Establishments, and which ones?

A: No.

Q: Can workmen at this place labour as many hours as at the Establishments at the Eastward? And if not, what is the cause?

A: I think they can.

Q: How is the welfare of the workmen affected generally by the Government owning the Dwelling houses?

A: I think it is for the advantage of the workmen for the Government to own the Dwellings.

Q: Are the Inspectors competent and faithful in the discharge of their duties?

A: I could hardly answer that question.

Q: Have you reason to suppose that any of them pass or approve work which they think or know ought to be condemned, under an improper influence of the workmen?

A: There are workmen who poke in any kind of work and the Inspectors meet with difficulties in the discharge of their duties.

Q: What is your opinion as to the degree of skill of the workmen at this Armory, compared with those at Springfield and other establishments for manufacturing Arms at the East?

A: From the best information I have, I think we have as good workmen here as there are there.

February 25, 1842

MR. GEORGE ZORGER, being called, answered as follows:

Q: What employment do you hold at this Armory & how long have you held it?

A: Inspector of finished lock work, and have been so since 1830.

Q: How long have you been engaged in the Gun-making business?

A: Almost all of my life; I have been here since 1808.

Q: Have you been employed at other Establishments, and what ones?

A: I worked one year at Augusta Arsenal, Geo., in 1825 & 1826, and three months at Springfield, during the last war.

Q: How many hours labour do the operatives generally perform per day at this Armory?

A: Some work 10 or 12 hours, some not more than 8.

Q: Can workmen at this place labour as many hours as at the Establishments at the Eastward?

A: Certainly they can.

Q: How many hours per day ought men at the Armory to work?

A: I think some might work from sunrise to sunset, except for Barrel forgers.

Q: Do the workmen, after losing time, endeavor by unusual exertion to make up their wages? and if so, what is the effect of such irregularity on the public interest?

A: They sometimes do. I do not think the interest of the United States is affected thereby.

Q: Have or have not interchanges of components in their various stages been made by the workmen, to the injury of the United States?

A: True.

Q: Do workmen attempt to impose bad work on the Inspectors? and do the Inspectors ever meet with improper behavior from the workmen in consequence of their strict performance of duty?

A: They do it if they can. The Inspectors sometimes meet eith [sic] bad treatment.

Q: Is there a great loss on Gun-barrels and other work? What is the cause? and how can it be avoided?

A: The principal loss on Barrels is from defects in the material.

February 25, 1842
MR. JOHN H. KING, being called, answered as follows:

Q: What employment do you hold at this Armory, and how long have you held it?

A: I am Inspector and Director at the Rifle Works—I have been Inspector about 5 years and about 3 1/2 years both Inspector and Director.

Q: How long have you been engaged in the Gun-making business?

A: About 27 years.

Q: Have you been employed at other establishments, and what ones?

A: I have worked at Hagerstown at Black—and White—Smithing.

Q: How many hours labour do the operatives generally perform per day at this Armory?

A: The piece workers work at the Rifle Factory from 8 to 14 hours; the difference in time being generally dependant on the disposition and habits of the men.

Q: How many hours per day are allotted for labour at similar work at private establishments, and what wages are allowed to workmen there of the various kinds?

A: Where I worked, we worked from sun to sun, in Summer, and in Winter to 9 P.M. The wages were rated from $1.25 to $1.50.

Q: How is the welfare of the workmen affected [sic] generally by the Government owning the Dwelling Houses?

A: I think it for the advantage of the workmen.

Q: Are the Inspectors competent and faithful in the discharge of their duties?

A: They are.

Q: Do the workmen to their own convenience or advantage run the machinery farther than ought to be done? If so what is the cause for such increase of velocity, and what is the effect on the Machines, and the Armory interest generally?

A: No.

Q: Have or have not interchanges of components in their various stages been made by the workmen to the injury of the United States?

A: There have been such things done.

Q: Do workmen attempt to impose bad work on the Inspectors, and do the Inspectors ever meet with improper behavior from the workmen, in consequence of their strict performance of duty?

A: Yes, some of them do.

Q: Are any instances known to you of partiality or preferment of persons employed, by the Superintendent or subordinate officers, in consequence of *political* opinions, and how have or how can their recurrance [sic] be avoided or obviated?

A: I have known none; there have been rumors. I think that such evils may be best remedied by the present system; that is by having a Military man as Superintendent, as he will be unswayed by political or personal considerations in this official acts.

Q: What is your opinion as to the degree of skill of the workmen at this Armory, compared with those at Springfield and other Establishments for manufacturing arms at the Eastward?

A: I think, on the branches at which they are employed, they are equal to those at other places.

Q: What means would you recommend for increasing your water power?

A: By throwing a Dam across the Shenandoah River, at the guard gates of the Shenandoah Company's works.

Q: Is the public interest in any way affected by the Winchester & Potomac Rail Road?

A: It is—It endangers the public buildings by fire—The evil could be remedied by the use of coal in the engines.

Note: This information is taken from HFNHP photostats (1842: 54–76).

References

Agnew, Aileen Button
    1988   Ceramics and the Sea Trade in Portsmouth, New Hampshire: 1765–1785. *Northeastern Historical Archaeology* 17:40–60.

Aitken, Hugh G.J.
    1985   *Scientific Management in Action: Taylorism at Watertown Arsenal, 1908–1915.* Princeton University Press, Princeton, New Jersey.

Anderson, Osborne
    1972   *A Voice from Harpers Ferry: The Black Heritage Library Collection.* Reprint of 1861 edition. Books for Libraries Press, Freeport, New York.

Anonymous
    1821   Manuscript. On file at Harpers Ferry National Historical Park, Harpers Ferry, West Virginia.

Anthony, Kate J.
    1891   *Storer College, Harpers Ferry, W.Va: Brief Historical Sketch.* Morning Star Publishing House, Boston.

Atwood, Albert W.
    1945   Potomac, River of Destiny. *National Geographic Magazine* July:49.

Barbour, Brian M.
    1979   Franklin and Emerson. In *Benjamin Franklin: A Collection of Critical Essays,* edited by Brian M. Barbour, pp. 25–29. Prentice Hall, Englewood Cliffs, New Jersey, New Jersey.

Barry, Joseph
    1988   *The Strange Story of Harpers Ferry with Legends of the Surrounding Country.* Reprint of 1903 edition. Shepherstown Register, Shepherstown, West Virginia.

Beaudry, Mary C., and Stephen A. Mrozowski
    1989   The Archaeology of Work and Home Life in Lowell, Massachusetts: An Interdisciplinary Study of the Boott Cotton Mills Corporation. *IA (The Journal of the Society for Industrial Archaeology)* 19(2):1–22.

Bender, Thomas
    1978   *Community and Social Change in America.* Rutgers University Press, New Brunswick, New Jersey.

Benét, Steven V. (compiler)
    1878   *A Collection of Annual Reports and Other Important Papers Relating to the Ordnance Department.* Government Printing Office, Washington, DC.

Bergstresser, Jack
    1988   Water Power on Virginius Island, Written Historical and Descriptive Data. HAER No. VW-35. Historic American Engineering Record, National Park Service, Washington, DC.

Blee, Catherine H.
1978   Archaeological Investigations of the Wager Block Buildings 1977–1978, Harpers Ferry National Historical Park, West Virginia. National Park Service, U.S. Department of the Interior, Washington, D.C.

Bodner, John
1992   *Remaking America: Public Memory, Commemoration, and Patriotism in the Twentieth Century.* Princeton University Press, Princeton, New Jersey.

Bond, Kathleen
1987   A Preliminary Report on the Demography of the Boott Mills Housing Units #33-48; 1838–1842. In *Interdisciplinary Investigations of the Boot Mills, Lowell, Massachusetts.* Volume I: *Life at the Boarding Houses,* edited by Mary C. Beaudry and Stephen A. Mrozowski, pp. 35–55. Cultural Resource Management Study No. 18, National Park Service, U.S. Department of the Interior, Washington, DC.

Bowen, Joanne
1990   Study of Seasonality and Subsistence in Eighteenth Century Suffield, Connecticut. Unpublished Ph.D. dissertation. Department of Anthropology, Brown University, Providence, Rhode Island.

Boydston, Jeanne
1990   *Home and Work: Housework, Wages, and the Ideology of Labor in the Early Republic.* Oxford University Press, New York.

Braverman, H.
1974   *Labor and Monopoly Capital.* Monthly Review Press, New York.

Brown, Stuart E., Jr.
1968   *The Guns of Harpers Ferry.* Clearfield, Baltimore.

Bumgardner, Stan
1991   Historic Structures Report, Building 48, Harpers Ferry National Historical Park, Harpers Ferry, West Virginia. National Park Service/University of Maryland Cooperative Agreement Historic Research Project. On file, Harpers Ferry National Historical Park, Harpers Ferry, West Virginia.

Burk, Brett J.
1993   Faunal Analysis of the Master Armorer's Assemblages. In *Interdisciplinary Investigations of Domestic Life In Government Block B: Perspectives of Harpers Ferry's Armory and Commercial District,* edited by Paul A. Shackel, pp. 9.1–9.36. Occasional Report No. 6, National Park Service, U.S. Department of the Interior, Washington, DC.
1994   An Armory Worker's Domestic Faunal Assemblage. In *An Archeology of an Armory Worker's Household: Park Building 48, Harpers Ferry National Historical Park,* edited by Paul A. Shackel, pp. 7.1–7.24. Occasional Report No. 12, National Park Service, U.S. Department of the Interior, Washington, DC.

Bushong, Millard K.
1941   *A History of Jefferson County.* Charles Town, West Virginia.

Campbell, Colin
1987   *The Romantic Ethic and the Spirit of Modern Consumerism.* Basil Blackwell, New York.

Carson, Hamilton H.
1963   U.S. Rifle Works, Harpers Ferry, West Virginia: Resistivity and Seismic Surveys and Excavations. On file, Harpers Ferry National Historical Park, Harpers Ferry, West Virginia.

Chickering, Patricia, and Michael Jenkins
1994   HAFE Package 116 Historic Structures Report, History Section: Block B, Lots
        2 and 3, Shenandoah Street, Park Buildings 32, 33, 33A, 34/35, 34A and 36,
        Harpers Ferry National Historical Park, Harpers Ferry, West Virginia.
        National Park Service/University of Maryland Cooperative Agreement.
        Harpers Ferry National Historical Park, Harpers Ferry, West Virginia.
Clawson, D.
1980   *Bureaucracy and the Labor Process.* Monthly Review Press, New York.
Colley, Sarah M.
1990   The Analysis and Interpretation of Archaeological Fish Remains. In *Archae-
        ological Method and Theory,* Vol. 2, edited by Michael B. Schiffer, pp. 207–253.
        University of Arizona Press, Tucson.
Cotter, John L.
1959   Preliminary Archeological Investigations: Harper House Garden & Building
        #23, Arsenal Area at Shenandoah and High Streets. National Park Service. On
        file, Harpers Ferry National Historical Park, Harpers Ferry, West Virginia.
1960   Completion of Archeological Test at Corner of Arsenal Building June 7, 1960.
        Harpers Ferry National Monument. On file, Harpers Ferry National Historical
        Park, Harpers Ferry, West Virginia.
Cowan, Ruth Schwarts
1983   *More Work for Mother: The Ironies of Household Technology from the Open
        Hearth to the Microwave.* Basic Books, New York.
Cressey, Pamela J., John F. Stephens, Steven J. Shephard, and Barbara H. Magid
1982   The Core–Periphery Relationship and the Archaeological Record in Alexan-
        dria, Virginia. In *Archaeology of Urban America: The Search for Pattern and
        Process,* edited by Roy S. Dickens, Jr., pp. 143–172. Academic Press, New York.
Cummings, Linda Scott
1993   Pollen and Macrofloral Analysis of Material for Package 116, The Late Nine-
        teenth-Century Privies and Possible Garden Areas Associated with the Early
        Nineteenth-Century Old Master Armorer's House at Harpers Ferry National
        Historical Park, West Virginia. In *Interdisciplinary Investigations of Domestic
        Life in Government Block B: Perspectives on Harpers Ferry's Armory and Com-
        mercial District,* edited by Paul A. Shackel, pp. 7.1–7.41. Occasional Report No.
        6, National Park Service, U.S. Department of the Interior, Harpers Ferry
        National Historical Park, Harpers Ferry, West Virginia.
1994   Diet and Prehistoric Landscape during the Nineteenth and Early Twentieth
        Centuries at Harpers Ferry, West Virginia: A View from the Old Master
        Armorer's Complex. In *An Archaeology of Harpers Ferry's Commercial and
        Residential District,* edited by Paul A. Shackel and Susan E. Winter. *Historical
        Archaeology* 28(4):94–105.
Cummings, Linda Scott, and Kathryn Puseman
1994   Pollen and Macrofloral Analysis on Samples from Park Building 48, Harpers
        Ferry National Historical Park, West Virginia. In *Domestic Responses to Nine-
        teenth-Century Industrialization: An Archeology of Park Building 48, Harpers
        Ferry National Historical Park,* edited by Paul A. Shackel, pp. 8.1–8.31. Occa-
        sional Report No. 12, National Park Service, U.S. Department of the Interior,
        Harpers Ferry National Historical Park, Harpers Ferry, West Virginia.
da Costa Nunes, Jadviga M.
1986   The Industrial Landscape in America, 1800–1840: Ideology into Art. *IA (The
        Journal of the Society for Industrial Archeology)* 12(2):19–38.

DeCunzo, LuAnn
   1982   Households, Economics and Ethnicity in Patterson's Dublin, 1829–1915: The Van
           Houter Street Parking Lot Block. *Northeastern Historical Archaeology* 11:9–25.
   1995   Reform, Respite Ritual: The Archaeology of Institutions; The Magdalen Society
           of Philadelphia, 1800–1850. *Historical Archaeology* 29(3).
Deyrup, Felicia
   1948   Arms Makers of the Connecticut Valley: A Regional Study of the Economic
           Development of the Small Arms Industry, 1798–1870. In *Smith College Studies
           in History,* Vol. 33, edited by Vera Holmes and Hans Kohn. Smith College,
           Northampton, Massachusetts.
Dickens, Roy S. (editor)
   1982   *Archaeology of Urban America: A Search for Pattern and Process.* Academic
           Press, New York.
Douglass, Frederick
   1881   *John Brown: An Address by Frederick Douglass at the Fourteenth Anniversary
           of Storer College, Harpers Ferry, West Virginia, May 30, 1881.* Morning Star Job
           Printing House, Dover, New Hampshire.
Drickamer, Lee C., and Karen D. Drickamer (editors)
   1987   *Fort Lyon to Harpers Ferry: On the Border of North and South with "Rambling
           Jour."* The Civil War Letters and Newspaper Dispatches of Charles H. Moulton
           (34th Mass. Vol. Inf.). White Mane Publishing, Shippensburg, Pennsylvania.
Dublin, Thomas
   1979   *Women at Work: The Transformation of Work and Community in Lowell Mas-
           sachusetts, 1826–1860.* Columbia University Press, New York.
   1977   Women, Work, and Protest in the Early Lowell Mills; "The Oppressing and, of
           Avarice Would Enslave Us." In *Class, Sex, and the Woman Worker,* edited by
           Milton Cantor and Bruce Ware, pp. 43–63. Greenwood Press, Westport, Con-
           necticut.
Everhart, William C.
   1952   A History of Harpers Ferry. On file, Harpers Ferry National Historical Park,
           Harpers Ferry, West Virginia.
Farmers Advocate, Charles Town, West Virginia. Newspaper on microfilm, Harpers Ferry
           National Historical Park, Harpers Ferry, West Virginia.
Fenicle, Diane
   1993   The Ties That Bind: A Social History of Block B, Lots 2 and 3. In *Interdiscipli-
           nary Investigations of Domestic Life in Government Block B: Perspectives on
           Harpers Ferry's Armory and Commercial District,* edited by Paul A. Shackel,
           pp. 3.1–3.22. Occasional Report No. 6, National Park Service, U.S. Department
           of the Interior, Washington, DC.
Fields, Barbara
   1985   *Slavery and Freedom on the Middle Ground: Maryland in the Twentieth Cen-
           tury.* Yale University Press, New Haven.
Foner, Philip S.
   1975   *American Labor Songs of the Nineteenth Century.* University of Illinois Press,
           Urbana.
Foner, Philip S. (editor)
   1977   *The Factory Girls.* University of Illinois Press, Urbana.
Ford, Benjamin
   1993   Health and Sanitation in Nineteenth-Century Harpers Ferry. In *Interdiscipli-
           nary Investigations of Domestic Life in Government Block B: Perspectives on*

    Harpers Ferry's Armory and Commercial District, edited by Paul A. Shackel, pp. 9.1–9.42. Occasional Report No. 6. National Park Service, U.S. Department of the Interior, Washington, DC.

1994   The Health and Sanitation of Postbellum Harpers Ferry. In *An Archaeology of Harpers Ferry's Commercial and Residential District*, edited by Paul A. Shackel and Susan E. Winter. *Historical Archaeology* 28(4):49–61.

Foucault, Michel

1979   *Discipline and Punish*. Vintage Books, New York.

Frye, Susan W., and Dennis E. Frye

1989   *Maryland Heights: Archeological and Historical Resources Study*. Occasional Report No. 2, National Park Service, U.S. Department of the Interior, Washington, DC.

Frye, Susan Winter, and Cari YoungRavenhorst

1988   Archeological Investigations on Virginius Island, Harpers Ferry National Historical Park, 198–1987. On file, Harpers Ferry National Historical Park, Harpers Ferry, West Virginia.

Gardner, William

1974   Excavation—Harpers Ferry, Backyards and Paymaster's Yard 1973–1974. On file, Harpers Ferry National Historical Park, Harpers Ferry, West Virginia.

Gilbert, Cathy, Maureen DeLay Joseph, and Perry Carpenter Wheelock

1993   *Cultural Landscape Report: Lower Town, Harpers Ferry National Historical Park*. National Park Service, U.S. Department of the Interior, Washington, DC.

Gilbert, Dave

1984   *Where Industry Failed: Water-Powered Mills at Harpers Ferry, West Virginia*. Pictorial Histories Publishing, Charleston, West Virginia.

1995   *A Walker's Guide to Harpers Ferry, West Virginia: Exploring a Place Where History Still Lives*. 5th Edition, Harpers Ferry Historical Association, Harpers Ferry, West Virginia.

Gutheim, Frederick

1949   *The Potomac*. Rhenehart, New York.

Halchin, Jill Y. (editor)

1994   *Archeological Views of the Upper Wager Block, Domestic and Commercial Neighborhood in Harpers Ferry*. National Park Service, U.S. Department of the Interior, Washington, DC.

Hanlan, James P.

1981   *The Working Population of Manchester, New Hampshire, 1840–1886*. UMI Research Press, Ann Arbor, Michigan.

Hannah, David H.

n.d.   Historic Structures Report, Part 1, for Historic Structures on Virginius Island. On file, Harpers Ferry National Historical Park, Harpers Ferry, West Virginia.

1969   Archeological Excavations on Virginius Island, Harpers Ferry National Historical Park, 1966–1968. Harpers Ferry Job Corps Civilian Conservation Center, Harpers Ferry, West Virginia. On file, Harpers Ferry National Historical Park, Harpers Ferry, West Virginia.

Hareven, Tamara

1978   *Amoskeag: Life and Work in an American Factory City*. Pantheon Books, New York.

1982   *Family Time and Industrial Time*. Cambridge University Press, Cambridge.

Harpers Ferry Free Press, Harpers Ferry, Virginia. Newspaper on microfilm, Harpers Ferry National Historical Park, Harpers Ferry, West Virginia.

Henry, Susan
1987   A Chicken in Every Pot: The Urban Subsistence Pattern in Turn-of-the-Century Phoenix, Arizona. In *Living in Cities: Current Research in Urban Archaeology,* edited by Edward Staski, pp. 65–74. *Special Publications Series,* Society for Historical Archaeology, California, Pennsylvania.

Herman, Bernard
1985   Multiple Materials, Multiple Meanings: The Fortunes of Thomas Mendenhall. *Winterthur Portfolio* 19(1):67–86.

Hershey, William D.
1964   Archeological Survey of the Lockwood House (Paymaster's House), Harpers Ferry, West Virginia. On file, Harpers Ferry National Historical Park, Harpers Ferry, West Virginia.

HFNHP microfilms. On file, Harpers Ferry National Historical Park, Harpers Ferry, West Virginia.
1807   Letter: Stubblefield to Dearborn, 22 May 1807. Miscellaneous letter and document file 18(3):280–281.
1810a   Letter: Annin to Eustis, 17 March 1910. Miscellaneous letter and document file 18(5):498–500.
1810b   Letter: Annin to Eustis, 15 March 1810. Miscellaneous letter and document file 18(5):496–497.
1813a   Letter: Annin to Armstrong, 24 June 1813. Miscellaneous letter and document file 13(1):16.
1813b   Letter: Annin to Armstrong, 2 November 1813. Miscellaneous letter and document file 13(1):30–32.
1815a   Letter: Anonymous to Crawford, 11 March 1815. Miscellaneous letter and document file 13(2):135–137.
1815b   Letter: Beale to Crawford, 15 December 1815. Miscellaneous letter and document file 13(2):138–139.
1816   Letter: Beale to Crawford, 13 February 1816. Miscellaneous letter and document file 13(2):147–150.
1817   Letter: Wadsworth to Graham, 14 October 1817. Miscellaneous letter and document file 13(2):178–184.
1818a   Letter: Stubblefield to Bomford, 16 May 1818. Miscellaneous letter and document file 21(3):244–245.
1818b   Letter: Stubblefield to Bomford, 2 March 1818. Miscellaneous letter and document file 21(3):229–230.
1819a   Letter: James Stubblefield to Colonel Decius Wadsworth, 27 March 1819. Miscellaneous letter and document file 21(4):303–307.
1819b   Letter: Stubblefield to Wadsworth, 28 January 1819. Miscellaneous letter and document file 21(3):297–298.
1819c   Letter: Wadsworth to Calhoun, 6 December 1819. Miscellaneous letter and document file 19(2):1184–1190.
1819d   Letter: Wadsworth to Stubblefield, 3 February 1819. Miscellaneous letter and document file 14(2):184–185.
1820   Letter: Wadsworth to Calhoun, 31 March 1820. Miscellaneous letter and document file 19(12):1201–1202.

1821a Letter: Wadsworth to Stubblefield, 31 March 1821. Miscellaneous letter and document file 14(3):232.

1821b Letter: Stubblefield to Bomford, 6 April 1821. Miscellaneous letter and document file 21(4):404–406.

1821c Letter: Stubblefield to Bomford, 18 April 1821. Miscellaneous letter and document file 21(5):417–418.

1821d Letter: Bomford to Stubblefield and Lee, 28 May 1821. Miscellaneous letter and document file 14(3):274–275.

1822a Notes of a Tour of Inspection, 10 December 1822. Miscellaneous letter and document file 21(6):573–601.

1822b Letter: Hall to Bomford, 5 January 1822. Miscellaneous letter and document file 21(5):467–470.

1822c Letter: Hall to Bomford, 5 November 1822. Miscellaneous letter and document file 21(5):480–483.

1822d Letter: Stubblefield to Bomford, 6 February 1822. Miscellaneous letter and document file 21(6):521–522.

1822e Letter: Bomford to Stubblefield and Lee, 22 February 1822. Miscellaneous letter and document file 14(4):302.

1823 Letter: Stubblefield to ordnance Department, 6 September 1823. Miscellaneous letter and document file 21(7):695–698.

1824a Letter: Stubblefield to Bomford, 30 July 1824. Miscellaneous letter and document file 21(7):749–751.

1824b Letter: Stubblefield to Bomford, 8 May 1824. Miscellaneous letter and document file 21(5):423–424.

1825 Letter: Bomford to Stubblefield, 23 November 1825. Miscellaneous letter and document file 14(5):446/

1826a Letter: Patch to Bomford, 25 January 1826. Miscellaneous 21(9):991–1003.

1826b Letter: Stubblefield to Bomford, 3 January 1826. Miscellaneous letter and document file 21(9):967–970.

1827a Extracts from the Proceedings of a Court of Enquiry convened at Harpers Ferry, 26 April 1927. Miscellaneous letter and document file 22(2):117–201.

1827b Letter: Wool to Brown, 16 November 1827. Miscellaneous letter and document file 18(13):1293–1314.

1827c Letter: Stubblefield Investigation, 5 May 1827, Miscellaneous letter and document file 22(3):218–220.

1827d Letter: Lee to Bomford, 3 January 1827. Miscellaneous letter and document file 22(1):37–40.

1828 Letter: Stubblefield to Bomford, 8 January 1828. Miscellaneous letter and document file 22(4):348–349.

1829a Letter: Staley to Eaton, 3 April 1829. Miscellaneous letter and document file 22(7):673–675.

1829b Letter: Roper to Jackson, 22 June 1829. Miscellaneous letter and document file 22(7):677–680.

1829c Letter: Symington to Eaton, 26 May 1829. Miscellaneous letter and document file 22(9):714–732.

1829d Letter: Stubblefield to Eaton, 1 June 1829. Miscellaneous letter and document file 22(8):736–739.

1829e Letter: Bomford to Stubblefield, 24 February 1829. Miscellaneous letter and document file 14(6):591–593.

1829f   Letter: Stubblefield to Bomford, 30 March 1829. Miscellaneous letter and document file 22(7):604–606.

1829g   Letter: Hall to Bomford, 7 December 1829. Miscellaneous letter and document file 22(6):564–565.

1829h   Letter: Dunn to Eaton, 7 December 1828. Miscellaneous letter and document file 22(6):568–569.

1831   Letter: Hall to Bomford, 24 March 1831. Miscellaneous letter and document file 22(11):1022–1025.

1832   Letter: Rust to Bomford, 15 September 1832. Miscellaneous letter and document file 22(13):1259–1261.

1835a   Letter: Bell to Bedinger, 25 May 1835. Miscellaneous letter and document file 14(11):1017–1019.

1835b   Letter: Moor to Bomford, 30 March 1835. Miscellaneous letter and document file 12(1):22–27.

1836   Letter: S. Cooper to Secretary of War, 11 October 1836. Miscellaneous letter and document file 25(3):334–340.

1839a   Letter: Brown to Lucas, 2 January 1839. Miscellaneous letter and document file 12(5):462.

1839b   Letter: Lucas to Talcott, 29 August 1839. Miscellaneous letter and document file 12(6):582–584.

1840a   Letter: Lucas to Talcott, 9 May 1840. Miscellaneous letter and document file 26(1):89–90.

1840b   Letter: Talcott to Lucas, 11 June 1840. Miscellaneous letter and document file 16(1):141A.

1841a   Sworn affidavit: William McClure, 9 March 1841. Miscellaneous letter and document file 23(1):48.

1841b   Letter: Smith, Coates, Lambaugh, Pine, Cross, Kirginu and Cross to John Bell, 26 October 1841. Miscellaneous letter and document file 23(1):45.

1841c   Sworn affidavit: Francis C. Melhorn, 8 March 1841. Miscellaneous letter and document file 23(1):51.

1841d   Letter: Talcott to Albert M. Lea, Acting Secretary of War, 23 September 1841. Miscellaneous letter and document file 23(1):89–91.

1841e   Letter: Talcott to Craig, 16 March 1841. Miscellaneous letter and document file 19(1):94.

1841f   Order from Craig, 29 April, 18 May, 7 June, 16 July, 10 August 1841. Miscellaneous letter and document file 23(2):137–147.

1841g   Petition to His Excellency John Tyler, 15 December 1841. Miscellaneous letter and document file 23(2):111–119.

1841h   Letter: Bomford to Spencer, 20 December 1841. Miscellaneous letter and document file 19(14):1378–1379.

1841i   Letter: Anonymous to Secretary of War, 27 June 1841. Miscellaneous letter and document file 23(1): 33–36.

1842a   Order from Craig, 18 March 1842. Miscellaneous letter and document file 23(2):137–147.

1842b   Craig to Talcott, 21 March 1842. Miscellaneous letter and document file 12(10):942–944.

1842c   Letter: Unsigned to President John Tyler, 28 March 1843. Miscellaneous letter and document file 23(2): 136–137.

1842d   Letter: Talcott to Spencer, 25 June 1842. Miscellaneous letter and document file 19(14):1388–1389.

1842e   Rules and regulations for the Workshops US Armory, 16 October 1842. Miscellaneous letter and document file 24(10):920–921.

1842f   Letter: Craig to Talcott, 22 March 1842. Miscellaneous letter and document file 12(10):946–948.

1843   Letter: Craig to Talcott, 14 September 1843. Miscellaneous letter and document file 12(11):1097–1099.

1844a   Letter: Symington to Talcott, 12 December 1844. Miscellaneous letter and document file 23(2):260–271.

1844b   Letter: Symington to Ordnance Department, 12 December 1844. Miscellaneous letter and document file 23(3):260–267.

1845   Letter: Symington to Talcott, 24 July 1845. Miscellaneous letter and document file 23(5):477–481.

1846a   Letter: Symington to Talcott, 29 June 1846. Miscellaneous letter and document file 23(6):57–60.

1846b   Letter: Symington to Talcott, 16 June 1846. Miscellaneous letter and document file 23(10):931.

1847   Rules for the Government of the Workmen employed in the Armory, 24 december 1847. Miscellaneous letter and document file 24(1):29–32.

1848a   Letter: Symington to Talcott, 16 June 1848. Miscellaneous letter and document file 23(10):940–943.

1848b   Letter: Symington to Maynadier, 14 April 1848. Miscellaneous letter and document file 23(10):927–929.

1848c   Letter: Symington to Talcott, 11 August 1848. Miscellaneous letter and document file 23(10):977–985.

1848d   Letter: Talcott to Symington, 7 January 1848. Miscellaneous letter and document file 19(4):322–323.

1849a   Letter: Symington to Maynadier, 12 July 1849. Miscellaneous letter and document file 24(1):10–17.

1849c   Letter: Symington to Talcott, 12 May 1849. Miscellaneous letter and document file 23(12):1149–1154.

1848d   Letter: Talcott to Symington, 10 November 1949. Miscellaneous letter and document file 19(5):411.

1850   Letter: Symington to Talcott, 23 July 1850. Miscellaneous letter and document file 24(2):145–146.

1852   Letter: Huger to Craig, 25 June 1852. Miscellaneous letter and document file 26(4):301–402.

1853   Letter: Craig to Dobbin, 3 September 1853. Miscellaneous letter and document file 20(1):134–135.

1954a   Letter: Craig to Davis, 17 March 1854. Miscellaneous letter and document file 20(2):158–167.

1854b   Letter: Roeder to Bell, 19 May 1854. Miscellaneous letter and document file 25(8):770–771.

1855a   Letter: Clowe to Craig, 25 July 1855. Miscellaneous letter and document file 25(8):748.

1855b   Letter: Craig to Clowe, 15 September, 1855. Miscellaneous letter and document file 19(8):797.

1855c   Letter: Maynadier to Clowe, 22 June 1855. Miscellaneous letter and document file 19(8):764.

1861   Letter: Ripley to Murphy, 25 April 1861. Miscellaneous letter and document file 20(4):405.

HFNHP photostats. On file, Harpers Ferry National Historical Park, Harpers Ferry.
West Virginia.
1795   Letter: Washington to Lear. 2 November 1795. In *The Diaries of George Washington 1748–1799.* edited by John V. Fitspatrick.
1810   Letter: Annin to War Department. 17 March 1810. "Public Buildings at Harper's Ferry in Virginia, 1st January 1810."
1832   Report: Wolcott to Bomford. 15 December 1832. R. G. 156 Ordnance Office, No. 28.
1835   Talcott: Inspection Report of Harpers Ferry Armory, 17–25 June 1835. R. G. 156 Ordnance Office, No. 28.
1836a   Talcott: Inspection Report of Harpers Ferry Armory. 21–25 June 1836. R. G. 156 Ordnance Office, No. 28.
1836b   Talcott: Inspection Report of Harpers Ferry Armory, 3 November 1836. R. G. 156 Ordnance Office, No. 28.
1842   Moor's Hoffman's and King's interview: Proceedings of a Board of Officers 1842. Inspection Report of Harpers Ferry Armory. 25 February 1842. R. G. 156 Ordnance Office, No. 28, c75.
1852   Inspection Report of Harpers Ferry Armory, 20 July 1852. R. G. 156 Ordnance Office, No. 28.
1859   Letter: Ripley to Craig, 14 April 1859. R. G. 156 Ordnance Office, No. 28.

Hindle, Brooke, and Stephen Lubar
1986   *Engines of Change: The American Industrial Revolution, 1790–1860.* Smithsonian Institution Press, Washington, DC.

Hinton, Richard
1894   *John Brown and His Men.* Funk and Wagnalls, London.

Hounshell, D. A.
1982   *From the American System to Mass Production, 1800–1932.* Johns Hopkins University Press, Baltimore.

Huntington, R. T.
1972   *Hall's Breechloaders: John H. Hall's Invention and Development of a Breechloading Rifle with Precision-made Interchangeable Parts, and Its Introduction into the United States Service.* George Shumay, York, Pennsylvania.

Independent-Democrat, Charles Town, West Virginia. Newspaper on microfilm, Harpers Ferry National Historical Park, Harpers Ferry, West Virginia.

Jefferson County, Virginia, Deed Books. On microfilm, Harpers Ferry National Historical Park, Harpers Ferry, West Virginia.

Jefferson, Thomas
1954   *Notes on the State of Virginia,* edited by William Peden. Originally published in 1789. University of North Carolina Press, Chapel Hill.

Johnson, Mary, and John Barker
1993   Virginius Island Community: Preliminary Social Analysis, 1800–1936. Draft. On file, Harpers Ferry National Historical Park, Harpers Ferry, West Virginia.

Joseph, Maureen Delay, Perry Carpenter Wheelock, Deborah Warshaw, and Andrew Kriemelmeyer
1993   *Cultural Landscape Report: Virginius Island, Harpers Ferry National Historical Park.* National Park Service, U.S. Department of the Interior, Washington, DC.

Kasson, John F.
1979   *Civilizing the Machine: Technology and Republican Values in America, 1776–1900.* Penguin Books, New York.

1990   *Rudeness and Civility: Manners in Nineteenth-Century Urban America.* Hill and Wang, New York.

Kelso, Gerald K., and Mary C. Beaudry

1990   Pollen Analysis and Urban Land Use: The Environs of Scottow's Dock in 17th, 18th, and Early 19th-Century Boston. *Historical Archaeology* 24(1):61–81.

King, Julia A.

1994   Rural Landscape in the Mid-Nineteenth Century Chesapeake. In *Historical Archaeology of the Chesapeake,* edited by Paul A. Shackel and Barbara J. Little, pp. 283–299. Smithsonian Institution Press, Washington, DC.

Klein, Terry H.

1991   Nineteenth-Century Ceramics and Models of Consumer Behavior. *Historical Archaeology* 25(2):77–91.

Kulikoff, Allan

1989   The Transition to Capitalism in Rural America. *William and Mary Quarterly* 46:120–144.

1992   *The Agrarian Origins of American Capitalism.* University Press of Virginia, Charlottesville.

Larrabee, Edward McMillan

1960a   Report of Archaeological Investigation of the Arsenal Square at Harpers Ferry National Monument, Harpers Ferry West Virginia, from July 20 through September 5, 1959. On file, Harpers Ferry National Historical Park, Harpers Ferry, West Virginia.

1960b   Report of Exploratory Archeological Excavations Conducted on the Lower Hall Island Rifle Factory, Harpers Ferry National Monument, Harpers Ferry, West Virginia, From August 25 through August 29, 1959. On file, Harpers Ferry National Historical Park, Harpers Ferry, West Virginia.

1961   Rifle Works Archeological Report: Report of the Second Season of Exploratory Archeological Excavations Conducted at the U.S. Rifle Works, Lower Hall Island, Harpers Ferry National Monument, Harpers Ferry, West Virginia, from June 23 through July 6, 1960. On file, Harpers Ferry National Historical Park, Harpers Ferry, West Virginia.

1962   Report of the Third Season of Exploratory Archeological Excavations Conducted at the U.S. Rifle Works, Lower Hall Island, Harpers Ferry National Monument, Harpers Ferry, West Virginia, from 25 August through 10 November 1961. On file, Harpers Ferry National Historical Park, Harpers Ferry, West Virginia.

Larsen, Eric

1993   "That Trying Climate": Health and Medicine in Nineteenth-Century Harpers Ferry. In *Interdisciplinary Investigations of Domestic Life in Government Block B: Perspectives on Harpers Ferry's Armory and Commercial District,* edited by Paul A. Shackel, pp. 11.1–11.64. Occasional Report No. 6, National Park Service, U.S. Department of the Interior, Washington, DC.

1994a   A Boardinghouse Madonna—Beyond the Aesthetics of a Portrait Created through Medicine Bottles. In *An Archaeology of Harpers Ferry's Commercial and Residential District,* edited by Paul A. Shackel and Susan E. Winter. *Historical Archaeology* 28(4):68–79.

1994b   Worker's Privilege: Metal Items from Park Building 48. In *Domestic Responses to Nineteenth-Century Industrialization: An Archeology of Park Building 48, Harpers Ferry National Historical Park,* edited by Paul A. Shackel, pp. 6.1–

6.12. Occasional Report No. 12, National Park Service, U.S. Department of the Interior, Washington, DC.

Larsen, Eric L., and Michael T. Lucas
1993   Mind Your Own Business: Residence/Businesses in 19th-Century Harpers Ferry. Paper presented at the Society for Historical Archaeology Meetings, Kansas City, Missouri.
1994   Minding Your Own Business: The Harpers Ferry Hotel of the 1830s. In *Archeological Views of the Upper Wager Block, a Domestic and Commercial Neighborhood in Harpers Ferry,* edited by Jill Y. Halchin, pp. 6.1–6.27. Occasional Report No. 11, National Park Service, U.S. Department of the Interior, Washington, DC.

Laurie, Bruce
1989   *Artisans Into Workers.* Noonday Press, New York.

Limp, W. Frederick
1979   An Economic Evaluation of the Potential of Fish Utilization in Riverine Environments. *American Antiquity* 44(1):70–79.

Linenthal, Edward Tabor
1993   *Sacred Ground: Americans and Their Battlefields.* University of Illinois Press, urbana.

Little, Barbara J.
1993   "She was . . . an Example to her Sex": Possibilities for a Feminist Historical Archaeology. In *Historical Archaeology of the Chesapeake,* edited by Paul A. Shackel and Barbara J. Little, pp. 189–204. Smithsonian Institution Press, Washington, DC.

Little, Barbara J., and Paul A. Shackel
1989   Scales of Historical Anthropology: An Archaeology of Colonial Anglo-America. *Antiquity* 63(240):495–509.

Lowenthal, David
1985   *The Past Is a Foreign Country.* Cambridge University Press, New York.

Lowrie, Walter, and William Franklin (editors)
1834   *American State Papers. Class V. Military Affairs,* Vol. 2. Gales and Seaton, Washington, DC.

Lucas, Michael T.
1993a   Ceramic Consumption in an Industrializing Community. In *Interdisciplinary Investigations of Domestic Life in Government Block B: Perspectives of Harpers Ferry's Armory and Commercial District,* edited by Paul A. Shackel, pp. 8.1–8.38. Occasional Report No. 6, National Park Service, U.S. Department of the Interior, Washington, DC.
1993b   Late Nineteenth-Century Material Goods from Lower Town Harpers Ferry: The Ceramic and Glass Evidence from Features 99, 132, and 21. In *Interdisciplinary Investigations of Domestic Life in Government Block B: Perspectives on Harpers Ferry's Armory and Commercial District,* edited by Paul A. Shackel, pp. 14.1–14.36. Occasional Report No. 6, National Park Service, U.S. Department of the Interior, Washington, DC.
1994a   An Armory Worker's Life: Glimpses of Industrial Life. In *An Archeology of An Armory Worker's Household: Park Building 48, Harpers Ferry National Historical Park,* edited by Paul A. Shackel, pp. 5.1–5.40. Occasional Report No. 12, National Park Service, U.S. Department of the Interior, Washington, DC.
1994b   A la Russe, á la Pell-Mell, or á la Practical: Ideology and Compromise at the Late Nineteenth-Century Dinner Table. In *An Archaeology of Harpers Ferry's*

Commercial and Residential District, edited by Paul A. Shackel and Susan E. Winter. *Historical Archaeology* 28(4):80–93.

Lucas, Michael, and Paul A. Shackel
1994   Changing Social and Material Routine in 19th-Century Harpers Ferry. In *An Archaeology of Harpers Ferry's Commercial and Residential District,* edited by Paul A. Shackel and Susan E. Winter. *Historical Archaeology* 28(4):27–36.

Maltby, J. M.
1979   *Faunal Studies on Urban Sites: The Animal Bones from Exeter 1971–1975.* Department of Prehistory and Archaeology, Exeter Archaeological Report 2. Sheffield University, Sheffield, United Kingdom.
1982   The Variability of Faunal Samples and Their Effects Upon Ageing Data. In *Ageing and Sexing Animal Bones from Archaeological Sites,* edited by B. Wilson, C. Grigson, and S. Payne, pp. 81–90. British Archaeological Reports, British Series 109, Oxford, England.
1985   Patterns in Faunal Assemblage Variability. In *Beyond Domestication in Prehistoric Europe,* edited by Graeme Baker and Clive Gamble, pp. 33–74. Academic Press, New York.

Marglin, S. A.
1974   What Do Bosses Do? The Origins and Functions of Hierarchy in Capitalist Production. *Review of Radical Political Economy* 6:60–112.

Margolis, Maxine L.
1985   *Mothers and Such: Views of American Women and Why They Changed.* University of California Press, Berkeley.

Marmion, Annie P.
1959 *Under Fire: An Experience in the Civil War.* Memoirs compiled and published by William Vincent Marmion, Jr. On file, Harpers Ferry National Historical Park, Harpers Ferry, West Virginia (HFB 206).

Marx, Leo
1964   *The Machine in the Garden: Technology and the Pastoral Ideal in America.* Oxford University Press, New York.

Mathews, Glenna
1987   *"Just a Housewife": The Rise and Fall of Domesticity in America.* Oxford University Press, New York.

McCoy, Drew
1980   *The Elusive Republic: Political Economy in Jeffersonian American.* University of North Carolina Press, Chapel Hill.

McCracken, Grant
1988   *Culture and Consumption: New Approaches to the Symbolic Character of Goods and Activities.* Indiana University Press, Bloomington.

McKendrick, Neil, John Brewer, and J. H. Plumb
1982   *The Birth of a Consumer Society: The Commercialization of Eighteenth-Century England.* Indiana University Press, Bloomington.

Miller, George L.
1980   Classification and Economic Scaling of 19th-Century Ceramics. *Historical Archaeology* 14:1–40.
1990   The Market Basket of Ceramics Available in Country Stores from 1780 to 1880. Paper presented at the 1990 Society for Historical Archaeology meetings in Tucson, Arizona, January 1990.
1991   A Revised Set of CC Index Values for Classification and Economic Scaling of English Ceramics from 1787 to 1880. *Historical Archaeology* 25(1):1–25.

Miller, George L., Ann Smart Martin, and Nancy S. Dickinson
  1994   Changing Consumption Patterns: English Ceramics and the American Marker
          from 1770–1840. In *Everyday Life in the Early Republic: 1789–1828,* edited by
          Catherine Hutching, pp. 219–246. Henry Francis du Pont Winterthur
          Museum, Winterthur, Delaware.
Mintz, Steven, and Susan Kellog
  1988   *Domestic Revolutions: A Social History of American Family Life.* Free Press,
          New York.
Mitchell, Robert
  1977   *Commercialism and Frontier: Perspectives on the Early Shenandoah Valley.*
          University Press of Virginia, Charlottesville.
Mrozowski, Stephen
  1984   Prospects and Perspectives on an Archaeology of the Household. *Man in the
          Northeast* 27:31–49.
  1987   Exploring New England's Evolving Urban Landscape. In *Living in Cities,*
          edited by Edward Staski. *Special Publication Series,* No. 5:1–9. Society for
          Historical Archaeology, California, Pennsylvania.
Mrozowski, S. A., E. L. Bell, M. C. Beaudry, D. B. Laudon, and G. K. Kelso
  1989   Living on the Boott: Health and Well Being in a Boardinghouse Population.
          World Archaeology 21(2):298–319.
Mueller, James W., Benjamin Fischler, and Susan W. Frye
  1986   Preservation and Discovery along the Shenandoah Canal at Harpers Ferry
          National Historical Park in 1983 and 1984. Draft report on file, Harpers Ferry
          National Historical Park, Harpers Ferry, West Virginia.
Myers, Bruce B.
  1965   Historic Grounds Report, Part II. Landscape Data Section and Portions of
          Shenandoah and Potomac Streets and the Arsenal Square. Manuscript on file,
          Harpers Ferry National Historical Park, Harpers Ferry, West Virginia.
Nassaney, Michael S., and Marjorie R. Abel
  1993   The Political and Social Contexts of Cutlery Production in the Connecticut Val-
          ley. *Dialectical Anthropology* 18:247–289.
National Archives
          Records of the Office of the Chief of Ordnance. Record Group 156, National
          Archives, Washington, DC.
          Records of the United States General Accounting Office. Record Group 217,
          National Archives, Washington, DC.
          Records of the Springfield Armory. Record Group 156, National Archives,
          Washington, DC.
Noble, D.F.
  1986   *Forces of Production: A Social History of Industrial Automation.* Oxford Uni-
          versity Press, New York.
Noffsinger, James P.
  1958   Harpers Ferry, West Virginia: Contributions Toward a Physical History. On
          file, Harpers Ferry National Historical Park, Harpers Ferry, West Virginia.
Oates, Stephen B.
  1970   *To Purge This Land with Blood: A Biography of John Brown.* Harper and Row,
          New York.
Ogden, Annegret S.
  1986   *The Great American Housewife: From Helpmate to Wage Earner, 1776–1986.*
          Greenwood Press, Westport, Connecticut.

Ostrogorsky, Michael
 1987 Economic Organization and Landscape: Physical and Social Terrain Altera-
       tions in Seattle. In *Living in Cities: Current Research in Urban Archaeology,*
       edited by Edward Staski. *Special Publication Series* No. 5:10–18. Society for
       Historical Archaeology. California, Pennsylvania.
Patterson, John
 1989 From Battle Ground to Pleasure Ground: Gettysburg as a Historic Site. In *His-
       tory Museums in the United States: A Critical Assessment,* edited by Warren
       Leone and Roy Rozenzweig, pp. 128–157. University of Illinois Press, Chicago.
Paynter, Robert
 1982 *Models of Inequality: Settlement Patterns in Historical Archaeology.* Academic
       Press, New York.
 1989 The Archaeology of Equality and Inequality. *Annual Review of Anthropology*
       18:369–399.
Paynter, Robert, and Randall H. McGuire
 1991 The Archaeology of Inequality: Material Culture, Domination and Resistance.
       In *The Archaeology of Inequality,* edited by Randall H. McGuire and Robert
       Paynter, pp. 1–27. Basil Blackwell, Cambridge, Massachusetts.
Pousson, John F.
 1985 Archeological Investigations, Harpers Ferry National Historical Park, Pack-
       age No. 110A, Wager Block Backyards. Northeastern team, National Park
       Service, U.S. Department of the Interior, Denver, Colorado.
Praetzellis, Adrain, Mary Praetzellis, and Marley Brown III
 1987 Artifacts as Symbols of Identity: An Example from Sacramento's Gold Rush
       Era Chinese Community. *In Living in Cities,* edited by Edward Staski. *Special
       Publication Series* No. 5:38–47. Society for Historical Archaeology, California,
       Pennsylvania.
Prude, Jonathan
 1983 *The Coming of Industrial Order: Town and Factory Life in Rural Massachu-
       setts, 1810–1860.* Cambridge University Press, New York.
Rainey, Reuban M.
 1983 The Memory of War: Reflections on Battlefield Preservation. In *The Yearbook
       of Landscape Architecture,* edited by Richard L. Austin, Thomas Kane, Robert
       Z. Melnick, and Suzanne Turner, pp. 69–89. Van Nostrand Reinhold, New York.
Reilly, Robert M.
 1970 *United States Military Small Arms: 1816–1865.* Eagle Press, Baton Rouge,
       Louisiana.
Reinhard, Karl J.
 1993 Parasitological Analysis of Latrine Soils from Harpers Ferry. In *Interdiscipli-
       nary Investigations of Domestic Life in Government Block B: Perspectives on
       Harpers Ferry's Armory and Commercial District,* edited by Paul A. Shackel,
       pp. 13.1–13.8. Occasional Report No. 6, National Park Service, U.S. Depart-
       ment of the Interior, Washington, DC.
 1994 Sanitation and Parasitism at Harpers Ferry, West Virginia. In *An Archaeology
       of Harpers Ferry's Commercial and Residential District,* edited by Paul A.
       Shackel and Susan E. Winter. *Historical Archaeology* 28(4):62–67.
Reitz, Elizabeth
 1986 Urban/Rural Contrasts in Vertebrate Fauna from the Southern Atlantic
       Coastal Plain. *Historical Archaeology* 20(2):47–58.

Ross, Steven J.
  1985   *Workers on the Edge: Work, Leisure, and Politics in Industrializing Cincinnati,*
         1788–1890. Columbia University Press, New York.
Rothschild, Nan A.
  1990   *New York City Neighborhoods: The Eighteenth Century.* Academic Press, New
         York.
Rovner, Irwin
  1993   Phytolith Analysis: Archaeological Soils from Lower Town Harpers Ferry, West
         Virginia. In *Interdisciplinary Investigations of Domestic Life in Government*
         Block B: Perspectives on Harpers Ferry's Armory and Commercial District,
         edited by Paul A. Shackel, pp. 6.1–6.13. Occasional Report No. 6, National
         Park Service, U.S. Department of the Interior, Washington, DC.
  1994a Floral History by the Back Door: A Test of Phytolith Analysis in Residential
         Yards at Harpers Ferry. In *An Archaeology of Harpers Ferry's Commercial and*
         Residential District, edited by Paul A. Shackel and Susan E. Winter. *Historical*
         Archaeology 28(4):37–48.
  1994b Phytolith Analysis of Selected Soil Samples from Park Building 48, Harpers
         Ferry, West Virginia. In *Domestic Responses to Nineteenth-Century Industriali-*
         zation: An Archeology of Park Building 48, Harpers Ferry National Historical
         Park, edited by Paul A. Shackel, pp. 9.1–9.10. Occasional Report No. 12,
         National Park Service, U.S. Department of the Interior, Washington, DC.
Ryan, Mary
  1981   *Cradle of the Middle Class: The Family in Oneida County, New York, 1790–*
         1865. Cambridge University Press, New York.
Sanborn, Franklin B.
  1885   *Life and Letters of John Brown: Liberator of Kansas, and Martyr of Virginia.*
         Roberts Brothers, Boston.
Scott, James
  1990   *Domination and the Arts of Resistance: Hidden Transcripts.* Yale University
         Press, New Haven, Connecticut.
Scott, Joseph
  1805   *A Geographical Dictionary of the United States of North America.* Archibald
         Bartram, Philadelphia.
Sadgwich, Catherine Marie
  1837   *Home.* James Monroe, Boston, Massachusetts.
Seidel, Ellen M.
  1985   Archeological Excavations for Package No. 115, Buildings 3, 37, 38, 39, 40, 43,
         and Lot 55B, Harpers Ferry National Historical Park, Harpers Ferry, West
         Virginia. National Park Service, U.S. Department of the Interior, Washington,
         DC.
Shackel, Paul A. (editor)
  1993a *Interdisciplinary Investigations of Domestic Life in Government Block B: Per-*
         spectives on Harpers Ferry's Armory and Commercial District, Occasional
         Report No. 6, National Park Service, U.S. Department of the Interior, Washing-
         ton, DC.
Shackel, Paul A.
  1993b Changing Meanings and Uses of the Landscape and the Built Environment. In
         Interdisciplinary Investigations of Domestic Life in Government Block B: Per-
         spectives on Harpers Ferry's Armory and Commercial District, edited by Paul

A. Shackel, pp. 5.1–5.24. Occasional Report No. 6, National Park Service, U.S. Department of the Interior, Washington, DC.

1993c   *Personal Discipline and Material Culture: An Archaeology of Annapolis, Maryland, 1695–1870.* University of Tennessee Press, Knoxville.

1993d   Prospects for an Archaeology of the People without History. In *Interdisciplinary Investigations of Domestic Life in Government Block B: Perspectives on Harpers Ferry's Armory and Commercial District,* edited by Paul A. Shackel, pp. 18.1–18.22. Occasional Report No. 6, National Park Service, U.S. Department of the Interior, Washington, DC.

1994a   A Material Culture of Armory Workers. In *Domestic Responses to Nineteenth-Century Industrialization: An Archeology of Park Building 48, Harpers Ferry National Historical Park,* edited by Paul A. Shackel, 10.1–10.7. Occasional Report No. 12, National Park Service, U.S. Department of the Interior, Washington, DC.

1994b   Interdisciplinary Approaches to the Meanings and Uses of Material Goods in Lower Town Harpers Ferry. In *An Archaeology of Harpers Ferry's Commercial and Residential District,* edited by Paul A. Shackel and Susan E. Winter. *Historical Archaeology* 28(4):3–15.

1994c   Memorializing Landscapes and the Civil War in Harpers Ferry. In *Look to the Earth: An Archaeology of the Civil War,* edited by Clarence Geier and Susan Winter, pp. 256–270. University of Tennessee Press, Knoxville.

in press   Town Planning and Nineteenth-Century Industrial Life in Harpers Ferry. In *The Archaeology of 19th-Century Virginia,* edited by Theodore R. Reinhart and John H. Sprinkle, Jr. Council of Virginia Archaeologists, Special Publication No. 35, Archeological Society of Virginia.

Shackel, Paul A., and David Larsen

in press   Labor and Racism in Early Industrial Harpers Ferry. In *Lines That Divide,* edited by James Dell, Robery Paynter, and Stephen Mrozowski. University of Massachusetts Press, Amherst.

Shackel, Paul A., and Barbara J. Little

1994   Archaeological Perspectives: An Overview of the Chesapeake Region. In *Historical Archaeology of the Chesapeake,* edited by Paul A. Shackel and Barbara J. Little, pp. 1–15. Smithsonian Institution Press, Washington, DC.

Shackel, Paul A., and Susan E. Winter (editors)

1994   An Archaeology of Harpers Ferry's Commercial and Residential District. *Historical Archaeology* 28(4):16–26.

Shackel, Paul A., and Cari YoungRavenhorst

1994   Summary of Excavations at Park Building 48. In *Domestic Responses to Nineteenth-Century Industrialization: An Archeology of Park Building 48, Harpers Ferry National Historical Park,* edited by Paul A. Shackel, pp. 3.1–3.17. Occasional Report No. 12, National Park Service, U.S. Department of the Interior, Washington, DC.

Shackel, Paul A., Cari YoungRavenhorst, and Susan E. Winter

1993   The Archaeological Record: Stratigraphy, Features, and Material Culture. In *Interdisciplinary Investigations of Domestic Life in Government Block B: Perspectives on Harpers Ferry's Armory and Commercial District,* edited by Paul A. Shackel, pp. 4.1–4.85. Occasional Report No. 6, National Park Service, U.S. Department of the Interior, Washington, DC.

Shelton, Cynthia
  1986   *The Mills of Manayunk: Industrialization and Social Conflict in the Philadel-phia Region, 1787–1837.* Johns Hopkins University Press, Baltimore.
Sigourney, Lydia
  1989   Home. In *Major Problems in American Women's History,* edited by Mary Beth Norton, pp. 113–114. Reprint of 1850 edition. D. C. Heath, Lexington, Massachusetts.
Smith, Merritt Roe
  1977   *Harpers Ferry Armory and the New Technology: The Challenge of Change.* Cornell University Press, Ithaca, New York.
  1985   Army Ordnance and the "American System" of Manufacturing, 1815–1861. In *Military Enterprise and Technological Change: Perspectives on the American Experience,* edited by Merritt Roe Smith, pp. 39–86. MIT Press, Cambridge, Massachusetts.
  1991   Eli Whitney and the American System of Manufacturing. In *Technology in America: A History of Individuals and Ideas,* edited by Carroll W. Pursell, Jr., pp. 45–61. The MIT Press, Cambridge, Massachusetts.
  1994   Technological Determinism in American Culture. In *Does Technology Drive History? The Dilemma of Technological Determinism,* edited by Merritt Roe Smith and Leo Marx, pp. 2–35. MIT Press, Cambridge, Massachusetts.
Smith, Philip R., Jr.
  1958a   History of the Methodist-Episcopal Church, 1818–1868, and the Free Church. On file, Harpers Ferry National Historical Park, Harpers Ferry, West Virginia.
  1958b   The Methodist Protestant Church and the Odd Fellow Hall. On file, Harpers Ferry National Historical Park, Harpers Ferry, West Virginia.
  1959a   History of the Evangelical Lutheran Christ Church, Camp Hill, 1850–1868. On file, Harpers Ferry National Historical Park, Harpers Ferry, West Virginia.
  1959b   History of the Public School: The Harpers Ferry Female Seminary, Armory Magazine, Camp Hill. On file, Harpers Ferry National Historical Park, Harpers Ferry, West Virginia.
  1959c   Protestant Episcopal Church. On file, Harpers Ferry National Historical Park, Harpers Ferry, West Virginia.
  1959d   St. Peter's Roman Catholic Church. On file, Harpers Ferry National Historical Park, Harpers Ferry, West Virginia.
Snell, Charles W.
  1959a   Extracts From National Archives Record Group 217, Records of the U.S. Treasury Department, Records of the Second Auditor, 1817 to 1841, Relating to the U. S. Armory, Vol I. On file, Harpers Ferry National Historical Park, Harpers Ferry, West Virginia.
  1959b   Historic Building Report Part II, Historical Data Section, Buildings No. 34–56, 32, 33, and 34A, The Samuel Annin House, Lot 3, Block B, Shenandoah Street. Harpers Ferry National Monument. On file, Harpers Ferry National Historical Park, Harpers Ferry, West Virginia.
  1959c   The Presbyterian Church. On file, Harpers Ferry National Historical Park, Harpers Ferry, West Virginia.
  1960a   Harpers Ferry Repels an Attack and Becomes the Major Base of Operations for Sheridan's Army, July 4, 1864 to July 27, 1865. On file, Harpers Ferry National Historical Park, Harpers Ferry, West Virginia.

1960b   The Fortifications at Harpers Ferry, Virginia, in 1861 and Jackson's Attack, May 1862. On file, Harpers Ferry National Historical Park, Harpers Ferry, West Virginia.

1973   The Business and Commercial Development of Harpers Ferry's Lower Town Area: 1803–1861. On file, Harpers Ferry National Historical Park, Harpers Ferry, West Virginia.

1979   The Acquisition and Disposal of Public Lands of the U.S. Armory at Harpers Ferry, West Virginia, 1796–1885: A Narrative History. National Park Service. On file, Harpers Ferry National Historical Park, Harpers Ferry, West Virginia.

1980   An Armorer's Dwelling House, Bldg. No. 48, on U.S. Lot No. 2 North of Shenandoah Street, Harpers Ferry National Historical Park, West Virginia: Historical Data Section. On file, Harpers Ferry National Historical Park, Harpers Ferry, West Virginia.

1981a   A Comprehensive History of the Armory Dwellings, Houses of the U.S. Armory at Harpers Ferry, Virginia, 1789–1884. Vol. I. A History of the Construction, Repair, Improvements, and Acquisition of Armory Dwelling Houses 1789–1841. On file, Harpers Ferry National Historical Park, Harpers Ferry, West Virginia.

1981b   A Descriptive Catalog and Directory of 187 Armory Dwelling Houses, 1841–1852, of the U.S. Armory at Harpers Ferry, Virginia. Including Rents Collected. Vol. II. A History of Armory Houses. On file, Harpers Ferry National Historical Park, Harpers Ferry, West Virginia.

SoJ *(Spirit of Jefferson)*, Charles Town, West Virginia. Newspaper on microfilm, Harpers Ferry National Historical Park, Harpers Ferry, West Virginia.

Spencer-Wood, Suzanne
1991   Toward an Historical Archaeology of Materialist Domestic Reform. In *The Archaeology of Inequality,* edited by Randall H. McGuire and Robert Paynter, pp. 231–286. Basil Blackwell, Cambridge, Massachusetts.

Stansell, Christine
1986   *City of Women: Sex and Class in New York, 1789–1860.* Alfred A. Knopf, New York.

Staski, Edward
1990   Studies in Ethnicity in North American Historical Archaeology. *North American Archaeologist* 11(2):121–145.

Strasser, Susan
1982   *Never Done: A History of American Housework.* Pantheon Books, New York.

Taft, Grace Jennings
1898   A Trip to Harpers Ferry. On file, Harpers Ferry National Historical Park, Harpers Ferry, West Virginia.

Thompson, E. P.
1967   Time, Work-Discipline and Industrial Capitalism. *Past and Present* 38:56–97.

Tilley, Louise A., and Joan W. Scott
1978   *Women, Work, and Family.* Holt, Rinehart, and Winston, New York.

Trigger, Bruce
1991   Distinguished Lecture in Archaeology: Constraint and Freedom. *American Anthropologist* 93(3):551–569.

United States Bureau of the Census
1830   *Population Statistics.* Harpers Ferry, Virginia. On microfilm, Harpers Ferry National Historical Park, Harpers Ferry, West Virginia; 164.

1840   *Population Statistics.* Harpers Ferry, Virginia. On microfilm, Harpers Ferry
        National Historical Park, Harpers Ferry, West Virginia; 241.

1850   *Population Statistics.* Harpers Ferry, Virginia. On microfilm, Harpers Ferry
        National Historical Park, Harpers Ferry, West Virginia; 411.

VFP (*Virginia Free Press*), Charles Town, Virginia/West Virginia. Newspaper on micro-
        film, Harpers Ferry National Historical Park, Harpers Ferry, West Virginia.

Villard, Oswald Garrison

1910   *John Brown, 1800–1859: A Biography Fifty Years After.* Houghton Mifflin, New
        York.

Vogel, Lise

1977   Hearts to Feel and Tongues to Speak: New England Mill Women in the Early
        Nineteenth Century. In *Class, Sex, and the Woman Worker,* edited by Milton
        Cantor and Bruce Ware, pp. 64–82. Greenwood Press, Westport, Connecticut.

Wall, Diana diZerega

1985   The Beginnings of the Family Consumer Economy: Toward the Archaeological
        Analysis of Social Change. *American Archaeology* 5(3):190–194.

1991   Sacred Dinners and Secular Teas: Constructing Domesticity in Mid-19th-
        Century New York. *Historical Archaeology* 25(4):69–81.

1994   *The Archaeology of Gender: Separating the Spheres in Urban America.* Plenum
        Press, New York.

Wallace, Anthony F. C.

1978   *Rockdale: The Growth of an American Village in the Early Industrial Revolu-
        tion.* Vintage Books, New York.

Washington Post, Washington DC.

1995   Headline: "Gain in Workers' Pay, Benefits Is Smallest Since at least 1981," 26
        July:A1

1995   Headline: "U.S. Finds Productivity, But Not Pay, Is Rising" 26 July 1995:A9.

Weber, Max

1930   *The Protestant Ethic and the Spirit of Capitalism,* translated by Talcott
        Parsons. Unwin University Books, London.

Wentzell, Volkmar

1957   History Awakens at Harpers Ferry. *National Geographics* CXI(3):402–408.

Whittlesey, Derwent S.

1920   *The Springfield Armory: A Study in Institutional Development.* Unpublished
        Ph.D. dissertation. University of Chicago.

Winter, Susan E.

1994   Social Dynamics and Structure in Lower Town Harpers Ferry. In *An Archaeol-
        ogy of Harpers Ferry's Commercial and Residential District,* edited by Paul A.
        Shackel and Susan E. Winter. *Historical Archaeology* 28(4):16–26.

Winter, Susan E., and Dennis E. Frye

1992   *Loudoun Heights Archeological and Historical Resources Study. Harpers Ferry
        National Historical Park.* Occasional Report No. 8., National Park Service,
        U.S. Department of the Interior, Washington, DC.

Wolf, Eric

1982   *Europe and a People Without History.* University of California Press, Berkeley.

Wyllie, Irvin G.

1954   *The Self-Made Man in America: The Myth of Rags to Riches.* Free Press, New
        York.

Zeder, Melinda
   1988   Understanding Urban Process through the Study of Specialized Subsistence
          Economy in the Near East. *Journal of Anthropological Archaeology* 7:1–55.
Zonderman, David A.
   1992   *Aspirations & Anxieties: New England Workers & the Mechanized Factory
          System, 1815–1850.* Oxford University Press, New York.

Index